THE PAST WITHIN US

THE PAST WITHIN US:
MEDIA, MEMORY, HISTORY

———————◆———————

TESSA MORRIS-SUZUKI

VERSO
London • New York

First published by Verso 2005
© Tessa Morris-Suzuki 2005

The moral rights of the author have been asserted

1 3 5 7 9 10 8 6 4 2

Verso
UK: 6 Meard Street, London W1F 0EG
USA: 180 Varick Street, New York, NY 10014-4606
www.versobooks.com

Verso is the imprint of New Left Books

ISBN 1-85984-513-4

British Library Cataloguing in Publication Data
Morris-Suzuki, Tessa
  The past within us: media, memory, history
  1. History – Philosophy 2. Mass media and history
  3. Representation (Philosophy)
  I. Title
  901

  ISBN 1859845134

Library of Congress Cataloging-in-Publication Data
Morris-Suzuki, Tessa.
  The past within us: media, memory, history / Tessa Morris-Suzuki.
    p. cm.
  Includes bibliographical references and index.
  ISBN 1-85984-513-4 (alk. paper)
  1. History in mass media. I. Title.

P96.H55M67 2004
900–dc22

2004020253

Typeset in Garamond
Printed in the UK by The Bath Press

Contents

Acknowledgements

It is common practice to acknowledge the help of various people 'without whom this book would not have been written'. Sometimes perhaps this is just a polite form of words. In my case, however, this book would really never have seen the light of day without the encouragement, persuasion and support of several colleagues, particularly Kojima Kiyoshi of Iwanami Publishing and Iyotani Toshio of Hitotsubashi University. Various sections of the manuscript benefited from the insightful comments of Yamanouchi Yasushi, Narita Ryûichi, Iwasaki Minoru, Nakano Toshio, Sakamoto Hiroko, Ôuchi Yoshikazu and others. Shimamoto Shûji of Shôgakukan Publishing and Morita Minako of Morita Shashin Jimusho provided invaluable advice on photographs, and Hilary Morris and Guido Granai introduced me to the joys of acquaintance with Alessandro Manzoni. My thanks also go to Vanessa Buffy Ward, Julia Yonetani and all in the Division of Pacific and Asian History at the Australian National University, and to Yoshimi Shunya and Kang Sangjung, for ideas and inspiration.

Last but not least, many thanks to Tim Clark, Jane Hindle, Andrea Woodman and all the staff at Verso for their editorial support;

to Hiroshi and Patrick; and to Hokari Minoru, for some particularly perceptive comments and suggestions, and for always daring to ask the really *big* questions about history. Even though I can't share this final version with you, I still want to say: Mino, this one's for you.

1

The Past is Not Dead

The Independence Hall of Korea, a massive edifice celebrating the triumph of nationhood, stands at the foot of a forested mountain some two hours drive south of Seoul. In front, a white marble monument to the sufferings and achievements of the Korean people soars skyward in the shape of two extended wings. Behind, a military radar station perched on top of the mountain provides a sharp reminder of the realities of nationhood in this still-divided land. Inside the cool cavernous museum, an array of national treasures (some real, some reproduced) unfolds before the eyes of the visitor. A reproduction of a wall-painting from seventh-century Samarkand depicts the arrival of travellers from the Kingdom of Silla in the south of the Korean peninsula, reminding viewers of the Silk Route connections which linked the ancient Korean kingdoms to the wider world. An array of beautiful celadon china recalls the country's long artistic and technological heritage.

But the Independence Hall, like most museums today, also utilizes more modern artistic and technological skills to bring the past to life. Huge wall-paintings and dioramas filled with waxwork figures depict the struggle of Korean patriots against Japanese colonialism. Vivid black-and-white photographs and reproductions of old newspapers record events like the uprising of March 1, 1919, which was fiercely suppressed by the Japanese authorities. The younger visitors to the museum queue with goggle-eyed curiosity to gaze at waxworks of the colonial period prisons where nationalists were tortured and killed – the grim scenes behind the keyholes enhanced by the recorded sounds of unearthly screams. Video monitors show grainy clips from films depicting the abduction of young women who were forced to satisfy the sexual demands of the Japanese military, and young men charging remorselessly to their deaths on the battlefields of the Korean War, while a 'Circle Vision Theatre' surrounds the viewer with more hopeful images from high-growth years of the late twentieth century and the 1988 Olympic Games. The Independence Hall also maintains a sophisticated web site in Korean, Chinese, Japanese and English, complete with 'cybergalleries', which give virtual visitors the illusion that they are walking through the museum room by room (http://www.independence.or.kr/).

The Crisis of History

Our visions of history are drawn from diverse sources: not just from the narratives of history books but also from photographs and historical novels, from newsreel footage, comic books and, increasingly, from electronic media like the Internet. Out of this kaleidoscopic mass of fragments we make and remake patterns of understanding which explain the origins and nature of the world in which we live. And doing this, we define and redefine the place that we occupy in that world. Often, in fact, it is the snippets of vision and sound – seconds of newsreel, stark caricatured faces – that continue to frame our picture of the past even when the details of the accompanying narratives have been forgotten. This book seeks to explore some of these varied encounters with history, and to reflect on the ways in which different media influence our understanding of the past. In writing it, I am impelled by the sense of a crisis in our relationship with the past – a crisis of history.

This crisis expresses itself in a paradox. On the one hand, our age is one of immediacy and constant change. New knowledge has economic value, while old knowledge sinks unvalued into the depths of the 'public domain'. Education increasingly stresses the relevance of contemporary topics and practical skills – assets which students (it is believed) will be able to convert into instant earning power. In this context, it is not surprising that history is in decline in the curricula of many countries. This loss of historical consciousness is the theme of repeated laments. More than three decades ago, in his essay the 'The Death of the Past', J. H. Plumb was already suggesting that 'the strength of the past in all aspects of life is far, far weaker than it was a generation ago; indeed, few societies have ever had a past in such galloping dissolution as this' (Lowenthal 1985, 364). More recently, David Marc's *The Bonfire of the Humanities* has specifically blamed the spread of mass media like television for contemporary society's 'stunning problems of shrinking attention span and lack of historical consciousness' (Marc 1995, 49).

But the past refuses to go away. Indeed, in recent years there have been moments when historical consciousness has seemed to well up like magma from between the shifting tectonic plates of an unstable world order, threatening to overwhelm us. Again and again we have been forced to confront the fact that (as William Faulkner once put it) 'the past is not dead; it isn't even past'.

Visiting the Independence Hall of Korea in April 2001, for example, I found myself thinking rather wryly about laments for the passing of the past. South Korea and Japan were at that point embroiled in a diplomatic incident which had just prompted the recall of the Korean ambassador from Tokyo. At several prominent points on the streets of Seoul, protestors had set up stalls with banners calling for a boycott of Japanese goods (Picture 1.1). The negative turn in relations between Japan and South Korea was a serious political embarrassment for President Kim Dae-Jung, whose achievements included an energetic and (until then) largely successful policy of improving relations with Japan. And all of this political and diplomatic turmoil was generated, not by the usual causes – trade friction, military concerns, border disputes and so on – but by a single history textbook, which the Japanese government had just approved for use in junior high schools. The Chinese and Korean governments and various protest groups argued that the text grossly distorted East Asian history, and in particular whitewashed the history of Japanese expansionism and colonialism in the region. In the weeks that followed, the escalating dispute was to lead to the temporary freezing of trade liberalization measures between Japan and South Korea, as well as to an incident in which a group of incensed Koreans publicly cut off their own fingers with meat cleavers as a gesture of protest.

East Asia's 'textbook wars' are just one instance of the way in which the spectre of history seems more than ever to intrude on public life, as questions of commemoration, historical responsibility and history education become focuses of impassioned national and international controversies. Historian Henry Reynolds poses the rhetorical question, 'Was there ever a time in the past when history was so central to the political debate, when Clio was consulted so readily?' (Reynolds 2000, 3). Reynolds is referring particularly to Australia, where political leaders increasingly mobilize history to support contending visions of the national identity, and where the question of responsibility for injustices inflicted on the Aboriginal community remains a sensitive political issue. But elsewhere too questions of commemoration, apology and historical responsibility have been just as politically salient. In recent years Czech and German governments have apologized to one another for prewar

and wartime misdeeds; the Norwegian King has apologized for wrongs done to the nation's minority Saami population; the Queen of England has signed a statement of regret to New Zealand's Maoris for their dispossession by the British; US Secretary of State Colin Powell's return to Vietnam, where he once served as a military officer, revived debate over US responsibility for events like the My Lai massacre; and some American politicians and activists have taken up the cause of the descendants of the victims of the Atlantic slave trade to demand reparations.

The issue is not simply one of judging the 'guilt of nations' for past wrongs (see Barkan 2000). History is also becoming a matter of public debate in other ways. In Southeast Asia, the start of the twenty-first century has seen a boom in the popularity of movies depicting formative moments in national history – particularly those events that involved conflicts with neighbouring countries. Thai historian Charnwit Kasetsiri points to the curious dichotomy between, on the one hand, the lack of interest in history within the formal curriculum and, on the other, mass public enthusiasm for these popular representations of historical consciousness.

The crisis of history, then, is not a simple matter of amnesia. Rather, it reflects a profound dilemma: in an age of global mobility and multiple, rapidly changing media, how do we pass on our knowledge of the past from one generation to the next? How do we relate our lives in the present to the events of the past? Which bits of the past do we claim as our own, and in what sense do they become our property? My concern with these questions has been stimulated by involvement in the history textbook debate in East Asia. Like disputes over apology and historical revisionism in other parts of the world, the Japanese textbook controversy highlights key problems of the intergenerational communication of historical knowledge, and the closely associated problems of historical responsibility. Here, I want to use some brief comments on this particular controversy as a point of departure for entering into a discussion of the more general crisis of history, and of the challenges that it creates for contemporary historians worldwide.

The 'Textbook Wars' and the Historiography of Oblivion

In Japan as elsewhere, the so-called age of globalization has been a time of fluidity, uncertainty and insecurity. Although the Cold War has lingered on in East Asia longer than anywhere else, the region is deeply affected by shifts in the global order. At a time of growing cross-border flows of finance and ideas, Japan has experienced a stagnating economy and a widespread sense of social malaise. For some sections of Japanese society, the response to such insecurities (replicated in many other parts of the world) has been to retreat behind the barricades of nationalist rhetoric – an effort to ward off the forces of global change by shoring up imperilled imagined communities. Interpretations of the past become a central feature of these strategies because, as Eric Hobsbawm once trenchantly put it, 'History is the raw material of nationalistic or ethnic or fundamentalist ideologies, as poppies are the raw material of heroin addiction' (Hobsbawm 1997, 5).

The history textbook dispute in East Asia is a vivid example of this process. Disputes between Japan and its neighbours over the teaching of history have surfaced intermittently over the past couple of decades, but the most recent and impassioned dispute originated in 1996, when a group of nationalist Japanese academics and others formed an association called the Society for History Textbook Reform [*Atarashii Rekishi Kyōkasho o Tsukuru Kai*]. The aim of the association was to combat the 'masochistic' view of Japan's past which, they believed, had been imposed on Japanese schoolchildren ever since the Pacific War (Ienaga 2001; McCormack 2000; Nozaki and Inokuchi 2000). The Society expressed particular outrage at the fact that junior high school textbooks in Japan now included references (albeit very brief ones) to the so-called 'comfort women' issue: the institutionalized rape and other sexual abuses of women (many of them from Korea and China) in 'comfort stations' established to serve the Japanese military during the war. A large part of their campaign has been devoted to denying that the 'comfort women' were victims of a deliberate military policy of institutionalized sexual exploitation, and to minimizing the significance of other instances of aggression such as the 1937 Nanjing Massacre, in which large numbers of Chinese civilians and prisoners of war were killed by Japanese forces.

In this sense, the work of the Society can been likened to the writings of European Holocaust revisionists such as Robert Faurisson and David Irving, and to the work of writers like Keith Windschuttle, who seeks to deny the reality of extensive massacres of Aborigines by European colonizers (Faurisson and Barnes 1985; Irving 1990; Windschuttle 2000). It is, in other words, part of a late twentieth-century 'historiography of oblivion', whose purpose is not simply to 'revise' understandings of the past, but specifically to *obliterate* the memory of certain events from public consciousness.

The Society for History Textbook Reform drew on the contributions of several prominent members to produce a series of publications expounding its view of the Japanese past and present: publications ranging from cartoons by comic-book writer Kobayashi Yoshinori (whose work is discussed in more detail in Chapter 5) to a stunningly turgid 774-page *History of the Nation's People* by Nietzsche scholar Nishio Kanji (Nishio et al. 1999). Then in 2001 the Society made its first bid for a direct role in the Japanese school curriculum by launching two junior high school texts: one on history and one on civics.

Textbooks in Japan are chosen by local education committees from a relatively restricted list of works approved by the Ministry of Education. The texts prepared by the Society were approved only after the Ministry had demanded numerous revisions, but their content still evoked an outcry from within Japan and abroad. In the case of their *New History Textbook*, which became the main focus of debate, controversy focused particularly on the inclusion (alongside more conventional historical material) of myths about the heroic deeds of early emperors, an emphasis on the unique glories of Japanese civilization, generally positive assessments of the impact of Japanese colonization on other parts of Asia, and the minimization of the oppressive aspects of Japan's prewar and wartime political regime (Nishio et al. 2001).

Within Japan the Society's textbooks prompted condemnation from many historians and other scholars. Nationwide campaigns to discourage education committees from adopting the texts were largely successful: in the end, less than 0.1 percent of Japanese junior high schools adopted the texts in 2001. However, the Society has since continued to campaign for their wider use, particularly in the rural regions of Japan. In a sense, then, the textbook affair highlights the continuing presence of a vigorous opposition to nationalist revisionism within Japanese society. But at the same time, the controversy revealed some underlying dilemmas facing those who – not only in Japan but also elsewhere – seek to resist and reverse the encroaching influence of historiographies of oblivion.

In Search of Historical Truth

Most of the intense criticism of the Society's history textbook, both within Japan and overseas, has focused on factual errors or omissions. The desire to point out the book's shortcomings was natural enough, but this strategy of criticism had some unintended consequences. Since the textbook covered a vast sweep of Japanese history, with blithe disregard for inconvenient facts, there were a very large number of points at which the authors' selection and presentation of events could be questioned. In concentrating on particular errors and omissions, however, the energies of critics were often dissipated into a host of divergent channels, and debate readily fragmented into detailed disputes about particular events or documentary sources, rather than addressing underlying issues of historiography.

More fundamentally, critics of the Society for History Textbook Reform faced a philosophical dilemma shared with many others around the world who seek to combat, in Pierre Vidal-Naquet's words, 'the assassins of memory' (Vidal-Naquet 1993). As US-based historian Yang Daqing observes, history writing in Japan, China and Korea is still strongly influenced by positivist notions of scientifically verifiable 'historical facts'. In China, this approach draws on materialist conceptions of history, but also in part reflects a reaction to the ideological passions of the Maoist era, when the notion that 'theory precedes history' exercised a powerful sway over Chinese images of the past. In Japan too, the study of history has been influenced by notions of dialectical materialism, but in both Japan and Korea there is also a strong tradition of positivist history derived from nineteenth-century Rankean ideas (Yang 2002).

More recently, though, postmodern and poststructuralist concepts have had a growing influence on intellectual life in Japan and South Korea (and also to a lesser extent in China). Indeed, many of the most outspoken opponents of the new nationalist historiography in Japan have been deeply influenced by these ideas. They have read their Foucault, Derrida and subaltern studies. They are conscious of the fact that all narratives are constructed and contestable, and wary of the contests for power concealed within claims to universal scientific truth. The dilemma they thus face is this: how can one mount an effective critique of the Society for History Textbook Reform without reverting to a simple positivism which seeks to replace the Society's 'incorrect' narrative of the national past with an authoritative, but still dubious, 'correct' alternative?

This problem is accentuated by the fact that some (though not all) of the Society's members use a kind of ersatz postmodernism to add substance to their nationalist view of the past. Nishio Kanji, for example, observes that 'history is not science ... history is a world which is brought into being only by words. It is a world of human interpretations: an uncertain accumulation of human wisdom formed from the fluid substance of language, and inseparable from the hopes and fears and desires that we, in the present, feel towards the future' (Nishio 1999, 41; see also Sakamoto 1994). These reflections provide the basis for the proposal that each 'nation' or 'ethnic group' or 'cultural zone' (the three terms being used interchangeably in Nishio's work) has its own distinct form of historical consciousness. A meaningful exchange of historical ideas between Japan and other places (such as China or 'the West') is thus precluded, since Japan's understanding of history is, according to Nishio, based upon a unique national consciousness which is 'remarkably different in type from both the European and Chinese versions', and is characterized by an 'unconscious sense of continuity' with the past (Nishio 1999, 42).

This historical relativism is carried over into the *New History Textbook* (of which Nishio is the chief author). Here students are instructed that

> different people, different ethnic groups and different ages have entirely different ways of thinking and feeling. Thus we can see that it is difficult to define a certain fact as simply being real. George Washington was commander-in-chief at the time when the US won its independence from Britain in the War of Independence (1775–1783), and was the first US president. In America he is regarded as a great founder of the nation. However, to Britain, which was defeated in the war, and thus lost its American colony, he is not necessarily a great figure at all. Even today, some British history textbooks exclude

Washington's name, or treat the independence forces as a rebel army. It is indeed perhaps obvious that history varies from one people to another. There is nothing really strange about the fact that there are as many histories as there are nations (Nishio et al. 2001, iii).

It is not difficult to demonstrate that Nishio's relativist view of the past, as well as being based on a fairly idiosyncratic reading of foreign textbooks, is also internally inconsistent. For example, while firmly admonishing students not to 'judge the past by the standards of the present', Nishio and his colleagues unhesitatingly use contemporary globalized aesthetic standards as a basis for asserting that various examples of early Japanese Buddhist art are 'on a par with the works of the great Italian sculptors Donatello and Michelangelo' (Nishio et al. 2001, 5). And, though he differentiates between Japan's unique unconscious historical identity and that of all other nations, Nishio evidently does not regard this national consciousness as equally shared by the entire Japanese population, since he proceeds to castigate all Japanese historians of 'the past half century or so' for being 'enmeshed in unbelievable superstitions and immured in ignorance and blindness' (Nishio 1999, 483).

Yet at the same time, this radical relativism does pose an intellectual and moral challenge to those who acknowledge the limitations of language, the constructed nature of narratives and the impossibility of a 'God's eye view' of the past. For if we are prepared to accept that all historical narratives are partial and contextual – that (to cite the powerful example used by Dipesh Chakrabarty) the account given by nineteenth-century Indian farmers who attributed their rebellion to the will of god is as much a valid historical narrative as the account given by a modern historian who attributes the same event to class conflict – how can we criticize the nationalist account of the Japanese past which, Nishio Kanji tells us, arises in his mind from its unconscious connectedness to his ethnic heritage (Chakrabarty 2000)?

As Eric Hobsbawm points out, the challenges of such relativism intensify as one approaches the large historical issues which still cast their shadow on our lives in the present: 'Few relativists have the full courage of their convictions, at least when it comes to deciding whether Hitler's Holocaust took place or not' (Hobsbawm 1997, viii). A relativist approach to atrocities such as the Holocaust (or to the Nanjing Massacre or the atomic bombing of Hiroshima and Nagasaki) seems grotesque for many reasons, not least of which are the material consequences of those deeds for the present. In other words, different narratives have different implications for the way in which we now take responsibility for addressing the legacies of past wrongs.

Analysing diverse narratives of the Holocaust, for example, Saul Friedländer observes that each narrative offers a distinct perspective on responsibility. The conventional 'liberal interpretation', which focuses on the political and ideological dimensions of the rise of Nazism, emphasizes the guilt of political leaders, while also to some degree acknowledging the responsibility of the mass of German bystanders who failed to resist the Nazis. Friedländer contrasts this to a 'structuralist' narrative, which 'puts a much greater stress on the continuity of social structures, rooted in nineteenth-century Imperial Germany, that offered the necessary breeding ground for Nazism in its rise and development, structures that, more often than not still exist within the [then] West German republic' (Friedländer 1988, 69). This approach at once broadens the social range of responsibility for the Holocaust, and in some respects makes the location of specific guilt more difficult to pin down. A third, 'symmetric' narrative focuses on parallels between the crimes of the Nazis and those of others, particularly the Soviet Union. This approach, exemplified by the work of writers like Andreas Hillgrüber, suggests a symmetry of responsibility between Germans and their enemies, while tending to emphasize a division within German society between a small group of 'evildoers' and the mass of ordinary soldiers and civilians, who are depicted as victims rather than aggressors. Lastly, a fourth narrative (which Friedländer identifies with the writings of Ernst Nolte) presents Soviet atrocities as pre-dating and, in a sense, providing a model for Nazi atrocities, and thus seeks to shift the focus of responsibility away from the German nation altogether (Friedländer 1988; Nolte 1993a; Nolte 1993b; Hillgrüber 1993).

In the same way, the narratives of the Japanese past presented by the Society for History Textbook Reform are clearly intended to relieve a contemporary generation of Japanese from any sense of responsibility for pre-1945 colonialism and military expansion in Asia. They are in this sense diametrically opposed to the approach of historians like Yoshimi Yoshiaki, who uses careful archival research to document Japanese military and state involvement in crimes such as institutionalized rape (for example, Yoshimi 1995). They are also in stark contrast to the postcolonial narratives of scholars like Tomiyama Ichirô, Komagome Takeshi and Kang Sangjung, who, in different ways, explore both the complexities of Japanese colonialism and the structural and intellectual continuities linking prewar empire to the postwar Japanese state (Tomiyama 2002; Komagome 1998; Komagome 2001; Kang 2002). Each of these approaches, it may be noted, has slightly different implications for our understanding of historical responsibility. Yoshimi's work places greater emphasis on the specific guilt of particular individuals and institutions, while the postcolonial approach (rather like Friedländer's 'structuralist' approach) sees historical responsibility as deeply embedded in enduring social structures. Though both draw attention to the need to address historical responsibility for wartime aggression and colonial expansion, the first directs that attention primarily towards the need for the punishment of wrongdoers and the payment of compensation, while the second highlights the need to think how we might undo the legacies of past violence and discrimination which survive in contemporary political and social institutions and modes of thought. It points, in other words, towards that sense of connection to history which I shall (later in this chapter) describe as 'implication' in the legacies of the past.

In relation to events like the Holocaust or Japanese military expansion in Asia, treating all narratives as equally valuable – denying that one may be 'better history' than another – implies that we forgo the possibility that anyone should take responsibility for the past. If all narratives are equally true/untrue, it becomes impossible to determine who should redress the legacies of past wrongs, and therefore impossible to act in ways that address that responsibility. This problem of language, truth and responsibility is one which many historians and other scholars have recently considered (for example, Appleby, Hunt and Jacobs 1994; Takahashi 2001). Yet it remains a central dilemma of contemporary historical thought. Later in the chapter I shall return to this dilemma, but first I want to highlight another inherent limitation of the textbook debate.

Beyond the Text

A second key problem of the textbook debate is that it is all about textbooks. In other words, it focuses on the content of formal school history education, and in so doing often conveys the impression that this is what determines historical consciousness. But today, more than ever, we learn about the past from a multiplicity of media. To understand the conflicting views of the past that exist, for example, in Japan, Korea and China, or to understand the changing ways in which the Holocaust is remembered within Europe and worldwide, it therefore seems vitally important to look beyond textbooks, to the ways in which images of the past are framed by popular culture.

In the past decade or so, a growing number of scholars have examined the presentation of history in various media, including novels, photography, film, museums and heritage sites. Often, though, these studies are relatively isolated from one another, confined within the boundaries of a particular branch of media studies: the historical novel is studied in the framework of literary studies (for example, Cowart 1989; Moses 1995; Price 1999); the historical film is examined from the perspective of the history of cinema (Grindon 1994; Rosenstone 1995; Sobchack 1996; Fujita 1997; Landy 2001); the museum display is considered from the perspective of heritage studies (Lowenthal 1985; Wallace 1986; Simpson 1996; Hong 1999), etc. But as the media of historical expression multiply, so they increasingly interact with one another. Historical novels are made into films and TV mini-series; historical dramas on television generate accompanying museum displays; Internet web sites are developed to accompany historical documentaries. In this context, there is much to be gained from exploring the ways in which a variety of popular media of historical expression coexist and relate to one another. How do images presented in one medium echo or amplify those presented in others? How do historical stories change when they are transferred from one means of communication to another?

Popular conceptions of the past are swayed by certain mass-marketed narratives of history. Thus, for example, substantial groups of people in late nineteenth- and early twentieth-century Britain understood the 1745 Rising in Scotland in terms of a narrative shaped by Scott's Waverley novels, just as generations of Americans (and others) have perceived the history of the Civil War though lenses coloured by the lush imagery of Hollywood's *Gone With the Wind*. Many people today recall the assassination of President John F. Kennedy in ways influenced by Oliver Stone's movie *JFK*, while many members of the current young generation of Japanese people perceive the events of the Asia-Pacific War through imagery influenced by Kobayashi Yoshinori's comic books. Examining the form and power of these individual mass-media narratives is therefore profoundly important.

But, in exploring popular representations of history, I also want to go beyond an analysis of how specific mass-marketed narratives impact on perceptions of the past. I am particularly interested in the subtle ways in which popular media, by their silences as much as by what they present, shape our imaginative landscape of the past. Popular culture tends repeatedly to return to certain events and images, making particular parts of history familiar and vivid, while rendering others distant or unknown.

To understand how these imagined landscapes are created, reinforced or transformed, we need to look both at the political and at the aesthetic economy of mass media. In other words, in choosing to represent specific historical events, novelists, publishers, filmmakers and others are constrained by the economic rules of the market in which they operate. In the competitive world of cultural capitalism, they tend to produce works that they think will sell to a reasonably wide and affluent audience, and are therefore influenced by their preconceptions of what that audience knows and is interested in.

But they are also constrained by aesthetic conventions. Novels and feature films, for example, generally conform to a fairly standard format in terms of length and structure. Popular culture works its effects by drawing on deep reservoirs of shared memory: we can readily make sense of the plot of a Hollywood western or a courtroom drama because it follows the pattern of already familiar narratives; we are moved by photographs because they remind us of other images already seen elsewhere; semi-conscious stores of musical memory teach us instantly to recognize, in a few notes of theme music, whether this ushers in a moment of triumph, tenderness or terror.

To understand how a knowledge of the past is communicated in an age of mass media, it therefore becomes necessary to understand something of the way in which these conventions have been formed, and the way in which they shape the stories that can be told about the past. Each medium has its own history, its own conventions, its own store of memories. Our understanding of events like the rise of Hitler or the outbreak of the Korean War depends, not just on who is telling the story, but also on whether we encounter the story in a history textbook, a historical novel, a collection of photographs, a TV documentary or a feature film. In the pages that follow, we will explore some of the ways that media and memories shape one another as new forms of popular culture emerge and evolve.

Fractured Images and Anti-Narratives

The two central problems of the East Asian textbook debate – the problem of confronting historical responsibility in a 'postmodern' world and the problem of going beyond a narrow focus on textbooks – are closely interrelated, and lie at the heart of dilemmas faced by historians in many parts of the world. Hayden White, for example, points out that the rise of modern historiography was deeply connected to the authority and logic of the written narrative. But today, more than ever, a knowledge of the past is conveyed through media which do not follow conventional narrative forms: through film, TV 'docu-dramas', CD-roms, comic-books, Internet web pages and so on. Citing the example of Oliver Stone's film *JFK*, White argues that such media often intercut the 'real' and the 'imaginary' (documentary footage and dramatization, for example), so that the distinction between the two dissolves: 'Everything is presented as if it were of the same ontological order, both real and imaginary – realistically imaginary or imaginarily real, with the result that the referential function of the images of events is etiolated' (White 1996, 19). The style of a film like *JFK* also breaks up the narrative form in other ways: through repeated cross-cutting, frequent and deliberately disorienting flashbacks and flash-forwards, and the use of blurred or disturbingly close-up shots. As a result it becomes more and more difficult to conceive the historical 'event' as a coherent story.

At the same time, White argues, the events of recent history themselves, events like the Holocaust or the atomic bombing of Hiroshima and Nagasaki, have acquired an immensity – an indescribable quality – which threatens to overwhelm the possibilities of narrative history. He therefore concludes that 'not only are *modern* post-industrial "accidents" more incomprehensible than anything earlier generations could possibly have imagined (think of Chernobyl), the photo and video documentation of such accidents is so full that it is difficult to work up the documentation of any one of them as elements of a single "objective" story' (White 1996, 23). The only solution, White suggests, may lie in abandoning the narrative and adopting varying forms of 'anti-narrative non-story' as a way of representing key events of the recent past.

I have some reservations about White's emphasis on the unprece-dented nature of the changes he describes. White suggests, for instance, that the blurring of the line between history and fiction in a docu-drama like *JFK* is radically different from anything found in nineteenth- or early twentieth-century historical novels (White 1996, 18). But as early as the 1820s a novelist like Alessandro Manzoni was already interweaving the romance of his novel *The Betrothed* [*I Promesi Sposi*] with long quotations from convincing (though invented) seventeenth-century 'historical documents', while, as we shall see in the next chapter, a novel like Tolstoy's *War and Peace*, in its struggle to confront the causes of the Napoleonic War, eventually slides from fiction into the non-fictional form of a historiographical essay.

Conversely, one may question how far a late twentieth-century docu-drama like *JFK* represents a real break from the traditional narrative form. Despite its deliberately fragmented cinematic style, with repeated use of jump cuts, close shots and unexpected camera angles, the dramatic structure of *JFK* faithfully follows the conventions of Hollywood drama, as the lone hero (New Orleans District Attorney Jim Garrison, played by

Kevin Costner) battles his way to a courtroom denouement where he defends his cause, watched by the wondering eyes of his wife and son, and proclaims his commitment to upholding the American values of freedom and truth. The dramatic climax is reached when Garrison, with shaking voice, quotes to the jury Kennedy's words 'ask not what your country can do for you, but what you can do for your country'.

More broadly, postmodern scepticism about the historian's ability to represent the truth is itself less radically original than some of its advocates and critics suggest. Ever since the nineteenth century, after all, historians and philosophers have engaged in intense historical debate about the contentious connection between the infinitely complex lived experience of history itself and the stories we tell about that experience. Writing in the 1830s and 1840s, for example, Alessandro Manzoni, although he criticized the confusion of fact and fiction in the historical novel, also acknowledged the impossibility of a complete representation of 'the truth' in history itself. History, he observed, 'not only openly confesses doubt but, when necessary, promotes it, sustains it, and attempts to substitute it for false convictions.' Where the historical novel creates confusion and uncertainty, history creates doubt as a positive form of understanding. 'History makes you doubt because it intends to have you doubt, quite unlike the historical novel which encourages you to believe while at the same time removing what is necessary to sustain belief. In the doubt provoked by history, the mind comes to rest – if not quite at its goal, at least at the limit of its possibilities' (Manzoni 1984, 74).

The epistemological impossibility of grasping and representing historical facts in their entirety, too, was highlighted in the early decades of the twentieth century by the work of scholars like Benedetto Croce:

> There are no immobile facts nor can such things be envisaged in the world of reality … for example, the perception that the object in front of me is a stone, and that it will not fly away of its own accord like a bird at

the sound of my approach makes it expedient that I should dislodge it with my stick or my foot. The stone is really a process under way, struggling against the forces of disintegration and yielding only bit by bit, and my judgment refers to one aspect of its history. (Croce 1949, 32.)

Problems of the relationship between the 'real' and the 'imagined' are, in this sense, long-standing, though constantly reinterpreted by each generation.

Though I would question White's emphasis on the novelty of post-industrial interminglings of the 'real' and the 'imaginary', I want to draw on some of his insights into the formative influence of media on the historical imagination. The structure and conventions of particular media do have significant implications for the way that historical knowledge is communicated. The framing power of media, of course, is not a rigid technological determinism. The inherent characteristics of a CD-ROM or docu-drama can be exploited and developed to quite different effects to tell contrasting historical stories. The inventive novelist, filmmaker or comic-book artist can push the boundaries of the medium, and at times break the mould of convention in ways that expand the limits of historical conceptions. In later chapters we shall encounter some examples of such a redefinition of boundaries, and also consider the ways in which creative *combinations* of diverse media can be used to tell new stories about the past.

Yet it remains true that the everyday practices of the popular media come to embody conventions and characteristics that have a profound influence on the way in which we, as audiences, consume notions of history. In a multimedia age, then, it becomes especially important, not simply to produce better history textbooks, but to encourage students to understand how the visions of the past which they encounter in popular media are moulded by the nature of the media themselves.

History as Identification and History as Interpretation

The internal dynamics of different media have a particularly significant bearing on a problem that has been the subject of much recent debate: the problem of the relationship between 'memory' or 'commemoration' and 'history'. Pierre Nora suggests that the past couple of decades have witnessed an explosive multiplication in the number of commemorations, memorials and heritage sites, a 'commemorative bulimia' that has 'all but consumed all efforts to control it' (Nora 1998, 609). Nora relates this explosion to a shift in attitudes to the past 'from the historical to the remembered and from the remembered to the commemorative' (Nora 1998, 626). History as an interpretative 'science of the past' (albeit, in Jacques le Goff's words, a science characterized by an endless process of reconstitution) comes to be replaced by a quest to re-establish a personal connection with a vanishing heritage: 'A search for the one thread in the social fabric of the present that will permit direct contact with the irrevocably dead past' (Nora 1998, 626; see also Le Goff 1988, 190).

Nora's analysis highlights an important tension between two dimensions of history. From one perspective, the study of history is about interpretation: it is a search for knowledge which will enable us to understand the causal relationships between events, the genealogy of ideas and institutions, and the forces which produce change in human societies. But on the other hand, history is also a matter of identification. Our relationship with the past is not simply forged through factual knowledge or an intellectual understanding of cause and effect. It also involves imagination and empathy. Museums, heritage sites, historical novels and films (as well as many academic history texts), invite us to enter into an empathetic relationship with the people of the past: to imagine their experiences and feelings, mourn their suffering and deaths and celebrate their triumphs. Often, this identification with others in the past in turn becomes the basis for rethinking or reaffirming our own identity in the present. By remembering a particular piece of the past, by making it our own, we create our sense of belonging to a certain group of people – whether a nation, local society, ethnic minority or religious group. In this way we also define our place in a complicated and changing world. Indeed, it is the very act of historical commemoration that calls group identity into being. As Jos Perry puts it, 'We recollect, therefore we are' (Perry 1999).

It could be argued, in fact, that representations of the past have *always* involved both an intimate interconnection and a certain tension between interpretation and identification. Even the most unemotional and 'scientific' of historical texts, in elaborating their explanations of the dynamics of the past, commonly assume some sort of personal connection between their readers and that past. Certainly the nineteenth-century writings of historians like Macaulay and Michelet, as well as the novels of Scott and Hugo, sought not just to explain the past but also to commemorate its joys and horrors, to persuade readers to project their imaginations into the landscapes and experiences of past eras, and thus to form an empathetic link of identity between past and present generations.

The precise relationship between 'history as interpretation' and 'history as identification' (as I shall call them here) has, however, varied over time, and has been influenced by changes in the media through which historical knowledge is created and communicated. Some media (for example, the written text) seem readily adaptable to the tasks of interpretation and analysis; others (for example, the monument, the heritage site, the museum display) seem more readily given to tasks of evoking identification with the experiences of the past. Images like photographs or newsreel footage often possess great power to convey the terror, elation or confusion of particular historical events; but without accompanying scripts or narration they seldom tell us much about causes or effects. A feature film like *Gone with the Wind* or *JFK* presents a forceful narrative of one particular version of a historical event. The structure of the feature film, however, is not easily adapted to the task of offering the means to assess the reliability of its own narrative in comparison with possible alternative versions of the same event. CD-ROMs and Internet web sites have the power to combine visual images (photographs and snippets of documentary film, for example) with short written documents. They are thus useful means for providing access to historical archives or collections of testimonies. Yet their non-linear structure and their tendency to fragment information into screen-sized pages mean that they provide less scope for extended explanatory narratives relating one piece of the archive to another.

Implication in the Past

My argument here is not that 'history as interpretation' is preferable to 'history as identification' (or vice versa). In suggesting that some media may more readily be adapted to tasks of commemoration, and others to tasks of interpretation, I do not mean to imply that this makes some media inherently 'better' at communicating a knowledge of the past than others.

Rather, I want to start by acknowledging that our understanding of history is never just an intellectual matter; any encounter with the past involves feeling and imagination as well as pure knowledge. Since our knowledge of the past is something from which we derive personal identity, it also helps to determine how we act in the world. Indeed, I would argue that academic history has tended to be too wary of emotions, too prone to treat historical knowledge as though it were a form of pure reason existing beyond the sullying realms of passion, fear, hope or sheer pleasure. Part of the power of some of the more alarming forms of popular nationalist historiography, as well as of many popular media representations of the past, comes from their capacity to touch the emotions which scholarly history often represses.

What matters, then, is from the start to recognize the affective dimensions, as well as the interpretive dimensions, of history. It is important, in other words, to recognize the way that our knowledge of the past engages with our emotions and identity – and influences and is influenced by our actions – while trying to reflect more deeply on the causes and implications of those affects. Why do we feel more involved with some narratives of the past than others? Why do some images of past events move us profoundly, and others leave us cold? How does this affective engagement influence the way that we interpret the causes and consequences of events? How, in other words, are 'history as identification' and 'history as interpretation' intertwined? How is their interaction influenced by the media through which we learn about the past? How do these media thus affect the way in which we understand our personal connection to past events? In posing these questions, we can start to see how our encounters with images of the past in many media mould our sense of historical responsibility; or, as I would rather put it, influence our consciousness of being 'implicated' in the processes of history.

The word 'implication' is intended to suggest that our relationship to the past is one that involves something slightly different from, and rather more far-reaching than, 'historical responsibility' in the commonly used sense of the term. The people who perform acts of violence or oppression clearly have, in the accepted legal and moral sense, responsibility for the consequences of those actions. But, for example, Germans born after 1945 do not bear a direct legal responsibility for the Holocaust in quite the same way: they did not cause this horror to happen. Similarly, Japanese people born after 1945 do not bear a causal responsibility for the Nanjing Massacre, any more than British people born after the 1960s bear responsibility for the violence of

British colonialism in Asia and Africa, or recent migrants to Australia bear responsibility for massacres of Aborigines by colonial settlers.

But at the same time, these later generations are profoundly connected to the events of the past for several reasons. In the first place, later generations, though they may not have been responsible for causing historical acts of violence or oppression, are often beneficiaries of the results of those actions. To take one particularly clear example, recent court cases have highlighted the fact that some of the large German companies whose growth fuelled Germany's postwar economic miracle had derived part of their wealth from the use of Jewish and other slave labour during the Second World War. Leading corporate players in Japan's postwar economic miracle, including such names as the Kajima Construction Company and Mitsubishi Heavy Industries, similarly profited from the use of Korean and Chinese forced labour during the Pacific War (Suh and Takahashi 2000, 103–104). In this sense, many of those who have benefited from the economic successes of these corporations are in an indirect way beneficiaries of wealth derived from historical violence. Recent migrants to Australia (myself included) live on land which they could afford to buy, in part, because it was, many decades ago, forcibly seized from Aboriginal occupants whose descendents, in many cases, continue to suffer the material and psychological consequences of that dispossession. We are, in this sense, implicated in the wrongs of the past: accessories after the fact.

But we are also implicated in the past in a wider sense. We live enmeshed in structures, institutions and webs of ideas which are the product of history, formed by acts of imagination, courage, generosity, greed and brutality performed by previous generations. Often we are quite unconscious of the way in which these structures and ideas have come into being. Our lives thus continue to be shaped by the oppressive institutions built on a history of violence, and will continue to be so unless we act to change them. The prejudices which sustained past acts of aggression also live on into the present, and lodge themselves in the minds of the present generation unless we take active steps to remove them. Though we may not be responsible for such acts of aggression in the sense of having caused them, we are 'implicated' in them, in the sense that *they* cause *us*. Popular media are an important means by which we are drawn into this web of inherited ideas and images: through the mass media, retold stories about the past, with their burdens of pride, compassion, mourning, grief and hatred, live on in our minds, and have subtle but real effects on the ways in which we respond, or fail to respond, to events, including international crises, in the present.

In Search of Historical Truthfulness

Reflecting on our implication in the processes of history does not produce a single authoritative 'historical truth'. But I want to argue that it does require 'historical truthfulness' – an open-ended and evolving relationship with past events and people. In emphasizing the word 'truthfulness' rather than the word 'truth', I am trying to shift debate away from the sometimes arid arguments about the existence or non-existence of historical facts, and towards a focus on the processes by which people in the present try to make sense of the past. Drawing on the tradition of Croce and many others, I accept the proposition that history (like the stone) has a life outside the mind of the observer, but that this life can never fully be captured and expressed by human imagery or language. Rather than debating how far a particular representation of the past is 'true' – in the sense that it approximates closely to an absolute and finite reality – it may be more useful to try to assess the 'truthfulness' of the processes by which people create meaning about the past.

From this point of view, the communication of historical knowledge can be seen as a series of relationships between historical events, the people involved in recording and representing the events, and the people who subsequently consume an account of the past through various media. Historical truthfulness involves an effort to understand this chain of relationships: to trace, as far as possible, the series of mediations through which narratives and images of the past reach us, and why we respond to them as we do. In doing this we are confronted with the recognition that the stories and images we receive about the past are shaped by the ideas and interests of the people who communicate them, by the nature of the media through which they are communicated, and by our own position in the present. Such chains of relationships may create obscurity as well as clarity, incomprehension as well as under-standing, indifference as well as empathy. Almost inevitably, they create diversity: a multitude of differing accounts and images of the past. An examination of varied representations of the same event enables us to understand the forces that shape the communication of historical knowledge, and to draw on a richer range of knowledge as we seek to comprehend our own implication in the processes of history. Historical truthfulness thus involves a kind of ongoing dialogue, through which we listen to an expanding repertoire of voices from the past, tell and retell the stories that we have heard, and so define and redefine our position in the present. In this sense I want to suggest that it provides a possible starting point for combating historiographies of oblivion while accepting the impossibility of any complete and perfectly 'correct' representation of the past.

Going to the Independence Hall of Korea in April 2001, for example, was for me an encouraging experience because I went in the company of a group of postgraduate students, who were enthusiasti-cally comparing the version of history presented in the museum with the varied versions they had learnt in school, seen on the cinema screen or read in comic books. Some of the students came from Japan, and were confronted with a depiction of the past which radically contradicted the narratives with which they were familiar. Some were Korean students, who had visited the hall before on school outings, but were starting to see its version of history presented in its exhibitions with more critical eyes. As one observed, when she and her friends had visited the hall as schoolchildren, they had come away filled with feelings of anger and hatred towards Japan, but returning as an adult researcher in the company of people from other countries, she was more interested in exploring the relationship between signifier and signified in the complex nationalist imagery of the hall's displays and architecture. One student, of South Korean nationality but brought up in Japan, recalled his ambiguous feelings about the contrasting versions of the past which he had encountered in a Japanese school and in the Korean media. Another, from the North Korean affiliated community in Japan, was able to add her comments on the versions of history that she had learnt in her school, with their emphasis on transmitting the ideas of Kim Il Sung. In other words what was valuable was that, in visiting the Independence Hall, we encountered not just its predictable nationalist narrative of the past, nor just two counterposed Japanese and Korean versions of history, but a series of cross-cutting accounts and questions which helped to break up those grand narratives of the nation. Listening to these stories as I walked round the museum, I saw the exhibits in a subtly different light from the way in which I would have seen them had I gone there alone.

There are two ways in which popular media impinge on this process of attending to varied accounts of the past, and thus on the processes of historical truthfulness. First, the media employed shape the memories that are transmitted. To read about the past in a textbook, for example, is different from encountering it in the artifacts, photographs and dioramas of a museum like the Independence Hall. Truthfulness about the past requires reflection on the role that such media play in moulding our understanding of history. Second, popular media have the potential to give us access to a diverse range of voices and images of past events; to stand in others' shoes, to see the same event from several different angles.

Crossing Borders: History and Globalization

This creative use of different media to communicate history across national borders is particularly important in an age haunted by the sometimes wearisome spectre of globalization. Many writers have reminded us that globalization does not mean the demise of the nation state; but it does mean that people around the world find their everyday lives influenced by forces and institutions whose origins lie outside their national borders. More than ever, we are expected to make judgments about actions which, though carried out by our own governments, have consequences in distant parts of the world. Fleeting televised images of desperate refugees or of the mangled victims of suicide bombings, for example, evoke calls for international intervention in wars whose historical origins most people in the intervening countries have no knowledge of at all.

The study of national history alone is obviously inadequate to provide the understanding needed to make sense of this world. Indeed, I would suggest that we can no longer confidently define the syllabus of historical knowledge which would equip the next generation with the necessary understanding of the forces that have shaped their world. How do we know which parts of the past will seem pressingly relevant in ten years' time? How many Americans, in the early 1990s, would have imagined the relevance of knowing the ethnic and political origins of Afghanistan's factional rivalries? How many Thais would have anticipated a need (arising from their military's leading role in international peacekeeping activities) to understand centuries of Portuguese colonialism and decades of Indonesian occupation in East Timor?

What is important, then, is not simply to learn the history of the other. The problem is how to equip people with the power to use various media creatively in an endless process of relearning and reimagining history. Contemporary mass media give us a greater potential than ever before to transcend the narrow frontiers of national history. But making use of that potential is no simple matter. For media and imagination are intertwined in a complex dialectical spiral. As we shall see in the next chapter, ever since the rise of the historical novel at the start of the nineteenth century, the politics of the imagination and the internal dynamics of media have worked together to shape accounts of the past.

The dynamics governing the interaction between society and mass media are themselves transnational. The novels of Tolstoy and Walter Scott have influenced the historical imaginations of readers in Africa, Asia and Latin America. Images captured by the Japanese photographer Yamahata Yôsuke (see Chapter 3) reappear in Australian history books, New York art museums and San Francisco based Internet web sites. Steven Spielberg's Hollywood movie *Amistad* has been criticized by Sierra Leonian viewers, who note the very different way in which the Amistad story has come to be incorporated into the cultural life of their West African nation (see Chapter 4).

For this reason, it no longer makes sense to examine these forces within the comfortable and familiar bounds of national frontiers. The journey through media and historical imagination which I embark on here is therefore also a journey across borders. It is, of necessity, a somewhat idiosyncratic journey, shaped by the trajectory of my own life experiences and interests. The examples which I draw on are derived from Britain, the United States, Japan, Russia, Australia, the Philippines and to a lesser extent other places as well. I do not want to obliterate the differences between these varied geographical locations. While observing these differences, though, I feel that it is important to address the dilemmas of twenty-first century historical consciousness, not from the security of a single fixed point on the face of the globe, but from the perspective of that constant mobility which is a key feature of contemporary being. As they participate in this journey, I hope that readers will glimpse some signposts which may help to them make sense of their own multitudinous trajectories through the unfolding landscapes of the ever-present past.

2

Unimaginable Pasts:
The Horizons of Historical Fiction

> On the 12th of June 1812 the forces of Western Europe crossed the frontiers of Russia, and war began: in other words, an event took place counter to all the laws of human reason and human nature. Millions of men perpetrated against one another such innumerable crimes, deceptions, treacheries, robberies, forgeries, issues of false money, depredations, incendiarisms and murders as the annals of all the courts of justice in the world could not muster in the course of whole centuries, but which those who committed them did not at the time regard as crimes.

These lines from the opening paragraph of Book Three of *War and Peace* capture the central problem which tears at the fabric of Tolstoy's novel: what is the relationship between individual responsibility and the flow of history? What is the force that can impel multitudes of ordinary people, apparently with little hesitation, to perform deeds which, seen across the narrow divide of a few decades, appear so evil? At the 'infinitesimal' level of our own everyday life we think of ourselves as free and responsible beings, capable of telling right from wrong and able to choose the course of our own actions. But when we look at the 'ocean of history', with its vast movements of peoples, revolutions and wars, each person seems caught up in a tide of events which can never simply be reduced to the sum of individual decisions (Tolstoy 1978, 1339). Yet if human history is really the product of social forces beyond an individual's control, how can we make an assessment of the individual's actions in the past, or give any historical meaning to the choices we make in the present? The narrative of *War and Peace*, in other words, struggles with the central problem of linking an interpretive under-standing of the events of history to an imaginative empathy for the people who participated in those events.

This problem came to obsess Tolstoy more and more as he wrote his sprawling narrative of Russia during the Napoleonic Wars. Originally conceived as an exploration of the manners and mores of early nineteenth-century civilian society, *War and Peace* gradually evolved, over the six years of its composition, into a novel whose dramatic focus lies in a sweeping depiction of the Battle of Borodino. This shift was influenced by the fact that Tolstoy was writing in the years immediately following the fiftieth anniversary of the battle. Just as the fiftieth anniversary of the end of the Second World War inspired intense controversies about the memory and meaning of that historical cataclysm, so too the fiftieth anniversaries of the events of the Napoleonic Wars provoked debate over the interpretation of a traumatic experience which was rapidly fading from living memory and becoming reinscribed in the realms of history (Gifford 1982, 27; Petrov 1960).

Tolstoy attempted to address the question of historical responsi-bility, on the one hand by entering imaginatively into the lives and thoughts of participants on both sides of the battle, but on the other also by searching on the grand scale for an understanding of 'the force that moves nations' (Tolstoy 1978, 1404). In the end, his struggle to forge these two dimensions of history into a logical whole forced him to go beyond the realms of fiction altogether, into the philosophical and historiographical musings which fill the epilogue to *War and Peace*. Here he attempted to find some resolution to the contradiction between his profound awareness of the complexity of individual human experiences and feelings, and his characteristically nineteenth-century intellectual faith in the existence of scientific laws governing human society.

The historical epilogue to *War and Peace* has failed to convince most readers, not just because of its rambling and ponderous style, but also because its conclusions seem so obviously at odds with the rest of the novel. Tolstoy's historical logic impels him towards the conclusion that Napoleon and Alexander I, as much as everyone else, were pawns caught up in the 'unconscious, universal, swarm-life of mankind' (Tolstoy 1978, 718). But as readers, we are transported to the battlefield of Borodino by the force of Tolstoy's imagination. We feel the prolonged agonies of death in war through the emotions of Andrei Bolkonsky, and experience the transforming moment when he recognizes a common humanity in the sufferings of his personal enemy Anatoly Kuragin. And on the very next page we enter into the reflections of Napoleon, surveying the carnage of battle, and fighting off a spontaneous impulse towards grief and compassion so that he can rejoice in the fact that among the piles of dead on the battlefield there are five Russians to every Frenchman (Tolstoy 1982, 968–969). Tolstoy, in other words, invites us to sense the infinite importance of the 'infinitesimal' personal experience of history, and to empathize with, or be repelled by, individual responses to particular historical events. David Price has argued that Tolstoy's search for a new philosophy of history in *War and Peace* ends in failure, 'but it is a glorious failure' (Price 1999, 5). It is also one which helps to illuminate both the power and the limitations of the realist historical novel.

History as Mass Experience

There was nothing new, of course, about reimagining the events of history in the form of a popular narrative. Epic poems and dramas in many parts of the world invited audiences to relive the joys and sorrows of half-remembered historical events, and explained (or, as Alessandro Manzoni argued, invented) the causes of these events in terms of human vices and virtues, destiny or the will of the gods (Manzoni 1984, 83). Epics like the Homeric tales, the mediaeval European tales of chivalry, the Chinese *Epic of the Three Kingdoms* or the thirteenth-century Japanese *Tale of Heike* were repeatedly passed on, retold and re-enacted in different social settings, helping to create a community of the historical imagination amongst a wide range of people. In Elizabethan England, the dramas of Shakespeare and his contemporaries drew on a stock of familiar historical tales in search of material to express a new fascination with individual character, motivation and moral dilemmas. The human vices and virtues – ambition, pride, determination, discretion – which the epics present as the origin of historic triumphs and tragedies, were now explored with far greater psychological depth. This link made between individual subjectivity and the great events of history foreshadowed the shape of the historical novel, and was to provide a major source of inspiration for early historical novelists like Walter Scott and Alessandro Manzoni.

But the nineteenth-century realist historical novel, which first appeared about half a century before Tolstoy wrote *War and Peace* – that is, at the very time of the Napoleonic Wars – reshaped the historical imagination in several profoundly important ways. First, as has often been pointed out, the historical novel tended to focus on the deeds and emotions of (usually fictional) 'ordinary people'. The great figures of history, if they appeared on the scene at all, generally came into view fleetingly on the periphery of the novel's action, as Napoleon does in *War and Peace*. The archetypal example is Scott's enormously influential novel *Waverley*, published in 1814, two years after the Battle of Borodino. *Waverley* offers its readers an unheroic hero, whose very name is chosen to sound ordinary. The novel creates an image of a past society (in this case, Scotland at the time of the 1745 Rising) peopled by a throng of thinking, feeling individuals whose lives, as much as the lives of great leaders, are entwined with the events of the age. Scott thus invites his largely middle-class readership, comprising those with the education and time to read his often convoluted prose, into a new relationship with the people of the past: here are individuals like you and me, with whom we can empathize, laugh and cry, whose ethics are open to our scrutiny, whose actions we can applaud or condemn.

But the issue is not simply the emerging focus on the historical role of the ordinary man (or, more rarely, ordinary woman); it is also the special ability of the novel to flesh out a picture of society. Here the contrast with Shakespearian drama is particularly telling. As George Lukács observed in his classic study of the historical novel, drama tended to 'reduce the world of human action to pure and direct relations of people to one another. The mediating role of things, institutions etc., is confined to a minimum; they appear simply as props, background etc., and play no dramatic part at all' (Lukács 1983, 119). The historical novel, on the other hand, provided a 'kind of concretization of the *here and now*' of a past age (Lukács 1983, 118). Its essence lay not just in its characterization of past emotions, but in a capacity to create word-pictures of society as a living totality: to evoke the sights and sounds, the feelings and structures, of a mediaeval town, an eighteenth-century highland village, or a Napoleonic battlefield in all their complexity. So, for instance, Victor Hugo's *Notre Dame de Paris* (1830) uses the vantage point of the tower of Notre Dame to offer his readers an extraordinarily detailed delineation of the social, as well as the spatial, landscape of fifteenth-century Paris. Similarly, Edward Bulwer Lytton turns the urban geography of Pompeii into a figurative image of the whole structure of ancient Roman society:

> Pompeii was the miniature of the civilization of that age. Within the narrow compass of its walls was contained, as it were, a specimen of every gift which luxury offered to power. In its minute but glittering shops, its tiny palaces, its baths, its forum, its theatre, its circus – in the energy yet corruption, in the refinement yet the vice, of its people, you beheld a model of the whole empire. (Lytton 1879, 10.)

This apprehension of the social whole is crucial because it is precisely this quality which allows the notion of *social change* to become integral to the historical novel. The sense of time in epics like the *Tale of Heike* and in Shakespearian drama is less a vision of change than an aching consciousness of transience. But for Scott, this grasp of the passing of time has taken on a quite different meaning:

> Like those who drift down the stream of a deep and smooth river, we are not aware of the progress we have made until we fix our eye on the now distant point from which we have been drifted. Such of the present generation as can recollect the last twenty or twenty-five years of the eighteenth century, will be fully sensible of the truth of this statement. (Scott 1829, 348.)

Earlier historical epics had used the fate of individuals, or meditations on the transience of life, to capture a sense of the past. But the realist historical novel embodies this perception of history in accounts of the changing material world of society, whether that society is presented as progressing or as lapsing into disorder and decay. The nation is thus seen as having a historical momentum which is intimately entwined with the private lives of the multitudinous human individuals of whom society is composed.

Lukács saw the origins of this transformation as lying precisely in the events of the French Revolution and the ensuing Napoleonic Wars. The key element in these events was broad social participation, first in the revolution itself, and then in the new mass armies created during the post-revolutionary wars: 'It was the French Revolution, the revolutionary wars and the rise and fall of Napoleon, which for the first time made history a *mass experience*, and moreover on a European scale' (Lukács 1983, 23; italics in original). The movement of enormous armies across the face of Europe allowed, or rather forced, many people to see themselves as participants in the shaping of national history. It also sharpened their sense of national belonging by exposing them to the experience of foreign places – 'hence the concrete possibilities for men to comprehend their own existence as something historically conditioned, for them to see in history something which deeply affects their daily lives and immediately concerns them' (Lukács 1983, 24).

But at the same time the period of the revolution and the Napoleonic Wars was also an age of interiority, when the arts in Western Europe were becoming increasingly concerned with exploring the inner workings of the mind. This convergence of a new vision of individual subjectivity and a growing consciousness of mass involvement in the flow of national history opened a space for the rise of the historical novel. For a growing stratum of readers in the nineteenth and twentieth centuries, then, the historical novel created a new form of empathetic identification with the events of the past. The novel presented the past as a social phenomenon – a process of change – in which the living experience of all individuals was bound up. This vision has two effects. It encourages people to project the processes of the past into the present, and to see their own lives as shaped by the forces of history. At the same time it also encourages them to direct their personal consciousness backwards in time, and to see the actions of ordinary people in the past, including those of their own ancestors, as contributing to the course of historical events in ways which are open to imaginative reconstruction and ethical scrutiny. In this way, it opens up all those dilemmas about the relationship between individual and national pasts which so troubled Tolstoy as he wrote *War and Peace*.

The realist historical novel, in other words, created a new form of imaginative link between its audience in the present and the people of the past. Rather than merely encouraging its readers to identify with the triumphs or suffering of historical heroes, it enabled them, by immersing themselves in the narratives of individual lives, to identify with the past of an entire – usually national – society, envisaged as a geographically bounded entity changing through time. By threading individual lives into the fabric of national social change, the historical novel exerted an influence which went beyond the bounds of the novel to influence (amongst other things) the writing of history itself. We can see its effects not just in the popularity of twentieth-century 'non-fictional novels' – dramatic reconstructions of historical incidents, like Cecil Woodham Smith's *The Reason Why* or Barbara Tuchman's *The Zimmerman Telegram* – but also in the style used by a new generation of romantic historians from the 1840s onward: a style exemplified by Thomas Babington Macaulay, whose *History of England* (1848–1861) reflects his profound admiration for Scott's novels (see Trevor-Roper 1986, 19). Consider, for example, Macaulay's account of the aftermath of the Battle of Sedgemoor in 1685. Here, as well as putting into practice his avowed aim of enlivening the factual narrative with 'the details which are the charm of historical romances', Macaulay, like any good nineteenth-century historical novelist, invites his readers to see the events of the past through the eyes of the imagined 'common citizen', the anonymous face in the crowd of history:

It was four o'clock: the sun was rising; and the routed army came pouring into the streets of Bridgewater. The uproar, the blood, the gashes, the ghastly figures which sank down and never rose again, spread horror and dismay through the town … During the day the conquerors continued to chase the fugitives. The neighbouring villagers long remembered with what a clatter of horsehooves and what a storm of curses the whirlwind of cavalry swept by. (Macaulay 1986, 100; see also Trevor-Roper 1986, 19.)

At the same time, though, the historical novel did not simply create a sense of imaginative empathy with the past, it also provided implicit interpretations of the causes, meaning and consequences of past events. Scott's *Waverley*, for example, despite its nostalgia for vanished Scottish Highland traditions, is ultimately an optimistic story of nation-building, in which the pain and cruelties of conflict between Scotland and England are to be transcended by a union between the two societies. The marriage of the Englishman Waverley to his Scottish bride Rose Bradwardine in the book's final pages prefigures the creation of a new Britain where 'the gradual influx of wealth, and extension of commerce' will totally transform the nature of Scottish society (Scott 1829, 348). In much the same way, Scott's later novel *Ivanhoe* depicts the mediaeval emergence of an English nation out of the conflict between 'the Saxons, by whom the soil was still cultivated, and the Normans, who still reigned as conquerors, reluctant to mix with the vanquished, or acknowledge themselves of the same stock' (Scott 1962, vii). Just as the marriage of the English hero and Scottish heroine in the closing pages of *Waverley* celebrates the eighteenth-century birth of the new Britain, so the marriage in the closing chapter of *Ivanhoe* celebrates the birth of a new England in the twelfth century. For although both Ivanhoe and his bride are Saxons, the wedding is blessed by the Norman king and 'the high-born Normans, as well as Saxons, joined with the universal jubilee of the lower order, that marked the marriage of two individuals as a pledge of future peace and harmony betwixt two races, which, since that period, have been so completely mingled that the distinction has become wholly invisible' (Scott 1962, 436).

The interpretations of past events embedded in the historical novel have, in a sense, particular power to influence the readers' understanding of history precisely because these interpretations remain implicit, inseparably interwoven into a narrative of fictional lives. In a history text, the historian's reading of the past is at the foreground of the narrative, and therefore more readily open to scrutiny and questioning. In a novel, our attention tends to be focused on the fates of individual characters, so that the background interpretations of history are often absorbed almost unconsciously. It is only with the coming of new and experimental forms of the historical novel in the twentieth century that some authors begin deliberately to expose their versions of the past to questioning, as John Fowles does in his novel of nineteenth-century England *The French Lieutenant's Woman* – a narrative which offers its readers the choice between two possible endings with different implications for our understanding of Victorian society.

Marking Time

Above all, the historical novel offers implicit interpretations of the past in the sense that it encourages its readers to become familiar with, and so to appreciate the importance of, particular eras and places rather than others. The action of a novel takes place in a circumscribed place and time. A few historical novels may explore the fortunes of families over several generations, and a handful attempt more ambitious temporal odysseys – one striking recent example being Adam Thorpe's *Ulverton*, which speaks through the voices of an English village across the course of three and a half centuries (Thorpe 1993). Most commonly, however, the narrative spans a few decades at most, and events occur in a clearly specified location or set of connected locations. In this way, the novel helps to construct a particular mental landscape of history, so that readers become more conscious of certain historical periods and places than others, more readily able to identify with some fragments of the past than with others.

In the introduction to *Waverley*, Scott offers an extended explanation, not only of the novel's title, but also of its subtitle: *'Tis Sixty Years Since*. The choice of this subtitle, he observes, required even more 'grave and solid deliberation' than the choice of the title itself, for its words 'may be held as pledging the author to some special mode of laying his scene, drawing his characters, and managing his adventures' (Scott 1829, 1). By placing the action of *Waverley* in events sixty years past, Scott was consciously attempting a radical experiment with the form of the novel. As he argues in the introduction, the events of sixty years ago are neither remote enough to seem romantically exotic, nor recent enough to appeal to the reader's interest in novelty and fashion. Choosing a setting sixty years in the past therefore makes it difficult for the novelist to offer a mere spectacle of fashions and manners, and instead channels attention towards the psychology of the main characters. It requires Scott to throw

> The force of my narrative upon the characters and passions of the actors;
> – those passions common to men in all stages of society, and which have
> alike agitated the human heart, whether it throbbed under the steel corslet
> of the fifteenth century, the brocaded coat of the eighteenth, or the blue
> frock and white dimity waistcoat of the present day. (Scott 1829, 3.)

In other words, by writing of historical upheavals experienced by the previous generation, and still remembered by some people in his own day, Scott feels able to express a vision of social transformation through the minds and personalities of characters with whom his readers can personally identify, and so to create a powerful sense of a continuum between past and present and between nation and individual.

James Cahalan, in his study of Irish historical fiction, points out that (like *Waverley*) many of Ireland's best-known historical novels are set in the time of the previous generation – that is, in a period about fifty to seventy years before the novel was written (Cahalan 1983, 21). The same can be said of many of the most influential historical novels. Tolstoy, of course, explored events sixty years past in *War and Peace*, while Dickens's *A Tale of Two Cities*, set during the French Revolution, was written in the 1850s. James Fenimore Cooper's *The Last of the Mohicans,* published in 1826, is, as its subtitle proclaims, 'A Narrative of 1757'. Writing in late 1920s and early 1930s Japan, Shimazaki Tôson chose to locate *Yoake mae* [*Before the Dawn*], his epic novel of the events surrounding the Meiji Restoration of 1868, precisely in the lifetime of the previous generation: its narrative is largely drawn from the life of his father Masaki, on whom the main character of the novel is based. One of the most influential of postwar Japanese historical novels, Shiba Ryôtarô's *Saka no ue no kumo* [*The Cloud Above the Hill*] published in serial form in the late 1960s, focuses on the period of the Russo-Japanese War of 1904–1905. In the West African context, Chinua Achebe's pioneering novel *Things Fall Apart*, published on the eve of Nigerian independence in 1959, deals with the coming of Western colonization in the 1890s.

Indeed, the literary critic Alfred Sheppart once argued that historical novels should ideally look back about half a century (Cahalan 1983, 21). Since the essence of the classic historical novel lies in its ability to persuade its readers to identify with the characters of a past age, there are obvious advantages to dealing with a period of the past which is recent enough to evoke reminiscences and emotions, but distant enough for intense antagonistic passions to have subsided. By choosing a setting half a century or so before the present, the creative writer can capture the elusive relationship between the individual and society at a moment when a particular fragment of the past is slipping over the horizon from memory into history.

But a sense of the connection to the past can also be aroused by more distant events. In the history of many nations, there are certain founding or transforming moments which remain subjects of continuing historical fascination, and whose raw material is mined by generation after generation of historical novelists as they, from their changing perspectives in the present, seek to rediscover the roots of their social being. So the Elizabethan era and the Civil War in England and the 1789 Revolution in France provide perennial themes for historical novels. In the United States, the American Civil War and the subjugation of native American society (whether presented as triumph or tragedy) have provided the setting for countless works of fiction. Similarly, the 1798 rising and the 1916 Easter Rising in Irish literature, the centralization of political power in the late sixteenth century and the events leading up to the 1868 Meiji Restoration in Japanese literature, and the 1890s revolution against Spain in Philippine literature appear again and again as the location for popular historical novels.

Maria Martinez-Sicat, in her study *Imagining the Nation in Four Philippine Novels*, shows how the events of the revolution against Spain and the subsequent resistance to US colonization in the 1890s have been retold and reordered by generations of Philippine novelists. Her study focuses on four influential writers, from Maximo Kalaw, whose 1920s novel *The Filipino Rebel* explored the social and psychological reasons for the failure of the struggle for independence, to Alfred Yuson, whose magical realist *Great Philippine Jungle Energy Café*, published in 1988, moves back and forth between the Marcos era and the 1890s, concluding with a transcendental reunion in a pseudo-tropical café where nineteenth-century nationalist heroes such as José Rizal and Leon Kilat sip Irish coffees with the likes of James Dean and John Lennon

(Martinez-Sicat 1994; Kalaw 1964; Yuson 1988). Despite their radically different treatments of the theme, though, these novels, Martinez-Sicat argues, share certain common elements. Not only are they all written in the language of the colonizer – English – they also all tend to focus on the role of the elite in the revolution, and to emphasize the struggle against a foreign enemy rather than the internal inequalities between exploiters and exploited (Martinez-Sicat 1994, 123–127). Equally important, the repeated return to the same moments of history helps to fix these moments in the minds of readers as familiar and readily recognizable events, part of a stock of shared historical knowledge which helps to bind together a particular reading public.

Though certain founding moments – revolutions, wars of independence – may provide enduring reference points for the historical novel, other settings are chosen neither because of their chronological relationship to the present nor because of their intrinsic position in national history, but because they suggest implicit analogies with contemporary political or social concerns. In many times and places, recorded history has been likened to a mirror. The triumphs and tragedies of the past offer reflections on the present. Reading about these past events helps us to step back from our own period and observe it with the eye of a historian, perceiving recurrent patterns in human behaviour across time. In a similar way, the pioneers of the modern historical novel soon discovered that the past was a rich source of metaphors for modern society.

The use of history as a trope helps to explain changing fashions in the setting for historical novels. In mid-nineteenth-century Britain, for example, imperial parallels encouraged a fashion for literature set in ancient Rome: exemplified by now little-read works like Macaulay's *Lays of Ancient Rome* and Edward Bulwer Lytton's *The Last Days of Pompeii*. It is no coincidence that a similar enthusiasm for imperial Roman themes was to characterize the Hollywood movies of the 1950s, nor that both

Macaulay and Lytton combined their literary activities with political careers which included significant roles as colonial administrators.

The impulse to use the past as a mirror for the present seems to intensify in particular eras – in times of imperial expansion, or in periods and places where restrictions on free expression encourage allegorical forms of fiction. Pushkin, for example, seeking discreet means to urge Tsar Nicholas I to adopt reformist policies in the wake of the failed Decembrist Rising of 1825, found a valuable metaphor in the reforms of Peter I – a subject which he explored in his unfinished but influential historical novel *Arap Petra Velikogo* [*Peter the Great's Moor*], which was posthumously published in 1837 (Petrov 1960, 52–53). One of the earliest studies of the historical novel in Japan, Iwakami Junichi's *On Historical Literature* [*Rekishi bungaku ron*], written at the height of the Pacific War, observes how changing cultural and political circumstances in Japan encouraged an increasing fashion for using the historical novel as a source of allegories for the present.

Pioneers of modern historical fiction in Japan, like Mori Ôgai, had drawn on the rich tradition of popular historical narratives consumed by the townspeople of the Edo period (1603–1867). Mori's work, while attempting to reconstruct and enter into the psychological world of the past, was marked by a scrupulous, indeed increasingly obsessive, attention to historical fact. His best-known historical tales, including novellas such as *The Abe Family* [*Abe Ichizoku*, 1913] and *Incident at Sakai* [*Sakai jiken*, 1914], deal with real people and incidents and are closely based on historical sources, although they also seek to explore the inner motives and emotions of their characters (Dilworth and Rimer 1977). Mori thus helped to establish a tradition of historical *shôsetsu* (the Japanese word *shôsetsu* in this context being similar but not precisely equivalent in meaning to the English word 'novel') closely resembling the historical reconstructions of English and American writers like Cecil Woodham Smith and Barbara Tuchman, who are usually regarded as writers of popular history rather than as historical novelists. (On the relationship between fact and fiction in Mori's work, see Ôoka 1974, 145–148; Bowring 1979, 217–224.) This tradition was, in the postwar period, to provide a basis for the immense popularity of the works of writers like Shiba Ryôtarô and Inoue Yasushi: historical reconstructions that are often based on the lives of real people and written in a form which persuades their readers that they are based on extensive historical research.

During the 1920s and 1930s, however, there was, as Iwakami Junichi points out, a growing tendency to contemporize the past – selecting and rewriting historical narratives in a way which echoed the political concerns of the day (Iwakami 1942, 201–206). Although Iwakami does not cite this particular instance, a striking example is Yoshikawa Eiji's best-selling samurai epic *Miyamoto Musashi*, serialized in a leading national newspaper between 1935 and 1939. Here Yoshikawa develops an account of the life of the noted seventeenth-century swordsman Shinmen Takezô, alias Miyamoto Musashi, into a parable which precisely fits the campaigns of 'spiritual mobilization' being promulgated by the government in the late 1930s against a background of the Japanese invasion of China and growing political tensions with the West. In the later sections of the novel, Miyamoto's rival Sasaki Kojirô becomes the representative of technology or physical skill (widely identified in late 1930s nationalist writings with the West), while Miyamoto (whose swordsmanship draws on Zen philosophies) becomes the representative of the superior power of the national spirit. In the concluding pages, Musashi triumphs over Kojirô because 'Kojirô had put his confidence in the sword of strength and skill [while] Musashi trusted the sword of the spirit' (Yoshikawa 1971, 970). The effect of this on readers was all the more intense because the final episodes of the novel, with their dramatic account of Musashi's voyage to Kojirô's island stronghold, were appearing in the *Asahi* newspaper at the same moment as, and alongside, reports of the Japanese invasion of Hainan Island in southern China and of the first clashes between Japanese and Soviet troops in Nomonhan (Aida 1986, 179–181). Through the writing of *Miyamoto Musashi*, Yoshikawa not only 'contemporized' the past but also helped to create the foundations for an enduringly influential set of myths about the nature of Japanese tradition – myths later taken up by some cultural theorists in Japan and abroad in the attempt to explain the sources of Japan's postwar economic expansion.

Landscapes of the Mind

The historical novel, then, creates a new form of empathetic link between past and present, between the lives of readers and an imagined image of the society of the past. But at the same time it also frames that society spatially, most often in terms of the nation state. In this way, it has been one of the chief vehicles through which the peoples of modern times were encouraged to imagine the past in national terms. Both modern history writing and the modern novel itself are inextricably linked to processes of nation-building. As Benedict Anderson shows with inimitable style, the nineteenth-century novel creates a sense of *simultaneity* – of multiple lives running parallel to one another, linked only by the fact that they are embedded in the same national society (Anderson 1991, 24–32). Novelists like Scott, Dickens, Tolstoy and Shimazaki, cutting back and forth from one parallel narrative to another within the pages of the same novel, build up a sense of the nation as a complex entity, made up of a multitude of coexisting layers and localities. This process of nationalizing 'history as identification' in turn subtly affects the scope and nature of the interpretations we bring to the epistemology of history.

In many cases, the historical novel is also a novel of travel, whose hero traverses the landscape, drawing together key points in the nation's history. The Japan of Shimazaki Tôson's *Before the Dawn*, for example, is a landscape held together by roads – the great highways of the Edo age, which form the sinews of his narrative and provide the background to much of the novel's action. The novel's plot centres on the life of one of the many post houses which acted as nodes of transport and communication along the highways. As Narita Ryûichi points out, this allows Shimazaki continuously to draw together the local and the national – the life of the mountainous rural community where the novel's main characters live and the events of the wider world, reported through the steady stream of news that travellers bring to the post house (Narita 2001, 34–35). The main characters of *War and Peace*, meanwhile, move along the trajectory of Napoleon's advance and retreat, and also traverse the landscape between Moscow and St. Petersburg, and between the two cities and the Russian countryside, represented by the Bolkonsky's estates of Bald Hills and Bogucharovo. This enables Tolstoy to develop a complex picture of the national space: the frivolous social life of the urban elite; the ordered rural world of Bald Hills with its 'English' park and ornamental garden; and the simpler village society of Bogucharovo – the world of 'steppe-peasants', of harsh but unpretentious lives and stubborn folk wisdom.

But the language of the novel also enables Tolstoy from time to time to perform a dramatic switch of perspective, an almost vertiginous ascent from the intimate details of the Moscow salon or the 'steppe-peasant's' cottage to a sweeping bird's eye view of the nation. All at once we step back from the infinitesimal level of individual lives and see the map of Europe unfurl before us:

> The invasion streams eastward and reaches its final goal – Moscow. The capital is taken: the Russian army suffers heavier losses than the enemy ever suffered in previous wars from Austerlitz to Wagram … A counter-movement follows, from east to west, bearing a remarkable resemblance to the preceeding movement from west to east … there is the same

coalescence into a group of colossal proportions; the same adhesion of the peoples of Central Europe to the movement; the same hesitation midway and the same velocity as the goal is approached. Paris, the ultimate goal, is reached. (Tolstoy 1978, 1347.)

This map transforms the characters of the novel into specks of life within the grand destiny of nations, but at the same time creates a distinctive vision of Europe. The landscape here is not the patchwork quilt of many nations that appears in the standard nineteenth-century atlas. Rather (as in so much nineteenth-century Russian social thought) it becomes a world divided by a single great boundary-line: the line between Russia and the West: a West whose centre of gravity lies in Paris. The peoples of central Europe, meanwhile, appear not as nations with their own tenacious sense of territory, but as shifting masses pulled back and forth between the magnetic forces of Russia and the West.

National maps play an important part in historical fiction, often appearing in the opening pages to fix the boundaries of the novel's action. One of the most memorable instances of this cartographical *mise en scène* is surely the opening passage of Shiba Ryôtarô's *The Cloud Above the Hill* [*Saka no ue no kumo*]:

A very small country begins to open itself to the world. One of the islands of this archipelago is Shikoku, which is divided into the regions of Sanuki, Awa, Tosa and Iyo. The chief town of Iyo is Matsuyama. Its castle is Matsuyama Castle. The castle town has a population (including samurai) of thirty thousand. In the centre of the town is a hill shaped like an inverted cauldron ... In ancient times, this castle was the largest castle in Shikoku, but because the surrounding landscape was extraordinarily beautiful, neither its stone walls nor towers looked stern or forbidding. The main character of this story might be said to be the small Japan of those times, but in any case, we will trace the footsteps of three people. One of these three was a writer of *haiku* poetry. Masaoka Shiki was the originator of a revival which brought new styles to the old Japanese forms of short poem, the *haiku* and *tanka*. In 1895, Shiki went back to his home town. (Shiba 1965, Vol. 1, 1–2.)

With a deliberately spare, almost childlike, simplicity of style, Shiba allows the reader's eye to travel inward from the outlines of the nation to region and town, and finally to the figure of Masaoka Shiki returning to his birthplace, Matsuyama. In the process, he not only equates his three main characters with the nation itself, but also gives Japan a particular location in global geography. It is a 'very small country': a tiny scattering of islands opening itself to the world. So the novel's opening words set up an image of Japan, not as the expanding empire which it was to be by the first decade of the twentieth century, but as the minnow which, by Volume 8 of the novel, is to take on and defeat the leviathan of the Russian empire. This particular image of the nation coincided rather readily with the dominant imagery of national identity in the postwar decades when Shiba was writing – decades when memories of imperial expansion were overlaid by the reinvention of Japan as a small and peaceable country poised on the divide between the great powers of the Cold War (Narita 1998).

Descriptions of place can create a sense of national unity, not just across space but also across time. In *Notre Dame de Paris* Victor Hugo draws his readers into the imagined world of the fifteenth century above all by his sense of the physical continuity of the city of Paris, and of its centrepiece the cathedral of Notre Dame, where 'every surface, every stone … is a page of the history, not only of the country but also of science and art' (Hugo 1902, 108). Paris, indeed, is as much the main character of Hugo's novel as Japan is the main character of Shiba's. Repeatedly overlaying his descriptions of mediaeval Paris with accounts of more recent changes to the city's architecture, Hugo is able both to lament the intrusion of the modern into the Parisian landscape, and to create an overwhelming sense of continuity, even of community, between past and present inhabitants of the city. His novel exhorts Parisians to *see* the past all around them:

> Conjure up the Paris of the fifteenth century; rebuild it in imagination; look through that amazing forest of spires, towers and steeples ... project sharply against an azure horizon the Gothic profile of old Paris; let its outline float in a wintry mist clinging round its numerous chimneys; plunge it in deepest night, and watch the fantastic play of light and shadow in that somber labyrinth of edifices ... let it stand out more rigid and jagged than a shark's jaw against a coppery sunset sky – and then compare. (Hugo 1902, 134.)

Crossable and Uncrossable Boundaries

Yet although national maps play a central role in historical fiction, it is also interesting to observe the way in which the historical novel at times *transcends* national boundaries. By considering which frontiers can, and which cannot, readily be crossed, we can gain a sense of the imaginative limits of historical fiction, and the political forces which shape the individual's feeling of relatedness to particular histories. Scott's novels – not just *Waverley* but also later bestsellers like *Rob Roy* and *The Bride of Lammermoor* – helped to create the nineteenth-century fashion for historical fiction and were, despite their Scottish theme, enormously popular on both sides of the Scots border, thus establishing the Scottish Highlands as a favoured setting for the British historical novel. During the nineteenth and early twentieth centuries many writers borrowed elements of Scott's Highland narratives and landscapes. Popular novels like Robert Louis Stevenson's *Kidnapped* (1886) and *The Master of Ballantrae* (1889) helped to fix the 'wild, bleak' landscape of the

Highlands, with its rocks, heather-clad hills and rushing mountain torrents, in the imagination of English as well as Scottish readers, and to make the events surrounding the 1715 and 1745 Risings familiar parts of the British historical narrative.

But nineteenth-century British historical novels also ventured beyond national boundaries, into, for example, the seventeenth- and eighteenth-century Paris of Stanley J. Weyman's *Under the Red Robe* (1894) and Dickens's *A Tale of Two Cities*. It is true that Dickens and Weyman depicted French history as unmistakably 'foreign', whereas a novel like *Ivanhoe* presents its characters as 'our forefathers' and the languages they speak as the precursors to 'our present English language' (Scott 1962, xxiii and 31). Yet it could still be assumed that the intrigues of Richelieu or the moral conflicts of the French revolutionaries would be sufficiently familiar to middle-class English readers to hold their interest, and sufficiently imaginable to evoke their emotions.

As well as seventeenth- and eighteenth-century France, mediaeval and Renaissance Italy and ancient Rome appear intermittently as settings for nineteenth and early twentieth-century English historical novels: settings which reflected wider currents in the historical imagination of English readers. Nineteenth-century education made middle-class English novel readers familiar with Roman history and society, and Roman ruins (including the recently unearthed ruins of Pompeii) were popular highlights on the itinerary of well-to-do Victorian travellers. Mediaeval and Renaissance Italy – the setting for works like George Eliot's *Romola* (1863) – was also made familiar through the nineteenth-century fashion for travelling to Italy, as well as through the poetry of Byron, Shelley and Browning and the growing enthusiasm for collecting and displaying Italian art in public art collections. The more recent French past, meanwhile, inevitably intruded on the British historical consciousness because of Britain's involvement in the Napoleonic Wars, and because French Enlightenment writings and revolutionary experiences provided a constant point of reference for British social thought. So the recurrence of these times and places in British historical fiction of the nineteenth and early twentieth centuries at once reflected and reinforced the vision of a civilizational trajectory which was seen as beginning in the classical Mediterranean and passing through Italy and France on its way to feed the stream of national culture which had produced modern Britain.

For a historical novel to succeed, in other words, it needs to evoke some sense of connection between readers and narrative. This is generally easier to do when the story is set in a time and place with which the readers have at least some faint familiarity, and when the events described can be seen in some way as causally or metaphorically related to the contemporary world. In the absence of this sense of connection, it requires extraordinary powers of construction or characterization to draw readers' sympathies into the novel's historical milieu.

The problem is vividly illustrated by Flaubert's *Salammbô*, which deliberately attempted to apply the techniques of the modern novel to the reconstruction of a history totally alien and remote from the novel's mid-nineteenth-century bourgeois French readership: Carthage at the time of its war with the surrounding 'barbarians' in the third century BC. *Salammbô*, indeed, might be seen as marking the outermost spatial and chronological horizons of the novel's possibilities. Flaubert's choice of his setting was made possible by French colonial expansion into North Africa, which allowed him to travel to Tunis and the ruins of Carthage in 1858. But at the same time, the novel reflects his disillusionment and weariness with the French society of his day, and his desire to escape imaginatively into an utterly exotic world. *Salammbô* is the product of meticulous historical research, and Flaubert devoted exhausting months of effort to polishing his breathtaking verbal pictures of the gardens and palaces of Carthage (King 1886, xv and xviii–xix). His lavish descriptions of the Carthaginian scenery evoke the dream-world of mid-nineteenth-century French orientalist art, and were later to capture the imagination of early Hollywood filmmakers. Yet the novel has been widely criticized (in Flaubert's day and since) both for its failure to create a compelling picture of the society which occupied this scenery, and for the inability of its characters to appeal to the imaginative sympathy of readers. As the comments of Charles Sainte-Beuve, Flaubert's most outspoken contemporary critic, suggest, the problem was not simply the chronological and spatial distance between nineteenth-century Paris and Hamilcar's Carthage, but the fact that readers possessed no imaginative framework for connecting the setting of the novel to more familiar parts of the past and present: 'What do I care about the duel between Tunis and Carthage? Speak to me of the duel between Carthage and Rome, that's a different matter! There I am attentive, there I am involved. In the bitter struggle between Rome and Carthage the whole future of civilization is at stake, our own depends on it' (quoted in Lukács 1983, 187).

But if some historical landscapes are difficult for the novel to occupy because they are seen as too remote, too disconnected from contemporary society, others are problematic because they are too intensely and disturbingly connected to the present. In this context, it is interesting to contrast the popularity of Scotland as a setting for nineteenth- and early twentieth-century British historical fiction with the relative absence of Ireland from the imagined landscapes of that fiction. This is not to say, of course, that there were no historical novels set in Ireland. Charles Maturin's *The Milesian Chief* (1812) 'straddled the divide' (as Katie Trumpener puts it) between national tale and historical novel, while the early nineteenth-century Irish historical novelists, brothers John and Michael Banim, consciously set out to emulate Scott by presenting fictional versions of Irish history which would appeal to an English audience (Trumpener 1997, 147; Cahalan 1983, 49–50).

John Banim's best-known novel, *The Boyne Water*, published in 1826, mirrors *Waverley* in attempting to present a sympathetic portrayal of both sides of a decisive military conflict, in this case the Williamite wars of the late seventeenth century. The narrative weaves together the destinies of an Irish Protestant brother and sister, Robert and Esther Evelyn, who fall in love with the Irish Catholic sister and brother Eva and Edmund M'Donnell. Through this relationship, both Robert and Esther are drawn into a romantically depicted Gaelic world filled (like Scott's Highlands) with mists and magic. As in *Waverley* so too in *The Boyne Water*, personal relationships become entangled in national destinies. In 1689 James II, the last Catholic king of England, was deposed and fled to Ireland, which became the site of a fierce military confrontation between James and his Protestant adversary William of Orange (who would become William III of England). Banim weaves his fictional narrative into these historical events. When James II's armies besiege the Protestant community of Derry, Esther Evelyn is trapped within the city walls and, like many of its defenders, dies of starvation. When the two armies meet in the decisive Battle of the Boyne, where James is defeated, Robert Evelyn and Edmund M'Donnell find themselves fighting on opposite sides (J. Banim 1976; Cahalan 1983, 49–54).

But the course of historical events themselves dictates that the ending of *The Boyne Water* will be very different from the ending of *Waverley*. The Williamite Wars culminated in the 1691 Treaty of Limerick, which promised freedom of religion to Irish Catholics and allowed Irish supporters of James to flee to the Continent. The final chapter of Banim's novel depicts Edmund M'Donnell joining this band of exiles, famous in Irish history as 'the wild geese': the first of many waves of exiles who were to carry a bitter nostalgia for a half-remembered homeland to all corners of the world. In Ireland, meanwhile, the terms of the Treaty of Limerick were promptly forgotten, and penal laws were introduced depriving Catholics of their land and civic rights. While

Waverley ends with a marriage celebrating the union of Scotland and England, *The Boyne Water* ends with the M'Donnell family torn apart and Robert Evelyn sadly writing to his exiled friend to report on the betrayal of the treaty. The only gleam of light in the gloom is Robert's forlorn hope that 'other times will naturally create another spirit ... Englishmen will yet repay their fathers' debt of faith to Ireland' (Banim 1976, 561–562).

The other decisive difference between Scott's works and Banim's is the fact that the former achieved national and international acclaim, while the latter received a very mixed reception in England, and are now remembered mainly by those with an interest in the history of Irish literature. (Rather tellingly, the only library copy of *The Boyne Water* that I could readily find was published in France.) Though the first edition of *The Boyne Water* sold quite well, and was likened by a number of commentators to Scott's bestseller, the media in England were scathing, a review in *The Times* newspaper describing Banim as 'childishly weak in historical judgment as to the political facts of which he treats', and his novel as 'a compendium of mad Popery' (Quoted in Escarbelt 1976, 13).

The appeal of Scotland as a setting for British historical literature, and the lack of interest in Ireland, suggests the different ways in which these spaces operate within the historical imagination. In the nineteenth century, the Highlands of Scotland had relatively recently been subdued and ruthlessly but effectively incorporated into the political order of Britain. As Scott repeatedly pointed out, it was still just possible to remember a time when the Highlands had formed a relatively independent and 'exotic' society with its own language and social hierarchies. Yet by the time he wrote *Waverley* the political incorporation of the Highlands was sufficiently thorough for the region to be a safe site, both for colonial nostalgia and for optimistic visions of the blessings of British unity (and thus also a site for the fantasy versions of

Highland life acted out by Queen Victoria and her successors on their private Scottish estate Balmoral).

Irish history, on the other hand, could not be addressed without raising the uncomfortable spectres of continuing political conflict: O'Connell's campaign for emancipation in the early nineteenth century, and later the famine in the 1840s; the home rule movement in the late nineteenth century; the Easter Rising; the fight for independence and the Civil War in the 1910s and 1920s. Ireland's landscape and customs may have been sufficiently exotic to provide a setting for romantic fiction, and its history was certainly deeply enough entwined with the English past, but its historical narratives offered little prospect for happy endings. So popular historical fiction in Britain evolved in a direction which tended to edit Ireland out of the imagined maps of the past, and rendered events like the 1715 and 1745 Jacobite rebellions in Scotland (and indeed the French Revolution) far more familiar to the English middle-class imagination than events like the Battle of the Boyne and the 1798 rising in Ireland. It was only in the very last years of the twentieth century, with growing Anglo–Irish cooperation to address the conflict in Northern Ireland, that novels and memoirs addressing the more painful aspects of the Irish past – such as Frank McCourt's *Angela's Ashes*, Roddy Doyle's *A Star Called Henry* and Seamus Deane's *Reading in the Dark* – began to find a large and enthusiastic English readership (McCourt 1996; Doyle 1999; Deane 1996).

A similar pattern of presences and absences is to be found elsewhere. In the landscape of Japanese historical fiction, for example, ancient China appears frequently, reflecting the importance of the classical Chinese romances in Japanese cultural life. During the 1910s and 1920s Akutagawa Ryûnosuke borrowed tales from the Chinese classics as a basis for short stories like 'Toshishun', in which he explores the eternal shadows that haunt the human mind (Akutagawa 1996). At a more popular level, Yoshikawa Eiji's works include a multi-volume reworking of the Three Kingdoms narrative, serialized from 1939 to 1943, while many of Inoue Yasushi's postwar bestsellers have Chinese settings – often, as in the case of novellas like *Rôran* [*Lou Lan* 1958], western Chinese settings, reflecting (and promoting) a fascination with the history of the Silk Route (Inoue 1981a). Yet despite equally powerful historical connections, Korea is less visible in this landscape, for reasons which resemble the explanation for the absence of Ireland from the landscape of popular British historical fiction: the Korean past was difficult for Japanese writers to address without raising the ghosts of a troubled colonial relationship. The absence is particularly noticeable in prewar Japanese historical fiction. After 1945, some works such as Inoue Yasushi's *Wind and Waves* [*Fûtô*], published in 1963, and several of Kajiyama Toshiuyki's novellas, including his *The Clan Records* [*Zokufu* 1961], deal with themes from Korean history, both ancient and modern (Inoue 1981b; Kajiyama 1995). It is worth noting, however, that in both cases, although the setting is entirely Korean, the narrative is able to appeal to Japanese readers at least in part because the dynamics of the plot are focused upon a key event in Japanese history. Kajiyama's works deal mainly with the Japanese colonization of Korea, while Inoue's novel focuses on the events leading up to the attempted Mongol invasion of Japan, and the destruction of the Mongol fleet by the 'divine wind' of a typhoon. Inoue challenges convention in the sense that he inverts the normal perspective of Japanese history, viewing the invasion, as it were, from the other side, but he also stays on safe ground in the sense that Japan remains the unspoken focus of the novel's narrative.

What I want to suggest here, then, is a rather complex and uneasy relationship between the historical novel and its readers' visions of the past. The novel emerged in a world increasingly obsessed precisely by 'novelty'. Unlike the retold historical epics of earlier centuries, the novel is expected to offer its readers new landscapes, new perspectives, new experiences. In this sense, it has the potential to change the frontiers of the historical imagination, and to arouse interest in events and places that were previously little known. But at the same time, this potential is limited by constraints on the willingness of the novel reader (who, after all, reads mainly for pleasure and relaxation) to be led into wholly unfamiliar or uncomfortably contentious territory. And it is also limited by the sheer hard economics of cultural production: by the fact that the novel is the mass product of print capitalism, and that publishers, book distributors and booksellers prefer to support and promote the production of novels whose subject matter and style, they believe, will sell. These limits, in turn, are connected to a wider network of systems for producing a knowledge of the past. People's willingness to read novels about a particular time or event is influenced by the historical knowledge they have acquired in schools, the artifacts they have seen in museums, the stories they have heard from their parents, and (more recently) by those other media of historical production which I shall discuss in later chapters – film, television and so forth.

Translated Tales, Imported Pasts

Examining the imaginative landscape of the historical novel is important to the process of determining historical truthfulness, to which I shall return in later chapters. The relationship between historical fiction and 'proper' history is often discussed in terms of the reality of the events and characters that appear in the novel. Debate, in other words, tends to focus on examining the novel's narrative and asking, 'Is this true?' But the pursuit of historical truthfulness also involves the wider process of considering why the novelist wants to write, and why readers want to read, about these events? What landscapes are absent from the novels we read? How do the landscapes of the past that we encounter in fiction influence our identification with and interpretation of particular parts of history?

Historical fiction elaborates our mental map of national history, and links this to a wider map of the histories of surrounding countries. But in doing so it also creates an uneven landscape, riven by invisible fissures. While it makes certain events and places in the past vividly memorable, its horizons stop short of other events and places, leaving them obscure and unimaginable. The picture is further complicated by the fact that novels themselves (as well as their subject matter) travel across boundaries: they may be read in locations other than the country where they were written. The process of the translation and international dissemination of novels is itself a strikingly uneven one, and creates, as it were, a very unequal balance of trade in historical imaginations.

The diffusion of the novel was an important element in the nineteenth-century colonial phase of that continuing process which is now known as 'globalization'. Emerging more or less simultaneously in various parts of Western Europe, the concept of the novel was gradually exported around the globe in the course of the nineteenth century. In new settings, imported ideas about the proper form and functions of the novel were reinterpreted in ways which reflected local circumstances and the continuing influence of indigenous genres of storytelling (see for example Kamei 1999). Early modern non-European novels, including works like Jose Rizal's *Noli Me Tangere* and *El Filibusterismo* and later Maximo Kalaw's *Filipino Rebel*, the writings of Mori Ôgai and Shimazaki Tôson, and Marcus Clarke's Australian historical novel *For the Term of his Natural Life* (published in 1874), used this global but constantly redefined form to express their vision of their own society in an age of cultural turmoil and imperial rivalries. Indeed, it is precisely the relatively standardized nature of the novel's format that makes it such a powerful vehicle for expressing visions of national distinctiveness. The commonalities of form – the possibility of comparing the works of writers like Clarke, Rizal or Shimazaki with those of contemporary European writers – made it all the easier to highlight the differences of content. So it becomes possible to observe, in distinctive uses of language and style or specific descriptions of landscape and depictions of social relationships, visions of national identity taking shape within the familiar structures of the novel's plot, characterization and dialogue.

But the intellectual elites of non-European societies did not just read the emerging national literatures produced by local writers: they also read *Ivanhoe* and *The Last Days of Pompeii*, *War and Peace*, *Notre Dame de Paris* and *The Last of the Mohicans*. Indeed, outside Western Europe and North America, the appearance of modern novels about the national past was often *preceded* by the translation and consumption of novels about unfamiliar and geographically remote pasts: the worlds of ancient Rome, mediaeval England or the French Revolution. The translation of historical novels therefore provides insights into the reshaping of historical imaginations brought about by European expansion, and into the problems and crosscurrents which this process of reshaping generated. Non-European readers of the European historical novel had simultaneously to come to terms with the unfamiliar form of the novel – its implicit notions of social totality and human subjectivity – and to make sense of a mass of relatively new historical detail.

In Japan, for example, up to the start of the 1890s the most widely translated works of English-language fiction were the plays of William Shakespeare and the novels of Edward Bulwer Lytton, Benjamin Disraeli and Walter Scott, many of which dealt with historical themes. For the translators of these works, one immediate problem was determining the form of language in which to render the translation, since the Japanese language itself was undergoing rapid change associated with the processes of modern nation-building. But even when issues of style had been decided, many dilemmas remained. How were nineteenth-century Japanese readers to be persuaded to *care* about the first-century destruction of Pompeii, or about the blending of

Saxon and Norman which (according to Scott's *Ivanhoe*) had produced 'our present English language, in which the speech of the victors and the vanquished have been so happily blended together' (Scott 1962, 31)?

Translation, in other words, had to be a work of imaginative creation. In the early stages, translators often abridged and rewrote the original texts, adding historical explanations, pruning some of the wealth of unfamiliar detail and incomprehensible dialogue, and producing works which were stylistically somewhere between more familiar forms of Japanese historical narrative and the literary forms of Scott or Lytton. The conceptual leaps involved in bringing these unfamiliar worlds to life are evident, not just from the texts of early translations but also from their illustrations. The emerging novelist and literary theorist Tsubouchi Shôyô, in translating Scott's *The Bride of Lammermoor* (published in Japanese in 1880 under the title *A Tale of the Spring Breeze*), begins by explaining to readers that 'this narrative takes place in a kingdom called Scotland. Scotland is in the northern part of the island of Great Britain, and was originally an independent kingdom. However, beginning from about the 1600s it united itself with the kingdom of England and accepted this kingdom's rule' (Scott 1880; Yanagida 1961, 234). Yet the pictures which accompany the text encourage readers to identify with the adventures and emotions of Edgar Ravenswood, Lucy Ashton and Scott's other seventeenth-century Scottish characters by recreating them in the more readily recognizable form of the heroes of the samurai romance (see Picture 2.1).

But if translators sometimes bridged the imaginative gap between author and readers by 'Japanizing' their subject matter, they were also inspired by an educational passion to make Western civilization, and thus the origins of contemporary European power, comprehensible to as wide an audience as possible. Indeed, it was precisely this obtrusively visible political and economic power of the nineteenth-century West which made the subjects of works like *Ivanhoe* or *The Bride of Lammermoor*

2.1 Edgar Ravenswood and Lucy Ashton. Illustrations from *Shunpû jôwa*, Japanese version of *The Bride of Lammermoor*, translated and abridged by Tsubouchi Shôyô, Tokyo, Nakajima Seiichi, 1879.

appealing to Japanese readers. Tamba Jun'ichirô, the first translator of Lytton's works, was able to point out to his readers in the opening pages of his version of *The Last Days of Pompeii* that

> The nation of Rome, part of the present-day country of Italy, created a great civilization before the time of Christ. The political system of this nation was at first a monarchy, but then it changed into a republic and then again into an empire with great wealth and a military strength which subjugated Europe. The period described in this book is that of the empire. When Rome subjugated Europe, the people of all countries went

there to pay tribute. People from Germany and England in the north, from Spain and Portugal in the south, from Greece, Egypt and Persia in the East and from the countries of the west needed trade and commerce with one another and so all these peoples travelled to Rome just as people of all provinces of Japan used to come to the capital. (Lytton 1879, 1–2.)

The image of Rome as the birthplace of contemporary European strength and civilization is enhanced by the illustrations to the Japanese version of *The Last Days of Pompeii*, in which the first-century Roman and Greek inhabitants of Pompeii are presented neither as samurai nor as the toga-clad figures of Victorian classical representations, but as relatively contemporary and unmistakably imperial Europeans (see Picture 2.2). Such illustrations offer an interesting counterpoint to the enthusiasm of eighteenth- and nineteenth-century European writers for illustrated accounts of travels among the Pacific Islands which depict the islanders clad in togas and laurel wreaths.

Translated novels, like the fashion for Roman, Italian and French settings in nineteenth-century British historical fiction, both reflected and sustained a particular sense of connectedness to certain parts of the past. Just as the choice of settings for the British historical novel reinforced a vision of the flow of civilization from the Mediterranean to the British Isles, so the worldwide diffusion of the classic European historical novels helped to make the history of ancient Pompeii, eighteenth-century Scotland, the Paris of the French Revolution and the colonization of America part of an implicit image of a 'universal' civilization whose history, however remote and foreign, had some causal connection with the modern destiny of non-European societies. Nineteenth-century Japanese readers of Scott's *Ivanhoe* (translated in 1886) encountered a text where Scott's references to 'our forbears' and 'our English language' had been rewritten, and the entire narrative recast

2.2 Illustration from *Kisô shunshi*, Japanese version of Edward Bulwer Lytton's *Last Days of Pompei*, Tokyo, Takahashi Gengorô, 1879.

into an abridged form which makes it both more distant and subtly different in emphasis from the original. The central importance of the coming together of Saxon and Norman is diluted, and the extended and tragic final farewell of the Jewish Rebecca, compelled to escape a realm in which there is (as she says in Scott's original) 'no safe abode for the children of [her] people', is rendered into the succinct statement that 'soon after, Rebecca and her father Isaac left England and went to Spain' (Scott 1962, 465; Scott 1910, 80). Scott's novel, in other words, is no longer a site for English retrospection on 'our origins', but has become a depiction of mediaeval chivalry and an account of the coming to power of Richard I. But despite these changes, the novel, and others like it, did help to give Sherwood Forest and the events of the Crusades (as seen from a Western European viewpoint) a place in the Japanese historical imagination.

By contrast, very few European readers ventured into the world of Jose Rizal's Manila, the mid-nineteenth-century Japanese inns and highways of Shimazaki's *Before the Dawn*, or even into the more readily accessible landscape of Marcus Clarke's Tasmania. In this sense, such evocations of the past tended to remain national and particular, rather than coming to be seen as part of an interconnected system through which world history was imagined. The worldwide diffusion of the novel, in other words, contributed to the creation of a sense of history in which certain parts of the past – the world of the Roman Empire, of mediaeval and Enlightenment Europe – acquired a certain global aura, a central place in the imaginations at least of educated elites around the world.

It was only in the last decades of the twentieth century that international exchanges of historical fiction began to become more complicated. Although the translation of European and North American novels for consumption in other markets still enormously exceeds the reverse flow of Asian, African, Latin American and

Oceanian literature into Europe and North America, the imbalance is no longer as overwhelming as it was in the nineteenth and early twentieth centuries. Meanwhile, the growth of diasporic literatures diversifies the space of memory on which European and North American fiction draws. So remembered moments of modern Chinese history enter US fiction via the writings of Amy Tan; and Rohinton Mistry's *A Fine Balance*, with its searing reconstruction of Indira Ghandi's India, becomes part of the literary tradition of Canada. Meanwhile, the burgeoning of world-literature classes in European and North American universities creates a new audience for works like Achebe's *Things Fall Apart* (of which more than two million copies had been sold in the United States by the 1990s). Such crosscurrents in the international flow of historical fiction disturb the assumptions about the relationship between reader, nation and history fostered by the classical nineteenth-century historical novel, and intensify that sense of a 'crisis of history' discussed in Chapter 1.

From the time of the Napoleonic Wars onwards, then, historical fiction gradually contributed to a worldwide reshaping of imaginings of the past. Most importantly, it created a new sense of an imaginative relationship between individual human lives and a constantly changing society, usually equated with the nation. The novel played a key role in the emergence of the modern sense of history as identification, while at the same time helping to shape the spatial bounds of that identification with the past. Yet in this process of reshaping the imagination, the novel also had implications for the interpretive frameworks through which history was understood. Ordinary individuals came to be seen as participating in the processes of national social change, and this sense of participation was to raise profound and persistent controversies about the relationship between individual human agency and the impersonal dynamics of social forces. The novel also created visions of the way in which national history was connected to the histories of other countries. It created flows of historical concepts which crossed national boundaries, but only certain boundaries proved to be easily transgressed. Besides, the influence of the historical novel was naturally limited by the fact that it appealed to a particular audience: primarily to a middle-class audience who possessed the education and time to read fiction. These limitations were particularly evident in the cases of writers like Kalaw and Achebe, who wrote about the history of colonized countries in the language of the colonizer, and whose work was therefore only accessible to a relatively small elite within their own countries.

By the end of the nineteenth century, however, new techniques for representing the past were emerging: techniques which in the end were to have a far wider social impact than the novel. The emerging technologies for recording vision and sound were to create further means to anchor personal memories in the broader narratives of national history. At the same time, new visual technologies had the capacity both to reach audiences beyond the largely middle-class realms of the novel-reading public, and to cross the borders of nation and language. The expanding possibilities for recording vision and sound would create fresh scope to capture the reality of history-as-it-happened, and convey that reality to wide audiences. But this potential, as it turned out, only served to blur further the dividing line between fact and fiction already evident in the emergence of the historical novel.

3

Shadows on the Lens:
Memory as Photograph

In November 1999 a major exhibition of war photographs, which had toured several cities in Germany, was closed after accusations that some of the exhibits were fakes. The collection had already attracted considerable controversy, and become the target of violent demonstrations by the far Right. Its subject matter and its title, 'War of Extermination: Crimes of the Wehrmacht, 1941–1944', disturbed the sensibilities of some German viewers, because it drew attention to war crimes committed by ordinary German soldiers. This challenged a popular belief that, while groups like the SS had committed atrocities, common soldiers, by and large, were not implicated in these acts, or had become involved only under duress. Criticisms of the exhibition were given extra force by the fact that they were voiced, not just by German historians, but also (most notably) by Polish scholar Bogdan Musial, who claimed that nine amongst more than eight-hundred pictures in the collection were fakes. These included photographs described as showing the corpses of Nazi victims, but in fact showing victims of the Soviet NKVD, and a picture of a firing squad which, according to historians, was actually Hungarian rather than German (Reuters, November 4, 1999).

Controversies about 'fake' photographs are, of course, nothing new. Accusations and counter-accusations of the faking of photographs were central to the propaganda battles of the twentieth century. One such dispute centred on a famous image from the Japanese invasion of China in 1937. This picture, taken by Hearst Corporation cameraman H. S. Wong, shows a small, semi-naked and injured child sitting alone and crying in the midst of the bombed ruins of Shanghai's southern railway station (Picture 3.1). The photo was widely reproduced in the US and elsewhere. *Life* magazine suggested that it may have been seen by as

3.1 Terrified baby on Shanghai Station, 1937. H. S. Wong/Getty Images. Courtesy of Getty Images.

many as 136 million people in the latter part of 1937 – and it is credited with having profoundly influenced US public attitudes towards the conflict in China.

Some US journalists at the time and since, however, have suggested that this image of the bombing of Shanghai was staged, in the sense that Wong deliberately excluded other people from the scene, and perhaps also moved the child in order to create a more striking image of abandonment and desolation. Other still shots and newsreel footage, including some also taken by Wong, certainly show the same child in the company of several people (Picture 3.2), though the claim that the infant was deliberately 'borrowed' and moved to a suitable location for

3.2 Shanghai Station, 1937. Source: J. Campbell ed., *20-Seiki no rekishi 15 – Dainiji Sekai Taisen (jô) – Senka no butai*, Tokyo, Heibonsha, 1990, p. 23.

the photograph remain controversial.[1] Whatever the case, suggestions of staging were quickly taken up by Japanese propaganda experts and used in an effort to discredit both the photograph itself, and more generally US and Chinese accounts of the bombing of Shanghai as a whole (see for example the *Japan Times and Mail* 1937, 18; Koyama 1942).

The same claims have recently been resurrected by the Japanese nationalist historian and founder of the Society for History Textbook Reform, Fujioka Nobukatsu, who employs them as a lynchpin in his efforts to cast doubt on the credibility of photographs of war atrocities in China (particularly of the photographs reproduced in Iris Chang's book *The Rape of Nanking*). Fujioka embellishes the earlier criticisms of Wong's photograph by adding an assertion that the smoke which appears in the image (and in newsreel footage also taken by Wong) was deliberately created by the photographer to enhance the scene.

It is important to notice here that Fujioka avoids any effort to distinguish between two quite different issues raised by the claim that the photograph is staged. The first is an issue of journalistic ethics. Deliberately moving an injured child around in order to create an effective photograph seems a heartless and ethically improper act. (It should be said, though, that while Fujioka quotes extensively from the 1937 *Life* magazine article which featured the photograph, he makes no mention of another picture in the same article which shows the child receiving medical attention.) The second and distinct issue is the

---

[1] For example, Arthur Rothstein of *Look* magazine, the journal which published the original claims of the 'staging' of the image, cites Wong's photograph as one of the great news photographs of the war, but states that 'the photographer "borrowed" the baby and set up the shot' (Rothstein 1956, 38). On the other hand, *Life* magazine's 1975 compilation of war photographs, which also features the image, says that 'it has been said that this [photograph] is staged, but it is evident from various points that this is no more than a fabricated rumour' (*Time Life Books* 1975, 26).

relationship between the image of the child and the fact that the Japanese bombing of the Shanghai South Station killed and injured Chinese civilians, including children. Fujioka does not explicitly question the facts of the bombing, but allows his presentation of the photograph as a piece of staged propaganda to imply doubt about the wider surrounding historical event (Fujioka 1999, 61).

In the ensuing discussion of the images of violence in *The Rape of Nanking*, Fujioka argues not simply that some pictures are misleadingly titled (which they apparently are[2]), but that all without exception are 'lies'. The grounds for this litany of denial vary widely. Some photographs are rejected because they conflict with the verbal testimony of Japanese participants in the invasion of Nanjing; others because of the uncertainty of their provenance; others again because of apparent inconsistencies within the image itself. In one photograph, for example, revisionist critics suggest that the shadows are pointing in divergent directions (Picture 3.3).

Likening these pictures to certain group photos of Chinese Communist Party leaders, which are known to have been altered after the event for ideological reasons, Fujioka writes:

> Everybody knows that words can lie. In contrast, the word 'photograph' [*shashin*] is written with characters which mean 'to reproduce the truth'. Ever since the development of the techniques of photography, this naïve

---

[2] In addition to minor mistakes, in the spelling of names and so on, the details of some photo captions in Chang's book are open to question. One gruesome photograph, for example, depicts a Japanese soldier bayoneting a human body, and is captioned with words which clearly imply that the victim is being bayoneted while still alive. However, when the same image was published in *Life* magazine in 1937, it was accompanied by a text which read: 'Bayonet practice, wherein Japanese soldiers used dead Chinese for targets, was photographed by an Associated Press photographer near Tientsin on Sept. 9' (*Life*, October 11, 1937, 30).

human belief that photographs reproduce facts has been repeatedly used throughout history to create propaganda for political purposes. In reality, far from 'reproducing the truth', when they become entangled in politics, nothing could be less reliable than photographs. Photographs tell greater lies than words. (Fujioka 1999, 54.)

3.3 This photograph by an unknown wartime photographer is reproduced in Iris Chang's *The Rape of Nanking*. Fujioka Nobukatsu and Tanaka Masaaki use internal evidence, including the fact that the shadows appear to be pointing in different directions, to claim that the image is faked. Source: Tanaka Masaaki, *What Really Happened in Nanking: The Refutation of a Common Myth*, Tokyo, Sekai Shuppan, 2000, p. 112.

The point I want to emphasize here is the way that Fujioka uses the notion of the fake to frame his argument. Under the heading 'Fabricating Photographs, Techniques of Violence: Not One Single Piece of Such "Photographic Proof" Exists', Fujioka presents his readers with an array of photographic images: pictures which have been deliberately altered after the fact for ideological reasons, photos that may have been carefully composed in such a way as to heighten the emotional impact of the scene, and instances where questions can be raised about the relationship between the photograph and the accompanying caption. Placing these images together, he defines all the objects of his attack as being equally faked or 'lying' photographs, and contrasts them with selected 'true' photographs (drawn from wartime Japanese magazines) whose provenance, composition and labels he subjects to absolutely no critical scrutiny whatever. The same dividing line is even more starkly drawn by fellow-nationalist Tanaka Masaaki in an English-language booklet distributed free of charge to scholars of Asia in the US and elsewhere. Tanaka paraphrases Fujioka's arguments under the heading 'Faked Versus Authentic Photographs: A World of Difference'. The 'authentic' photographs in question come from the *Asahi* newspaper's coverage of Nanjing in December 1937, which, Tanaka argues, 'present a true picture of life in Nanking at the time, and demonstrate that there was absolutely no basis for accusations of a massacre' (Tanaka 2000, 110–111).

These accusations of photographic 'fraud' can serve as a starting point for thinking more broadly about questions of photographic representation and historical truth. While some members of the Society for History Textbook Reform, such as Nishio Kanji (see Chapter 1) adopt a form of historical relativism, suggesting that historical narratives inevitably vary from one nation to another, Fujioka and Tanaka go to the opposite extreme, drawing an absolute and impermeable line between true and false images. Their approach, like other debates over fake photographs, points to some deep-seated assumptions about the relationship between image and narrative. It is worth reflecting on the fact that, for example, paintings of war scenes or verbal descriptions of a battle may be criticized for being inaccurate, but are seldom accused of being faked. The notion of the fake is precisely the other side of the coin of a belief in absolute reality. Photographs are accused of being fakes because we implicitly assume that the camera should present an unmediated image of reality, and that dishonesty is being practised if it does not do so.

The passions stirred by debates about 'fake photographs' also reflect the special power of the photographic image to touch our deepest emotions. The graphic, dramatic nature of photographs makes them a focus for history as identification – they readily engage our feelings. For the photograph is, as Susan Sontag observes, 'not only an image (as a painting is an image), an interpretation of the real; it is also a trace, something directly stenciled off the real, like a footprint or a death mask' (Sontag 1973, 154). Its graphic presence seems to confront us with the substance of the past itself. This sense of reality has a special power to stir our imagination. We respond with instinctive emotion to the expressions of joy or terror, the fleeting moments of triumph or disaster captured on celluloid and projected through time into the present moment. For that very reason, we also feel profoundly cheated if we discover that our emotions have been roused by an image which is not what it appears to be.

Picturing Nagasaki

The problems raised by Fujioka and Tanaka's crude dichotomy between true and fake photographs illuminate the need to go beyond a simple debate about the truth of the image, and rather to address more complex questions of the truthfulness of the evolving relationship between event, photographer and viewer. To explain this more clearly, I shall focus on the example of two other black-and-white photographs which present famous images of war.

The first is a close-up of a small child, about four years old, wearing a hooded coat and clutching a rice ball in one hand. It is impossible to be sure whether the child is a girl or a boy, but I think this is a boy. His forehead and cheeks are scored by cuts and scratches, and he stares unblinkingly into the camera with an expression of totally blank helplessness (Picture 3.4).

3.4 Child with a rice ball, photographed by Yamahata Yôsuke in Nagasaki, August 10, 1945. From Iizawa Kôtarô ed., *Nihon no shashinka 23: Yamahata Yôsuke*, Tokyo, Iwanami Shoten, 1998, plate 20.

The second photograph is of a young woman in a loose robe, breast-feeding her baby. The background is obscure, but it is clear that the woman is sitting out of doors, and she appears to be surrounded by a tangle of twisted metal and vehicle parts. Her baby's head and face are covered with dark marks, as though singed by fire, and the woman's cheek is similarly marked. As she cradles the baby, she gazes into the middle distance with an unfocused look of great sadness (Picture 3.5).

3.5 Mother and baby, photographed by Yamahata Yôsuke in Nagasaki, August 10, 1945. From Iizawa, op. cit., plate 27.

Both photographs were taken in Nagasaki on August 10, 1945, the day after the atomic bomb was dropped on the city, by war photographer Yamahata Yôsuke, and both have been very widely reproduced in subsequent accounts of the atomic bombings. The provenance of these photographs is profoundly important. It seems absurd and slightly obscene to suggest that we should treat them as pure 'images', detached from any reference to outside events. They are famous and historically significant images because they are photographs of Nagasaki on August 10, 1945, and in this case, as it happens, there is little controversy about the circumstances in which they were taken.

Yamahata's negatives survive intact, placing these two images in the context of an unfolding series of scenes of appalling destruction, where the rigid outlines of blackened corpses protrude from the chaotic ruins of the city. Yamahata was a war photographer attached to the Japanese army's News and Information Bureau, who had worked on assignment in China before returning to Japan in 1944. He was dispatched to Kyushu on August 5, 1945, and on his way passed through Hiroshima on the day before the first atomic bomb was dropped. In his written account of the events of August 1945, Yamahata described how he was in Fukuoka, north of Nagasaki, when reports came in that a second 'New Style Bomb' (as it was then described by the Japanese government) had exploded there. Together with writer Higashi Jun and artist Yamada Eiji, he was immediately sent to Nagasaki to record the effects of the blast, and arrived in Nagasaki just before dawn of the following day.

For hours, Yamahata walked around the city, numbly and remorselessly recording the horrors around him. As he recalled afterwards, 'At the time I was completely calm and composed. In other words, perhaps it was too much, too enormous to absorb ... Even when I think back on it now, that composure seems very strange. Walking through the tragedy of Nagasaki at the time, all I thought of was the photographs I had to take, and of how to avoid being killed if another New Style Bomb were to fall' (Jenkins 1995, 103; Iizawa 1998).

Yamahata's photographs, then, are clearly 'true', in the sense that they were actually taken in Nagasaki immediately after the atomic bombing. But to say this tells us very little about the way in which they communicate an understanding of the devastation to those who did not experience it. For people living far removed in time and space from the event, it is important, I think, to look at Yamahata's photographs, to be receptive to the power of their images. But at the same time it is also important to be conscious of the reasons why these images have such power, and to consider how the feelings which they arouse in viewers flow into interpretations of the historical causes and significance of the atomic bombings.

Family Albums

Like many of the most memorable historical photographs, these two images are deeply individual and personal. They focus on the faces of particular, though for the moment nameless, people. They inspire an effort to imagine who these people were and how they felt. Working outside the constraints of language, the photograph (far more than other media like the novel) is able to convey some sense of individual experience across national boundaries. The face of the small bewildered child, captured by Yamahata on August 10, 1945, for example, still speaks to people born long after the bomb was dropped and living many thousands of miles from Nagasaki. But the power of the photograph to convey that sense of individual empathy is not determined by the technology of the camera itself. Rather, it is something that has been shaped by an interplay between photography and social memory. Photographs influence the way people remember and understand the past; but the way we take, see and respond to photographs is in turn also shaped by social forces. With the worldwide spread of the camera came the creation of worldwide conventions about the social uses of photography, and it is these shared conventions which make it easy for viewers to feel empathy for what is portrayed in photographic images taken in times and places very different from their own.

This evolution of photography was profoundly influenced by the circumstances of the camera's invention in the context of nineteenth-century European and North American society. Since the eighteenth century, the emerging European upper-middle classes had sought to cement their social status by acquiring cultural trappings once associated with the aristocracy – and among the most symbolically significant trappings were portraits, either of individual members of the household or of the whole family group. During the eighteenth and early nineteenth centuries, simplifications in artistic techniques had made painted portraits cheaper and more readily accessible to middle-class families (Lalvani 1996, 44–45). This passion for portraiture was part of the emerging culture of the individual and the nuclear family which also sustained the rise of the historical novel.

Photography flowed readily into the channels created by such traditions, and portrait photography became the main source of income for the first photographic studios. Initially, portrait photography had much in common with earlier forms of portraiture. Early daguerrotypes and ambrotypes, like painted portraits, were unique and non-repro-ducible, and their expense put them beyond the reach of all but wealthy families. Portrait photography still required sittings, in which the subject would be posed in front of studio sets – often arrangements of drapery and colonnades designed to suggest the neo-classical mansion. The results were static and solemn images. As late as 1886 the Japanese professional photographer Matsuzaki Shinji, in a handbook for studio photographers, felt it necessary to warn his readers that 'including smiles in photographs is almost impossible, and it is better to ensure that the subject does not move' (Iizawa et al. 1999, 17). In the early days of the camera, the same considerations made it virtually impossible to photograph small children.

By the time Matsuzaki was writing, however, technological changes were rapidly removing these constraints. The gelatin dry plate, developed in the 1870s, needed only to be exposed to light for a fraction of a second, and so helped to encourage the European and American fashion for family photographs, with the smallest members of the family seated on their parents' knees. Reproducible photographs, which first appeared in the 1850s, were also cheaper than the early daguerrotypes. Meanwhile, the production of smaller and lighter cameras was making it possible for commercial photographers to move out of the studios. In Europe and North America, travelling photographers brought the new technology to rural households, taking portrait photographs not in arranged studio settings, but in front of or within the home.

Photography therefore worked its way into existing patterns of social interaction. But it also had the power to open up new possibilities and to create new traditions. In Japan, for example, there was no existing history of child portraiture. And yet, as improved photographic techniques made it possible to photograph the very young, well-to-do families eagerly seized on the opportunity to record the arrival of new additions to the family (Picture 3.6). An extraordinary collage produced in the 1890s, for example, records the faces of the 1,700 babies photographed at Ezaki Reiji's Asakusa photographic studio in the three years from 1891 to 1893 (Morita 1986).

The profound appeal of such pictures, of course, lay in the fact that they capture the fleeting substance of life itself: they are 'a way of imprisoning reality, understood as recalcitrant, inaccessible; of making it stand still' (Sontag 1978). Or, as film critic André Bazin once wrote, photography and cinema possess the power to 'embalm time, rescuing it

3.6 Early twentieth-century Japanese family photograph; subject and photographer unknown. Author's collection.

from its proper corruption' (Monaco 1981, 329). This passion to possess – to embalm – time was intensified by the changes which were overwhelming everyday life from the late nineteenth century onwards. Urbanization was weakening the roots which had held families for generations within the same village community. As people moved into towns and cities, or migrated across national frontiers, connections with grandparents, uncles, aunts and cousins often became diffused across space. Relatives (particularly relatives other than parents and siblings) might now be seen, if at all, only once or twice a year for special celebrations.

At the same time, the individual's and the family's place in the flow of time was changing. For many people in rural communities, stories of the past were grounded in the landscape all around which bore traces of the ancestral past. Fragments of family narrative were infused in the physical scenery: in graveyards, or in the fields, roads or hills which had been the sites of particular ancestral adventures. With migration and urbanization, on the other hand, increasing numbers of people found themselves living in environments to which they had no historical ties. Photographs created a portable past, which travelled over space as well as time, enabling mobile individuals to surround themselves with fragments of personal history. These fragments became all the more vital to the construction of a sense of identity because of the speed of change.

Even for families who did not migrate to the cities, the surrounding landscape was changing, obliterating traces of the personal and ancestral past. For them, too, the photograph would play a growing role in reconstructions of personal history. An early manual for young amateur photographers proclaimed that

> as printing makes the result of thinking immortal, so the camera has made lasting the result of seeing; as books tell us what men thought in the past, so will the camera in the future tell us what men saw in the past. All over the world the camera shutters are snapping … They are noting for our children how their fathers and mothers lived, what were their surroundings, what they did. They are saving from forgetfulness types of men and women, quaint happenings, occurrences both commonplace and strange. (Jenks 1908, vii.)

The use of the camera as a vehicle for recording the realities of personal life was not predetermined from the beginning. The mid-nineteenth-century enthusiasm for photography also stimulated a boom in the sale of staged tableaux in which models acted out scenes from fiction or history. Drawing on the tradition of painted magic lantern slides, entrepreneurs created series of 'life model' photos which presented viewers with dramatized tales: from sentimental melodramas like *Jessica's First Prayer* (based on an 1870s religious novel) to visual versions of bawdy songs (Crompton, Henry and Herbert 1990, 8 and 54–59). Most popular of all, in the 1850s and 1860s, were the boxed sets of stereographic photographs, which could be viewed though a specially designed stereoscope to produce a three-dimensional effect. But with the advent of the movie camera at the end of the nineteenth century the use of still photography to reconstruct fiction lost its appeal. This dichotomy between still photograph and film reinforced the identification of the still photograph with reality, and helps to explain why viewers today sometimes experience a more powerful sense of the presence of the past from viewing a still photograph than from observing the same event recorded on moving film.

The power of photography to record everyday life was enormously increased from the 1880s onwards, with the emergence of cheap, light snapshot cameras. By 1900, with the advent of the Kodak Brownie camera, photography had become widely accessible to well-to-do families in the US (Coe and Gates 1977, 23). From the early days of mass photography, enthusiasts recognized the potential of the snapshot camera to strengthen the individual's sense of connectedness to the past. It was the snapshot camera that made it possible for the photograph album to become a focus of family memories. Since photography was a new art and few families, in the early stages, possessed photographs that went back much more than a decade or so, the earliest photographic albums tended to be synchronic: they located the family's place in the contemporary social order, rather than in the flow of time. In the 1850s and 1860s, the albums of middle-class families might typically contain photographs of famous figures (political leaders, artists and so on) in the front, followed by photographs of family members and of those friends who added their photographic *cartes-de-visites* to the album when they came to call (Henisch and Henisch 1994, 157). But from the start of the twentieth century, as photography matured and diffused throughout society, the photograph album evolved into a chronological record of family life.

The family album did not simply preserve the narrative of the family past: it recast it into new forms. As parents and children, siblings and friends, turned its pages together, the album became the focus of a new sort of family narrative, a new way of passing on the inherited past to the next generation, and so of shaping a sense of personal identity that could span many years. This is a linear narrative marked at regular intervals by certain milestones of change and growth: birth, going to school, family outings, graduation, travel, marriage, moving house. The album, by and large, edits out distant relatives, chance acquaintances and the familiar routine of everyday life. These, if captured on film at all, become part of the detritus of miscellaneous and forgotten snapshots that litter the bottom of drawers and cupboards. What are retained are moments of transformation and achievement – the arrival of the first child, the long-awaited holiday, the move to a new and bigger home. Here, as so often, the albums cast the family narrative into the modern metanarrative of progress, in Pierre Bourdieu's words 'solemnizing and immortalizing the high points of family life' (Bourdieu 1990, 19; see also Hirsch 1997, 49–54). Divorce, unemployment, poverty and boredom must, for the most part, be looked for in the absences: the blank pages, the missing faces, the photographs removed from their frames.

In reconstructing our memories around the photo album we almost imperceptibly change their quality. Events are now no longer remembered only from within – from interior experience – but are also objectified. We see ourselves from the outside, and superimpose this objective and fixed image of ourselves in the photograph onto the interior memories of the delight or pain or confusion which infused particular moments of our lives. In the process we come to observe ourselves and our families as part of a constant transformation. For it is only when we look at our own face in the fading photograph that we understand how much we, and the world we live in, has altered with the passing of the years. The photograph album historicizes memory.

Family albums, and the memories they evoke, help us to respond to photographs of people whose names and circumstances we do not know. Yamahata's photographs of Nagasaki evoke images of portrait photography, indeed also (in the case of the photograph of the mother and her baby) of the more ancient religious iconography of Madonna and child. They connect in our minds with familiar pictures of the new member of the family, or the child at a picnic. But here such images are suddenly transposed into a landscape of devastation that extends beyond the realms of our imagination. I cannot look at the photograph of the child with the rice ball without seeing, somewhere at the back of my mind, photographic images of my son aged about two, wearing a rather long jumper with a hood, his pose and dress somehow recalling that of the child in the picture. In Nagasaki, however, instead of 'immortalizing the high points of family life' the camera was carried in the hands of a stranger whose remorseless gaze captured families and individuals in a moment of agony and despair. The semiconscious superimpositions of these drastically dissonant images are the starting point from which we begin to extend the imagination towards the experience of the atomic bombing.

Composing Reality

Years later, Yamahata was to write of the atomic bombing of Nagasaki:

> Since many experts and victims of the blast have published articles on the
> military might of atomic weapons, and on the cruelty of the harm which
> they inflict, I have no intention of speaking about this. But from my
> position I believe that my task is to encourage absolutely everyone to
> think freely about these photographs, and to form their own criticisms on
> the basis of the data starkly recorded by the camera. (Yamahata 1959, 23.)

Here Yamahata speaks of his photographs almost as though they were
an unmediated representation of reality – data 'starkly recorded' by an
impersonal camera without human intervention. But in fact, of course,
even confronted with the numbing horror of the aftermath of the
bomb, Yamahata remained a professional photographer, consciously
using his camera in an effort to communicate the enormity of the event
to others. He chose his angles and his focus, often taking several shots
of the same scene in the effort to capture the image which he wished to
convey to viewers. He took four photographs of the young woman at a
makeshift first aid centre breastfeeding her badly injured baby. In one,
her face is turned away as a doctor bends down to attend to the baby's
injuries. In another, she looks down anxiously towards her child, and
the expression on her face is indistinct, while in the third she stares
blankly into the distance. But in the fourth and most widely reproduced
image, Yamahata has caught, perhaps almost by chance, a fleeting
and profoundly moving expression of mingled concern and despair on
her face.

There are two surviving pictures of the child with the rice ball. One,
taken from further away, shows the child standing with a woman
(presumably his mother) whose head is heavily bandaged (Picture 3.7).

3.7 Child with a rice ball, accompanied by adult, photographed by Yamahata Yôsuke in Nagasaki, August 10, 1945. Source, Iizawa, op. cit., plate 19.

It is the close-up image of the child's expressionless yet deeply expressive face, however, that impresses itself on our memories and imagination.

Does this mean that Yamahata's photographs of Nagasaki were staged? To pose the question instantly highlights the fact that there is no simple dividing line between the genuine and the staged image. Even in the heat of battle, photographers choose their angle of vision and frame their shots, using imagery (as historians use words) in an always-incomplete effort to express their feeling and understanding of events. And after the battle is over, they edit their own work, selecting, developing and enhancing the images which most successfully communicate the messages they wish to convey to viewers.

Instead of a sharp line between the real and the staged, what exists is an endlessly contested moral question of the extent to which a photographer may legitimately intervene in shaping the images of historically significant events. The question has many dimensions, and is not susceptible to simple or universal answers. In moments of death and destruction, how should the photographer balance the importance of recording events for posterity against the dangers of violating the privacy of personal suffering? Is it justifiable to rearrange the scene: to clear away rubble, or ask bystanders to step back in order to obtain a more effective shot? May the photographer use the technologies of development (or, more recently, the techniques of digital enhancement) to remove or highlight parts of the image?

Much of the film which Yamahata used in Nagasaki, for instance, was damaged, possibly by the effects of radiation. In the photograph of the child with a rice ball, the dark mood of the scene is intensified by a shadow on the film which obscures the lower part of the image. The photo of the child with his mother is also damaged by small burn-like blemishes on the film. Curators preparing prints of the photos for exhibition therefore face the dilemma of whether, or how far, to use contemporary technology to 'correct' this damage. Does restoration enable us to see the scene as Yamahata himself saw it, or are the shadows and burns themselves part of the inherent reality of the photograph? Such questions profoundly complicate the distinction between the true and the fake photograph. The processes of historical *truthfulness*, however, require above all that we should be sensitive to these questions, be conscious of the presence of the eye behind the lens, and take time to think through the problems of vision and representation that a particular photographer confronts in a particular historical moment.

To elucidate some of these problems, we might consider Yamahata's Nagasaki photographs in the wider context of his life's work and of their subsequent destiny. On the one hand, we can contrast the stark immediacy of Yamahata's Nagasaki photographs with the very different quality of the pictures he took while on assignment with the army in China and Southeast Asia in the early 1940s. Here Yamahata was operating within the confines of a strict censorship system which, amongst other things, banned 'press photographs disadvantageous to our army' and 'press photographs which may risk giving an impression of cruelty during the arrest and interrogation of Chinese soldiers and civilians' (Mainichi Shinbunsha ed. 1998–99, I, 199). In practice, the wartime Japanese media tended to avoid representations of death and destruction in battle altogether, preferring instead to publish inspiring images of the military happily cooperating with civilians in the building of the Greater East Asia Co-Prosperity Sphere. Yamahata's photographs from the 'front' therefore include very few actual images of fighting, and instead offer a range of rather static, sunlit images carefully composed for aesthetic effect (for example, Picture 3.8).

Censorship, moreover, did not end with Japan's defeat. Among the early acts of the Allied occupation of Japan was the reimposition of press censorship (albeit with less drastic punitive sanctions than those imposed by the wartime Japanese military). At the same time, with little

3.8 Soldier with children, photographed by Yamahata Yôsuke, China,1940. From Iizawa, op. cit., plate 5.

visible sense of irony the occupation authorities used these press controls to promote the values of liberal democracy and to silence criticism of the occupation, and particularly of its leader, General Douglas MacArthur (Dower 1999, 405–440).

One aspect of this censorship was the banning of images showing the effects of the atomic bombs. Yamahata, who had developed his photographs of Nagasaki himself rather than handing them over to the army's news and information sections, managed to publish a few of the pictures in newspapers immediately after Japan's surrender. But after the return of censorship in September 1945 pictures of the death and injury caused by the bomb disappeared from view, and it was not until after the San Francisco Treaty of 1951 that Yamahata's Nagasaki photographs could again be seen by the public.

Like the wartime Japanese government, SCAP (Supreme Command Allied Powers – the label usually applied to the occupation administration) was conscious of the power of photography to move public opinion. As well as censoring undesirable images, therefore, they also encouraged prominent Japanese photographers to take and publish images which represented their vision of the society they sought to create in postwar Japan. One striking example was a series of portraits of the Emperor Hirohito and his consort, taken at SCAP's request by Yamahata Yôsuke.

As John Dower has eloquently demonstrated, the occupation authorities' postwar vision for Japan was complex and often contradictory (Dower 1999). Deeply idealistic aspirations to create a democratic and peaceful Japan – embodied in the postwar Constitution's emphasis on equality, freedom, human rights and pacifism – went hand in hand with increasing Cold War fears of subversion. At the centre of these postwar paradoxes was the role of Emperor Hirohito. Already before the surrender of Japan, General MacArthur and his psychological warfare experts had worked out a plan for the occupation of Japan which involved maintaining the emperor in a symbolic role while absolving him of culpability for the events of the war. A senior advisor to MacArthur was later to remark that the occupation forces had 'requisitioned the services of the emperor', using what they saw as his 'mystic hold' on the Japanese people to secure their own control over the defeated nation (Dower 1999, 283 and 299). To requisition imperial charisma for postwar use, however, it was necessary both to draw a clear dividing line between Hirohito and other military leaders, and to change the emperor's image from that of a military leader to that of a peace-loving family man (Bix 2000).

During the war, published photographs of the emperor (some of them taken by Yamahata Yôsuke's father Shôgyoku) generally presented him in martial dress and pose. One year after his assignment to Nagasaki, however, Yamahata was invited by SCAP to visit the imperial palace and create a very different portrait of Hirohito. Rather than presenting the emperor as the remote and revered leader of wartime ideology, this image was to evoke the homely traditions of the family album, depicting, for example, the emperor and empress reading a magazine together in the garden. A shot taken by an unknown photographer shows Yamahata painstakingly setting up this scene. In the carefully composed final picture, the pile of books beneath the table reminds the viewer of the emperor's scholarly interests (Picture 3.9). The emperor himself points a gently didactic hand to a magazine, helping his wife to keep up with

3.9 Yamahata Yôsuke at work photographing Emperor Hirohito and Empress Nagako, photographer unknown. Source: Rupert Jenkins, *Nagasaki Journey: The Photographs of Yosuke Yamahata, August 10 1945*, Tokyo, Charles E. Tuttle Co., 1995, p. 107.

current events in the new climate of democratization and emerging women's rights.

What do these transitions in Yamahata's career tell us about the nature of photography as a record of history? All the photographs taken by Yamahata – in China, in Nagasaki and in the Imperial Palace gardens – are equally true in the sense that they record events that really occurred and scenes that really existed. But the truthfulness of the relationship between photographer, event and image is a different and more complex matter. In terms of the power of the photograph to evoke an identification with the events of the past, there is an inescapable difference between a photographer's encounter with a sudden and catastrophic event like the bombing of Nagasaki, and the orderly, prearranged circumstances of official portrait photography. In the first instance, there is little room for the careful preparation or the composition of scenes. The photographer seizes the images that can be snatched from the moment of disaster. The results are usually confused or imperfectly focused, but for that very reason often have a raw immediacy that conveys the reality of the event to the viewer. The controversy surrounding H. S. Wong's photograph of the child on the Shanghai station arises not simply because the scene may have been arranged, but because it was taken in such a moment of disaster: circumstances where we expect the photographer to minimize direct intervention in the shaping of the scene, and where the deliberate composition of an image, which might be quite appropriate elsewhere, seems somehow distasteful and disingenuous.

In Nagasaki, Yamahata responded with shock and compassion, recognizing the victims of the bombing as people who might have been his own family, or himself. His skill as a photographer allowed him to communicate his feelings through the camera. These qualities, together with the overwhelming devastation of the scenes he recorded, created unforgettable images which retain the power, more than half a century later, to tear a fissure in the comforting temporal walls around our everyday reality, allowing a cold dark instant of the past into the present moment we occupy.

It is not surprising that the more consciously staged and static image of the emperor and empress should lack that capacity to engage the feelings of the viewer. The problem of the imperial portrait, however, forces us to consider not just how far a photograph engages our emotions, but also how it conveys implicit interpretations of the meaning of historical events. Yamahata was reticent about his political views, and it is difficult to tell whether his work with the imperial family reflected a conscious desire to disassociate the emperor from the events of the war and its disastrous conclusion, or whether he simply did not see any connection between his photographs of China, his Nagasaki photographs and his images of the emperor. Yet his postwar portraits of the emperor clearly formed part of an implicit interpretive narrative about the war and its aftermath. In this narrative, Hirohito's image as a martial leader in whose name thousands had fought, killed and been killed, was obscured by the superimposition of a new domesticated, peaceable image of the emperor. Yamahata's willingness to participate in the creation of this new image suggests a rather disturbing failure to consider, or at least publicly to acknowledge, the links between the images which his camera had singled out for inscription in the historical record: the relationship between the violence in China which he had been unable to photograph and the horrors of Nagasaki which he had so vividly depicted; or between the disastrous events of the war (including the atomic bombings) and the person of the wartime figurehead who was allowed so very easily to reinvent himself in the postwar period as an amiable family man.

If we place Yamahata's Nagasaki photographs in the context of the photographer's own career, then, they seem to be part of an interpretive narrative which runs roughly as follows. The atomic bombings were a terrible and disastrous event, which must be remembered forever in order that human beings may avoid the possibility of annihilation through nuclear war. Yet this event had no very direct connection to the history of Japan's own imperial expansion in Asia; nor did it have much bearing on the postwar reintegration of Japan into a new, US-dominated East Asian order.

The pursuit of historical truthfulness makes it important for the viewer to think carefully about the feelings which photographic images evoke. It is also important, as far as possible, to look critically at the implicit interpretations through which the photographer understood the historical meaning of these images, and to compare this with other possible interpretive frameworks. Yamahata's Nagasaki photographs, as they have been circulated and reproduced in many countries and in many media, have been incorporated into a multitude of diverse narratives of the past. The production of historical truthfulness, then, goes beyond the relationship between photographer, event and image to encompass the role of editors and exhibitors, who select, label and arrange the photographs for historical display, and us, the viewers, who encounter these displays and use them to construct our own interpretations of the past – interpretations that may be radically at odds with those of the photographer himself.

National Albums

The way we identify with and interpret photographs is shaped by the context in which the image is seen: by the pictures and text which surround it. Seen singly and without a caption, Yamahata's pictures of the woman and her baby and of the child with the rice ball would undoubtedly be moving; but they possess a special and potent emotional force only when we see them in the company of a text which tells us that they were taken in Nagasaki the day after the atomic bomb was dropped.

In fact, they generally reach us not just with a caption attached, but also in the company of other pictures and words that help to frame our response. In the commemoration of the atomic bombings, photographs and drawings have played a particularly important role. As Lisa Yoneyama points out, survivors of the bombings are caught between an intense concern that the experience of atomic warfare be remembered and communicated, and a world where language often seems inadequate to the task of communicating the enormity of the event (Yoneyama 1999, 85–92). Both because of their quality as photographs and because they are among the very few photographic records of the immediate aftermath of the atomic bombings, Yamahata's photos have been repeatedly reproduced in collections of historic images in many parts of the world. Of the one hundred or more photographs which Yamahata took in Nagasaki on August 10, 1945, these two are chosen for repro-duction with particular fequency, in part, no doubt, because they convey something of the human tragedy of the event without confronting the viewer with the more grotesquely disturbing scenes of violent death contained in many of the other photographs.

Like family albums, published collections incorporating Yamahata's photographs are the product of social forces which influence the way we see and respond to the photographic image. The mass consumption of photographs in newspapers, magazines, exhibitions and books has in some ways mirrored the evolution of the family album. Like the earliest family albums, the first published collections of photographs were inevitably synchronic. They brought together contemporaneous images of a multitude of different people and places to create a total image of a nation, an empire or a specific dramatic event. The apparent authenticity of the photographic collection endowed it with a special capacity to compress infinitely complex and spatially dispersed reality into a manageable, visible form. The photographic book gave the readers a sense of *seeing* the society to which they belonged, even though that society extended far beyond the bounds of their actual lived experience.

This potential was thoroughly understood, for example, by the editors of one of Britain's first major collections of printed photographs: a lavish two-volume production entitled *The Queen's Empire: A Pictorial and Descriptive Record, Illustrated from Photographs*, produced in 1897 to mark Queen Victoria's diamond jubilee. The significance of the collection was that it 'brought the Empire home', presenting the reader with glimpses of *reality* from every corner of the colonies, and yet at the same time it allowed that reality to be arranged into a particular moral order. As the editors remind their readers in the book's introduction:

> The pictures in this work are all authentic representations of the realities of life and scenery, of men and manners, of the works of man and the wonders of nature throughout the Empire. Every picture is a photographic reproduction, executed with the perfection which has only become possible in very recent years … In every part of the Empire we shall find some trace of the work Britain is doing throughout the world – the work of civilizing, of governing, of protecting life and property, of extending the benefits of trade and commerce. (*The Queen's Empire* 1897, x.)

The photographic collection, in this way, became a means of presenting the imperial order to the large sections of the domestic population who would never be directly involved in the creation and running of the colonies. It gave them a sense of participation in the processes of empire, and at the same time reassured them of their superior status in the racialized hierarchies of the colonial order (Picture 3.10).

With the passage of time and the accumulation of the photographic record, however, it began to be possible to publish photographic narratives which charted the movement of society across the course of decades. After the First World War, the advent of the rotary press,

HOMES OF WHITE MEN AND BLACK MEN.

Of the four illustrations on this page two are of special interest, as showing how our countrymen house themselves when they leave the town for the country, and plant themselves on the edge of civilisation. The square, well-built wooden house of the settler on the shores of Lake St. John looks as comfortable and roomy a home as a man could wish for. The cottage of the Queensland labourer is smaller, but is not unattractive, and the occupant, no doubt, takes a legitimate pride in a home which is really his own. The mud huts of the Koto Krata natives of the Gold Coast, and the circular, wattle-built, grass-thatched cabin of the Kaffir, present a strong contrast to the homes of the Anglo-Saxons, a contrast, happily, wholly in favour of the latter.

3.10 Image from *The Queen's Empire: A Pictorial and Descriptive Record*, London, Cassell and Co., 1897. Photographers unknown.

which made it possible for words and photographic images to be printed cheaply on the same page, encouraged a boom in the popularity of photographic magazines. These created a powerful vehicle for conveying visual images of social change. By the 1930s, for example, the British journal *Picture Post* was commemorating the twentieth anniversary of the end of the First World War with a published collection of sixty-nine photographs portraying 'twenty years of peace'. The message accompanying this record of the peace years was a sombre one, reflecting the mood of a moment of resurgent international tensions: 'What have we done with the last twenty years? Where have they gone to?... Look back over what has happened since that last Armistice Day. It is one long tale of human weakness – of ideals thrust aside in favour of "common sense". Today we ask ourselves, where has this "common sense" led us?' (*Picture Post*, November 12, 1938, 14).

It was in the years immediately after the Second World War, however, that photographic history would really come into its own. By now, many newspaper and magazine publishers had accumulated archives of photographs going back half a century or more. The immensity of the war itself, and of the postwar struggle for recovery, created a hunger for visual recollections of shared experiences of suffering and survival. At the same time, the growth of mass consumption and the mass media, as much as the experience of total war, created common memories which provided a basis for the publication of chronologically organized 'collective family albums' of the nation. By 1947, for example, enough people in the USA could remember smoking Chesterfield cigarettes, buying their first Model-T Ford or watching *Gone with the Wind* for it to seem possible to produce a book like Agnew Rogers and Frederick Lewis Allen's *I Remember Distinctly*, which bore the subtitle *A Family Album of the American People in the Years of Peace: 1918 to Pearl Harbor*. Unlike the *Picture Post*'s 'Twenty Years of Peace', which focuses on photographs of statesmen and major political events, *I Remember Distinctly* is a record of a particular vision of 'everyday life': a vision centred around consumer products, sporting heroes, movie stars and fashion.

In Japan, the late 1950s and early 1960s witnessed a particularly dramatic boom in the popularity of photo-histories. The trend was set in 1956, when the *Mainichi* newspaper published a celebration of 'thirty years of the Showa age'. The public response was so good that they soon followed this up with a second pictorial volume on the Meiji and Taisho eras. Other publishers followed. In 1960, Kodansha published a three-volume photographic *Hundred Year Record of Japan* [*Nihon hyakunen no kiroku*] depicting the transformation of national society since the opening to the West in the 1860s, while Heibonsha's ambitious five-volume photo collection *We Japanese* [*Warera Nihonjin*] included a volume on *The History of Life* [*seikatsu no rekishi*] from the Meiji Restoration to the present day (Konishi ed. 1960; Heibonsha ed. 1960). In the *Asahi* newspaper's 1960 publication, *An Album of Fifteen Postwar Years*, the pages seem to overflow with a mass of images – some one thousand in all – of life in Japan from the moment of defeat. Photographs of famous people or events jostle with pictures of the black-market, overcrowded trains, political demonstrations and hungry children devouring school dinners, yet the overall message is of collective triumph against the odds:

> Some people, seeing these [photographs] will remember their own painful postwar life … Some people, on the other hand, may be made to think again about Japan's position, caught in the midst of the conflict between the US and Soviet blocs … But whatever the case, we have a resilient life-force … Enduring the winds and the rains, at least we have come this far. (Asahi Shinbunsha 1960, 1.)

It is perhaps appropriate, therefore, that the book should open, even before presenting the first image of defeat in war, with a double-page spread depicting the consumer products of the postwar world.

By forging a link between individual and family memories, on the one hand, and national memories, on the other, these collections contributed to the mid-twentieth-century process of the 'national mobilization of memory' (see Morris-Suzuki 1998). The pictures in the published collections of photos, and even their design and layout, invite comparisons with the personal family album. Individuals (for example) draw a connection between pictures of the common soldier at war and the photographs that great-uncles or grandfathers brought back from the front. In this way, family stories can be reimagined as threads in the far bigger story of national society. But such a mobilization of memory is of course also a process of exclusion. As readers are invited to remember 'the way we lived', and to make comparisons between the published national albums and the pictures in their own family albums, invisible boundary lines are drawn, excising those who have no family photographs, or whose photographs fail to fit the favoured narrative of the national past. (Looking at Rogers and Allen's *Family Album of the American People*, for example, one cannot help being struck by the fact that this American family contains no Asian or other non-European migrants, no Native Americans and no Black people except for jazz performers, who seem to be presented as objects of consumption rather than as members of the remembering community.)

Editing the Archive

As the gulf of years separating us from the atomic bombings of Hiroshima and Nagasaki has widened, the iconic status of Yamahata's photographs as representations of those events has increased, and the photos themselves have come to be reproduced in an increasing diversity of publications which seek to create bonds of memory between viewer and subject. In some, the photographs are still used in an effort to keep alive the raw, immediate experience of the event. The volume *That Day in Hiroshima and Nagasaki* [*Ano hi, Hiroshima to Nagasaki de*], published in 1994 by the Japan Peace Museum, focuses exclusively on the experience of the bombings themselves, beginning with images showing clocks stopped at the moment when the two bombs exploded. The front cover of the volume shows Yamahata's photograph of the child with the rice ball; the back cover, his picture of the young woman nursing her baby. The captions of the photographs speak directly, in simple language, to the young people of the present. The picture of the child with the rice ball, for example, is reproduced again in the main body of the volume, accompanied by the following text: 'I am a child of Nagasaki. I am four years old. I want you to know what happened before my eyes on that day. And I want you know about that day in Hiroshima too. I want you to know, the children of Japan to know and the people of the world to know' (Heiwa Hakubutsukan o Tsukuru Kai ed. 1994, 6).

Elsewhere, however, the photographs have come to be presented in a more distanced way as part of national, or global, collective memories of the twentieth century. Kyôdô Tsûshin's fin-de-siècle collection, *Memory of the Twentieth Century: A Hundred Years of Japan and the World as Told by the Newspapers,* provides one instance of the way in which Yamahata's photographs have become part of national memory. It reproduces Yamahata Yôsuke's photo of the mother and baby in its account of the closing stages of the Pacific War. Although (as the title suggests) this book includes some events of global significance, among them the Holocaust and the US civil rights movement, the focus is primarily on Japan. The mother and child are seen against the background of a series of images depicting the massive destruction of Japanese cities through firebombing followed by the atomic blasts. Here, then, the atom bombs are just one part of the wider communal experience of Japanese wartime suffering. Yet the suffering is also distanced by being placed in a narrative in which bombing and defeat give way to peace and reconstruction. The caption reads, 'Mother and child wait for medical treatment: This photograph, which was taken by a cameraman with the western army stationed in Fukuoka, and published after the lifting of reporting restrictions in 1952, vividly shows the victims of atomic weapons' (Kyôdô Tsûshin 2000, 201).

The atomic bombing, however, is central to the pasts of many nations, and Yamahata's images therefore also figure in quite different ways in other national albums. A celebratory volume published by the Australian War Memorial to mark the fiftieth anniversary of the end of the Pacific War – and entitled *Victory: 1945 – War and Peace* – places his images of the nursing mother and of the child with the rice ball into a narrative of war whose shape is radically at odds with that presented in *Memory of the Twentieth Century*. Here, the story of the war – a European as much as a Pacific war – begins in 1939, and is told above all in terms of the heroism and suffering of Australian soldiers. In the opening words of the volume, 'Australia was one of the few nations to have fought from the beginning of World War II in September 3, 1939, to its end on August 15, 1945' (Fitzgerald 1945, 6). The book's images of national masculinity and mateship are reinforced by a cover photo showing a group of smiling Australian soldiers posing arm-in-arm in front of the Sydney Harbour Bridge.

In *Victory* rather small reproductions of the photos of Yamahata's two iconic photographs are presented, uncaptioned, on a page which also shows pictures of the bombing of Hiroshima. Highlighted excerpts from the longer accompanying text emphasize the key points of the narrative. On this page, the words singled out for emphasis express the compassion felt by one former Australian prisoner-of-war who visited Hiroshima soon after Japan's defeat: 'Our brother man went by crippled and burned, and we knew only shame and guilt' (Picture 3.11). But turning the page the reader is at once presented with the smiling faces of newly-released Australian prisoners of war, and the reassuring statement that 'the fact that the bomb would bring the war to a speedy end was sufficient justification' (Picture 3.12). In this context, the visual melding of the atomic bombs of Hiroshima and Nagasaki into a single event is also significant; since it obscures the fact that the decision to drop a second atomic bomb on Nagasaki is even harder to justify than the profoundly questionable decision to drop the first bomb on Hiroshima.

AWM 131583

AWMP1234/13/10

"We felt no sense of either history or triumph. Our brother man went by crippled and burned, and we knew only shame"

AWM 44329

◄   cabin of the US Army Air Force Super Fortress, named Enola Gay after the pilot's mother, with the cargo which would deliver a devastating new dimension to modern warfare.

He was discharged from the Air Force several years later and after a troubled life ended his days in a mental hospital. The pilot Colonel Paul Tibbets and co-pilot Captain Robert Lewis suffered no remorse and went on to become successful businessmen.

Response in the Allied nations was generally in favour of its use but with the hope that the new technology would be used only for peaceful purposes. The fact that the bombs would bring the war to a speedy end was sufficient justification for their use.

On August 9, President Truman said the US had used the atomic bomb "against those who attacked us without warning at Pearl Harbour, against those who have starved and beaten and executed American prisoners of war, against those who have abandoned all pretence of obeying international laws of warfare. We have used it to shorten the agony of war, in order to save the lives of thousands and thousands of young Americans".

Three Sydney Methodist clergymen, the Reverends R.F. Sutton, B.R. Wyllie and Alan Walker, contested the general mood of congratulation. The bomb's use, they said, was a "devastating blow" to the Allies' claim "to the moral leadership of the world".

In response, one person claimed the wonder weapon was "the most humane act of either war. It saved countless lives and untold misery". Others drew attention to Japanese atrocities with the implication that Japan suffered no more than it deserved.   ➤

3.11 Photographs by Yamahata Yôsuke, reproduced in Alan Fitzgerald, *Victory 1945 – War and Peace*, Sydney, Gore and Osment/Canberra, Australian War Memorial, 1995, p. 66.

The self-congratulatory national narrative of *Victory* allows the text to end with the image of a 'world at peace': an image in which the continuing shadow of the atomic bomb in the postwar world has become completely invisible. This perspective differs from that of another collection of images of the same year: the *Mainichi* newspaper's volume *1945 – The Fall of Totalitarianism in Japan and Germany*. Here too, Yamahata's picture of the mother and child is reproduced within the context of an account that spans European and Asian experiences of war, and that celebrates the downfall of the Axis powers. Yet in this case, the image is accompanied by a quotation from Bertolt Brecht's

3.12 Newly liberated Australian prisoners of war, Yokohama, 1945. Reproduced in Fitzgerald op. cit., p. 68. Australian War Memorial image no. 019202. Courtesy of the Australian War Memorial.

journals which points to an entirely different relationship between past and future: 'The atom bomb, in which atomic energy makes a timely first appearance, strikes "normal folk" as simply awful. To those impatiently awaiting their sons and husbands, the victory in Japan seems to have a bitter taste. This superfart is louder than all the victory bells' (Mainichi Shinbunsha ed. 1999; English translation of the quotation is from Brecht 1993, 354–355).

The Family of Man

In 1955, Edward Steichen's exhibition *The Family of Man* opened at New York's Museum of Modern Art. *The Family of Man*, which contained some 500 photographs by 273 photographers from 68 countries, was billed as 'the greatest photographic exhibition of all time', and was certainly one of the most controversial. More than 270,000 visitors saw *The Family of Man* at its original showing at MoMA, and millions more as it toured the United States, Canada, Europe, Japan, Australia and elsewhere during the late 1950s and early 1960s. By 1978, some five million people had bought one of the three book versions of the exhibition (Berlier 1999).

Steichen's selection of photographs drew on the conventions of the family album, evoking echoes which helped the viewers to link their own memories and experiences to images of a world of strangers. The exhibition, innovatively displayed to present the viewer with a kaleido-scopic maze of images, followed the human family on a life course through the stages of love; marriage; childbirth; growing up; labour in the home, the field and the factory; the enjoyment of music and dance; the sharing of meals; study and contemplation; ageing and death; suffering and religious faith; to an apotheosis of peace embodied in the ballot box and the United Nations (Picture 3.13). The pictures focused on the expressions of the human face and body, and bore just the

3.13 Installation view of Edward Steichen's exhibition *The Family of Man*, Museum of Modern Art, Jan 24–May 8, 1955. ©PhotoSCALA, Florence/Museum of Modern Art 1955/2004. Courtesy of Scala Group.

simplest of captions giving the name of the country where they were taken and of the photographer and copyright owner. The only other inscriptions were quotations, interspersed throughout the exhibition, from philosophy, poetry or folk wisdom.

In a sense, the exhibition could be seen as an eloquent expression of postwar humanism. It spoke of a reaction against war, a vision of human equality and fraternity, which had widespread force in the postwar world – not only in the United States and Europe but also amongst the political and intellectual elites of newly independent countries. This was the vision that inspired enthusiasm for the creation of the United Nations, and it is no coincidence that Steichen's exhibition should have concluded with a giant photograph of the UN General Assembly at work. In Steichen's own words, his hope was to express 'the essential oneness of mankind throughout the world' (Museum of Modern Art 1955, 3).

At the time and since, however, Steichen's vision of the human family attracted criticism as well as praise. A particularly outspoken critic is the visual theorist Allan Sekula, who argues that Steichen's glorification of a Western, middle-class model of the family and of the triumph of electoral democracy was in perfect harmony with the demands of US consumer capitalism in the early Cold War years (Sekula 1984). Steichen himself also recognized that the sense of common human identity projected by *The Family of Man* was achieved at the cost of an ambivalent and problematic approach to historical interpretation. His global family moved through the eternal cycle of birth, growth, decline and death, but was abstracted from the detail of historical vicissitudes which might complicate the viewer's sense of shared humanity with the viewed. So, for example, the unforgettable image (labelled, of course, 'Israel'), of a Palestinian woman one hand raised to the sky in a gesture of rage or despair, is detached from any historical meaning, as is the image of weeping and angry Korean women confronting a barbed-wire barricade (Picture 3.14).

3.14 South Korean youths demonstrating. Michael Rougier/Getty Images. This image appears in the *Family of Man* exhibition simply labeled 'Korea. Michael Rougier'. Courtesy of Getty Images.

We are invited to share these people's grief or passion, but not to know anything about its cause.

And yet, despite this apparent denial of history as interpretation, *The Family of Man* in fact made certain implicit judgments about the narrative of the recent past. One such judgment became visible when Steichen chose to remove from the MoMA exhibition a photograph showing the lynching of a Black man in the southern United States, arguing that it would be excessively disturbing to viewers (Berlier 1999). Another is evident from the exhibition's treatment of images related to the atomic bomb.

A composite image, exhibited in the final sections of *The Family of Man*, shows a cosmopolitan group of faces of all ages and nationalities. The face in the middle is that of the child with a rice ball. The image is accompanied by a quotation from Bertrand Russell: 'The best authorities are unanimous in saying that a war with hydrogen bombs is quite likely to put an end to the human race ... there will be universal death – sudden only for a fortunate minority, but for the majority a slow torture of disease and disintegration'.

The design of *The Family of Man*, indeed, focused attention on the ever-present threat of atomic warfare, which Steichen described in a press release as 'one of the greatest challenges of our time'. In addition to Yamahata's photograph, the exhibition space also included a darkened room containing a single massive image of an atomic mushroom cloud. But as Lili Bezner observes, Steichen's treatment of atomic warfare remained 'distanced, safe and general' (Bezner 1999, 154 and 157). The atom bomb was pictured as a threat to the human family, but not as the product of human hands and a weapon made and used as a result of deliberate political decisions. US visitors to the MoMA's showing of *The Family of Man* were not explicitly challenged to reflect on their government's responsibility for the dropping of the first atomic bombs, or to confront America's role in the continuing development of nuclear weapons. Although they saw the image of the child with the rice ball, they were spared the sight of Yamahata's other Nagasaki photographs, with their gruesome images of charred bodies and the barely recognizable remnants of human forms: photographs which might have compelled a more painful reassessment of the decision to drop the bomb.

Steichen's choice and use of photographs was determined both by his overall political message and by the aesthetic design of the exhibition. He wanted to convey to viewers an essentially optimistic image of the common experience of the human family, and was reluctant to include graphic or controversial images of violence which might draw the focus of attention away from this overarching theme (Sekula 1984).

This tension between the *The Family of Man*'s overall humanitarian message and more direct issues of responsibility for violence and injustice became even more sharply visible when the exhibition moved to Japan, where it was shown at the Takashimaya Department Store's exhibition space in Tokyo in 1956. Here, after consultation between the Japanese designers and Edward Steichen, about fifty photographs by Japanese photographers were added to the display (Kanamaru, Ishida and Nakajima 1956, 123). These included some of Yamahata's most harrowing images of Nagasaki. It was, in other words, apparently considered acceptable to show these visions of destruction to a Tokyo audience, but not to show them to a New York audience. In Takashimaya, a large wall display superimposed pictures of the child with the rice ball and other injured victims of the bombing upon a background of another massively enlarged photograph showing a scene of utter devastation, where rigid blackened corpses lie amongst the pulverized buildings (Picture 3.15).

However, when Emperor Hirohito paid an official visit to the exhibition, this scene was concealed from his eyes by a specially installed curtain. The act of concealment, at once shielding the imperial gaze from the disturbing realities of the bombing and drawing a symbolic

3.15 Image from the Takashimaya showing of the *Family of Man* exhibition. Source: *Asahi Graph*, April 29, 1956.

barrier between the imperial persona and the memories of war, provoked outrage in some sections of the Japanese media. The *Asahi Graph* magazine devoted the first page of one edition to a visual presentation of this censorship incident, as well as to a second incident involving the removal of exhibits concerning the bombing of Nagasaki when the exhibition was visited by Hirohito's second son, Prince Yoshi, in the same year. The *Asahi Graph* article confronts the viewer with the censored items next to a headline reading: 'Your Highnesses the Emperor and Prince Yoshi, Please Look at These'. Soon after the incident, Steichen and the local organizers removed the most graphic scenes of atomic destruction from the show altogether. As in the case of the decision to withdraw the photograph of the lynching in the United States, it was argued that the controversy surrounding these pictures would become an undesirable focus of attention, and disrupt the 'flow' of the exhibition as a whole (*Kamera Mainichi*, June 1956, 122–123).

Yamahata did not comment directly on the drawing of the curtain over his photographs during the emperor's visit. However, referring to the removal of some of his pictures from the exhibition he observed:

> The reason given was that it was undesirable to show such 'exceptional events' in an exhibition on the theme of human dignity. But, whatever the rights and wrongs of the debate, I think that, in the sad situation where peace is disrupted, these are far from being 'exceptional events'... what has actually become of the abandoned brothers and of the mother and child whose photographs I took? At that moment, those people still seemed fortunate compared with the others. Their injuries were slight and they were still very much alive. But the tragic question is whether they managed to avoid the terrible radiation sickness which came later. (Quoted in Iizawa 1998, 64.)

The use of Yamahata's images in *The Family of Man* illuminates the point that the truthfulness of photographs does not simply reside within the individual photograph itself, but is also a matter of the process in which the images are combined with one another, and with written and other texts. And the issue here is not only what is shown, but also what is absent or concealed. A war photographer evokes the agony or triumph of a particular point in time, but it is only as we put images together into sequences that we begin to create an account of the causes and effects of that moment. Yamahata's photographs may be used to create a Japanese national collective memory of wartime suffering, to present the atomic blast as an inescapable part of the horrors of war, or to warn of the terrors of a worldwide nuclear future. They can be used as a starting point for reflections on the chains of human responsibility that led to the nuclear bombing, but they can also be edited and presented in ways which seek to avert the eye of the beholder from the problems of responsibility.

The Eye of the Beholder

Finally, historical truthfulness is also a matter of the relationship between image and viewer: of the way in which we, as observers, approach photographs. Here, too, the relationship between empathy and interpretation matters. The intimate nature of photography makes the photo both an extraordinarily powerful medium of historical communication, and one whose use is fraught with problems. When writing and presenting academic papers about photographs, I feel uncomfortably conscious of the fact that displaying and looking at photographic images can violate the dignity of those who have died as the victims of war, a violation less readily perpetrated by, for example, those who view only paintings of a battle scene. Yet to exclude such photographs, to focus only on images of survival, would obviously create a euphemistic image and obscure the horrors of war. The historical use of photos always works along the margins of this delicate tension between the personal and the public, between the need to know, the need to feel and the need to respect. It raises, in other words, a problem of the visual representation of particularly traumatic historical events – a problem of representing the unrepresentable, to which we shall return in later chapters.

Conventionally, historians – accustomed to operating in the medium of the written word – have tended to use photographic images simply as appendages to text, confirming the truth of the narrative and adding to its emotional force. But an encounter with photographs of the past can do far more than this. In an age of retreat from the written word, photographic images may become an increasingly important starting point for engaging with the past (see http://www.geocities.jp/pastwithin). In us, the viewers, photographs can evoke empathy and identity, but can also be a starting point for reflecting on our sense of identity. They may be seen, in other words, less as pieces of evidence to be labelled true or fake, than as question marks which set in motion a procession of speculations: that persistent reflection which forms the core of the process of historical truthfulness. What other photographs were on that reel of film? What images are missing: discarded by the photographer, thrown out by the editor or the censor, or absent simply because, at the crucial moment, the photographer could not bear to release the shutter? How are image, text, spoken words and other fragments of memory woven together into a story that explains what is happening in the photo and why it is important? What varied narratives can be built around this picture to explain the reasons for the event it depicts? Why do I feel more for this image than for that? How do others in different times and places respond to these images? And what happened after the photograph was taken?

4

Moving Pictures:
The Filming of History

It is autumn. The camera moves slowly across a golden rural landscape. Rolling fields of wheat are bathed in a light that shines through the gathering clouds of late afternoon. But already we sense that there is something wrong with this landscape. In the background a drum beats with insistent menace. And as the camera pans down to rest on the jagged barbed-wire fence in front of the field, the soft voice begins its litany: 'Even a peaceful landscape ... even an open field ... even an ordinary road ... even a resort town with a steeple and a marketplace ... can lead to a concentration camp'.

Alain Resnais's film *Night and Fog* [*Nuit et Brouillard*, 1955] begins with such ordinariness. Architects draw up plans of the camps, lavishing on them the attention to detail that they would give to the design of a suburban villa. Watchtowers are to be constructed in 'Alpine' or 'Japanesque' style; gateways embellished with wrought-iron decorations. The military bureaucrats enumerate and record deportees as they are loaded onto cattle trucks.

Resnais moves back and forth from present to past – the present of 1955, when the camps stand rusting and ruined amongst rolling wheat and resurgent weeds; the past of black-and-white documentary footage: a face stares mutely out from the door of a truck for a moment, before the train is sealed and begins to move. Present counterpoints past, while the almost lyrical words of Jean Cayrol's text contrasts with the increasingly unbearable visual images; and all are woven together with the sounds of Hanns Eisler's musical score. Discordant notes heighten images of the deserted camps. Yet the music accompanying the film's most terrible scenes is sometimes suddenly gentle.

Resnais's narrative drags the viewer forward with a remorselessly accelerating tempo. The camera moves impassively over the ruined huts with their countless wooden shelves in place of beds, the endless row of holes in a bare wooden board which served as latrines, the sign that reads 'cleanliness is health'. The documentary footage offers glimpses of elderly men and women huddled naked before the gaze of the armed and uniformed guards who will be their executioners. The gathering momentum of the film is punctuated only by the milestones of years: 1942 – Himmler plans the extermination.

And now I want to stop watching. I want to close my eyes, but I am supposed to be a historian and Resnais spares the viewer nothing – not the piles of suffocated bodies in the newly opened cattle truck; not the mountains of eyeglasses and shorn hair; not the skeletal corpse of the naked woman whose face, for a moment, is almost beautiful as she is dragged like a sack of potatoes to a mass grave; not the dehumanized, dismembered, distorted human bodies; not the images too difficult to turn into words.

And in almost thirty minutes we have reached the end. The guards and the officers stand in the dock in sullen defiance of their accusers. "'I am not responsible," says the Kapo. "I am not responsible," says the officer. "I am not responsible." Then who is responsible?' Finally Resnais brings us back to his present – to the present of the 1950s, the present of the Algerian war, the present of the autumnal colours of rusted and mouldering camp ruins, but also to a present which is extended into the future – into *our* present and beyond – by Jean Cayrol's narrative: 'We pretend to take hope as the image recedes, as though one could be cured of the concentration camp plague; we pretend to believe that all this happened only once, at a certain time and in a certain place, and we refuse to look around us, we who do not hear the endless cry.'

Locomotive Cinema

How is it possible to stand back from a film like *Night and Fog*, to view it as an object of detached scrutiny? Its message is too powerful and too painful. I rented it from a video store thinking of it as research material which I would use as part of an academic project, but at the end of the thirty minutes I am reduced to despair at the scenes I have just watched. A film like *Night and Fog* cannot simply become an object of media studies, from which I can detach my feelings as a viewer. But it can perhaps become a departure point for thinking about the extraordinary power of film as an expression of the past.

From the very beginning, the creators of the motion picture had at least an inkling of this power. When the Lumière brothers shot the famous few minutes of footage which would become one of the first publicly exhibited movies – *The Arrival of a Train at la Ciotat* – they deliberately chose to film the moving train not from the side but from the front, so that it appears to viewers as though it is heading straight towards them. At the first public showing, on December 28, 1895, some members of the audience are said to have fled from their seats in terror as the train approached (Barsam 1992, 3). Their feelings are reflected in the words of the novelist Maxim Gorky, who watched the film when (in telling testimony to the global reach of the Lumière brothers' project) it was shown in his home town of Nizhni Novgorod just four months later:

Suddenly, something clicks … and a train appears on the screen. It speeds straight at you – watch out! It seems as though it will plunge into the darkness in which you sit, turning you into a ripped sack full of lacerated flesh and splintered bones, and crushing into dust and into broken fragments this hall and this building, so full of women, wine, music and vice. (Gorky 1996, 8.)

The Lumière brothers already understood that film draws viewers into its own world, so that we cease to be aware of our immediate surroundings, and become immersed in the landscape on the screen. Other pioneers of the moving picture were to put this sense of immersion to their own uses. From the early twentieth century onward, for example, travel films became one of the most popular forms of documentary movie, and entrepreneurs like William Keefe and George C. Hale in the United States created 'cinema trains' where 'passengers' would sit in a remodelled railway carriage and watch filmed shots of exotic scenery flowing past on screens designed to replicate train windows (Barsam 1992, 29).

As in a train journey, so too in the cinema, the passengers/audience lose control over the speed and trajectory of the journey. Once the opening scenes have appeared on the screen, we are caught up in a continuous flow which cannot be stopped or reversed. Cinema-goers not only lose consciousness of their own spatial surroundings as they are drawn into the visual world of the film, they are also displaced from the mundane flow of time and absorbed into what Robert Gessner termed the 'continuous present' of the movie: 'Cinema is unique among the arts in its projection of time primarily as the continuous present, the immediate moment being both of utmost importance and the accumulation of all that has gone before' (Gessner 1968, 273). When reading a book or turning the pages of a photo album, we choose where to stop, and can turn back pages to remind ourselves of what has come before.

But as movie audiences we become prisoners of the director's sense of time, carried relentlessly along with the flow of film until the closing credits. It was only with the diffusion of home videos from the 1970s onward that audiences would begin to obtain a new form of control over cinematic time: rewinding, replaying, freezing frames to scrutinize them more closely or skipping unwanted sections.

The moving picture is also a medium which engages the senses of sight and hearing simultaneously. For Gorky, viewing the Lumière brothers' film in 1896, one of the most disorienting aspects of the movie was that its vivid representations of movement were presented in total silence: 'Noiselessly, the locomotive disappears beyond the edge of the screen. The train comes to a stop, and grey figures silently emerge from the cars, soundlessly greet their friends, laugh, walk, run, bustle and ... are gone' (Gorky 1996, 8). But by the first decades of the twentieth century, even silent movies were being accompanied by the atmospheric music of the cinema organ or, in some places, including Japan and India, by the voice of a narrator. With the coming of talkies in the 1930s sound and vision came to be far more closely interrelated. A work like Alain Resnais' *Night and Fog* uses this interweaving of image, voice and music to intense effect. In this particular case, the effect of sound is not so much to dramatize, but rather to soften the impact of image. By itself, the documentary footage that Resnais shows is so appalling that the mind wants to deny it, to block it out. The quiet voice of the narrator and the sounds of the musical score seek to create a place in the viewer's mind that may house even such scenes.

Like the photograph, then, the moving picture creates a powerful sense of identification, but the quality of the emotions evoked by a movie is different from that of the emotions evoked by still pictures. Viewing Yamahata Yôsuke's photographs of Nagasaki, for example, we are confronted with unforgettable frozen images: the fleeting expressions of unknown human faces captured for eternity by the camera's lens. When we place these faces back into the flow of time, however, we see them in a different light which is no less moving, but which moves us in a different way.

Fifty years after Yamahata took his photographs, the Japanese broadcasting company NHK commemorated the anniversary of the bombings by making a programme which sought out the survivors pictured in the photographs. In the final sections of the documentary, we see a scene of a long country road outside Nagasaki, and walking slowly towards us down the road comes the tiny figure of an old woman, bent double as she pulls the cart of vegetables which she sells to neighbouring villagers. Her name is Tanaka Kiyo, and her leathery face is furrowed by a maze of deep wrinkles. Only a certain luminosity in her eyes enables us to connect this face to the face of the young woman photographed by Yamahata as she breastfed her baby in the ruins of the city on August 10, 1945. In a rather tired and resigned voice, which seems to crack more with old age than emotion, she recalls how she was working in the fields when the bomb fell. She rushed back to her ruined house to find that her baby, Yoshihiro, had been flung across the room by the force of the blast. She tried to nurse him back to health, but his injuries were beyond recovery, and although he barely cried, he died ten days later, at the age of four months (NHK 1995).

The still images of photography are often those that we remember most clearly, burning themselves into our memories, but it is the moving film, and its combination of sound with changing human moods and expressions, that is more likely to move us to tears. This emotional charge means that the images which moving pictures – both documentaries and feature films – present of past events are likely to have a deep impact in shaping shared feelings of identification with those events. For large numbers of people around the world, their understanding of the American Civil War has been subtly coloured by the imagery and textures of *Gone with the Wind*, although for some people these may also have been overlaid with the rather different imagery of the Ken Burns documentary *The Civil War*. Many British people derive their entire knowledge of the Zulu Wars, one of the key events in the history of colonial South Africa, from Cy Endfield's 1964 movie *Zulu*, and just as many Americans (and others) derive their entire knowledge of the Amistad case from Steven Spielberg's film of that name.

Inventing Reality: Fact and Facsimile in *The Birth of a Nation*

In the early days of the camera, as we have seen, still photography was sometimes used not just to record reality, but also to create photographic images of reconstructed scenes, including scenes from plays or novels and of famous historic events. With the coming of moving pictures, however, the role of the still photograph in recreating imagined events was superseded by film, and photography was redefined as a technique, not for the dramatizing of fiction, but for the recording of reality. The motion picture, meanwhile, came to occupy a dual role in the creation of images of history. On the one hand, it shares with still photography the ability to capture the real. So the urge to record dramatic and catastrophic events for posterity stimulated the emergence of documentary filmmaking, just as it stimulated the development of photography. In Japan, for example, the great earthquake of 1923 became the subject not only of some of the most widely sold collections of news photographs, but also of the first educational documentary sponsored by the Ministry of Education. The gradually accumulating archive of footage of such historical events would provide a resource to be mined by later generations of documentary filmmakers.

But, on the other hand, film also shares with the novel the ability to reconstruct the past in ways that engage the empathy of the audience. Reality and reconstruction, indeed, come to be closely intermingled. Documentary films use reconstructions of past events as well as archival footage, while some feature films (like *JFK*) cut archival footage into a dramatized reconstruction of the past. This complex relationship between the real and the reconstructed is not new, but has haunted the cinematic representation of history from the early days of the moving picture, and has inspired intense and unending debates over the line between fact and fiction on film.

The complexities are, for example, vividly illustrated by the very first historical spectacular, D. W. Griffith's *Birth of a Nation* (1915): a film whose brilliance of cinematic technique is exceeded only by the grotesqueness of its racist message. Recreating and rewriting the story of the American Civil War (in which his father had fought on the losing side), Griffith was obsessed with the desire to convey a sense of reality. Vast armies of extras were brought in to reconstruct the battle scenes, in which Griffith used techniques reminiscent of nineteenth-century romantic art to capture the panorama of war, destruction and death. A fleeing Confederate family huddles on a mountaintop while, far below, an unending line of soldiers snakes its way across the devastated landscape of the South; the smoke of battle creates a double image in which, in the foreground, individuals fight and die while, in the background, a distant city burns to the ground.

The Birth of a Nation was, on its release, the longest US feature movie ever shown to the public, and it helped to establish the tradition of the two-to-three hour movie as the standard form of the Hollywood blockbuster. Drawing on the techniques of the realist novel (particularly on the works of Dickens), Griffith, for the first time in movie history, made extensive use of parallel montage to create a total image of society (Gessner 1968, 332; Eisenstein 1949, 200–201). The narrative cuts back and forth between the lives of the Northern Stoneman family and the Southern Cameron family, and between the domestic life of the increasingly impoverished Southern planters and the drama of the battlefield. Brief glimpses of the deliberations of politicians, debates in state legislatures, street scenes and images of life on the plantation give the audience the sense that they, like the fleeing Confederate family, are perched upon a high vantage point from which they can see the whole of US society in the 1860s unfurling below them. Just as Tolstoy uses the techniques of the modern novel to soar from the minutiae of domestic life to panoramic visions of Russian and European destiny, so in Griffith's film 'the movement of camera perspective from distant shot to medium and close range ... provided an avenue from the most private reaction to a vista of immense scale' (Grindon 1994, 16 – Picture 4.1). The society which Griffith unfurls before the viewer's gaze is one which reflects his central message – the message that, to quote the film's titles, 'the bringing of the African to America planted the seeds of disunion', and that the Ku Klux Klan were the true saviours of America's 'Aryan birthright'. This narrative culminates in an extraordinary apotheosis

4.1 Scene from *The Birth of a Nation*. Dir. D. W. Griffith, 1915.

where, with peace restored, the figure of Christ appears to pour his blessings on a celestial realm inhabited (of course) exclusively by 'Aryans' – a vision of paradise which bears an uncanny resemblance to a US small-town society cocktail party.

Griffith drew not just on cinematic technique but also on academic history in his efforts to persuade the audience of his contentious interpretation of American history. While the film's narrative is based on a justly uncelebrated popular novel, Thomas Dixon's *The Clansmen*, its title frames are laden with citations from supposedly serious historical works. Bob Katz observes of the film *JFK* that 'Hollywood has never been the land of footnotes' (Staiger 1996, 42). Yet the format of the silent movie, with its abundant use of written text, in fact allowed Griffith to attempt to introduce the authority of the footnote into his film. Early titles in the film present extended quotations from Woodrow Wilson's *History of the American People*, including the statement that, in response to the abuses of the Reconstruction era, 'the white men were aroused by a mere instinct of self-preservation ... until at last there had sprung into existence a great Ku Klux Klan, a veritable empire of the South, to protect the Southern country'. (Wilson, who occupied the White House when the film was released, arranged for *The Birth of Nation* to become the first movie to receive an official White House sceening, and reportedly commented afterwards that Griffith's film was 'like writing history in lightning. My only regret is that it is all so terribly true' (quoted in Litwack 1995, 136).)

This emphasis on 'scholarly history' was one of the main selling points of the movie. In an interview published in 1916, Griffith claimed that 'sets were all constructed according to elaborate research which had been conducted for some time previous to starting work on the picture. The result of this research was the installing of the first research library in the picture business' (Vardac 1971, 85). On the basis of this research, Griffith was able to induce an illusion of realism by punctuating the film with scenes which he described as 'historical facsimiles'. In other words, in the absence of archival footage to insert into his film, he creates tableaux which he claims to be exact reconstructions of a particular place and event. So the scene of Lincoln's assassination is prefaced by the text: 'AN HISTORICAL FACSIMILE of Ford's theatre as on that night, exact in size and detail, with the recorded incidents, after Nicolay and Hay in *Lincoln, a History*'. And the politics of the Reconstruction era are represented by a scene titled: 'The Riot in the Master's Hall. The Negro party in control in the State House of Representatives, 101 blacks against 23 whites, session of 1871. AN HISTORICAL FACSIMILE of the State House of Representatives of South Carolina as it was in 1870. After a photograph by "the Columbia State"'.

These ambiguous claims to realism offer the audience no hint of the point at which facsimile fades into interpretation and fiction. So fictional film characters occupy the foreground of the assassination scene, and the South Carolina House of Representatives becomes the scene for Griffith's vicious lampoons of the behaviour of liberated slaves (Picture 4.2). Griffith, in other words, exploits to the full the capacity of cinema to convey to the audience a sense that they are immersed in historical reality itself, while at the same time moulding that reality into a fictional narrative which conveys a particular interpretation of past events. The seamless flow of film back and forth between reconstructed reality and pure imagination is ideal for his purposes. Griffith advertised the historical truth of his interpretation by offering $10,000 to anyone who could prove that an incident in the movie was historically untrue. But when the president of the National Association for the Advancement of Colored Peoples responded with the obvious point that there is absolutely no basis in history for a key element in the film's central narrative – involving the abduction of a White woman, and an attempt to force her into marriage, by the Black Lieutenant Governor of a southern state – Griffith refused to pay, apparently because he had 'meant to limit claims to scenes of nonfictional representation' (Simmon 1993, 110).

4.2 Scene representing the 'South Carolina House of Representatives', from *The Birth of a Nation*. Dir. D. W. Griffith, 1915.

Present at the Making of History

In April 1915, as *The Birth of a Nation* was attracting crowds to cinemas across the United States and provoking race riots in several cities, D. W. Griffith predicted that 'the time will come, and in less than ten years … where the children in public schools will be taught practically everything by moving pictures. Certainly they will never be obliged to read history again.' The movie, in Griffith's vision, would offer viewers an entirely new way to *experience* the past:

Imagine a public library of the near future, for instance. There will be long rows of boxes or pillars, properly classified and indexed, of course. At each box a push button and before each box a seat. Suppose you wish to 'read up' on a certain episode in Napoleon's life. Instead of consulting all the authorities and wading laboriously though a host of books ... confused at every point by conflicting opinions about what did happen, you will merely seat yourself at a properly adjusted window, in a scientifically prepared room, press the button, and actually see what happened.

There will be no opinions expressed. *You will merely be present at the making of history.* (Griffith 1971, 34–35, emphasis added.)

It is unlikely that many academic historians fully shared Griffith's vision of film as a substitute for text, but the publicity surrounding *The Birth of a Nation* certainly helped to persuade them to pay serious attention to the impact of the cinema on the public's understanding of the past. US history educator Henry Johnson, for example, was later to cite the launch of Griffith's film, along with the coming of the Nickelodeon and the invention of the talkie, as one of the milestones which marked the emergence of film as a popular medium with the power to 'approximate reality itself' (Johnson 1940, 170–171).

The obvious influence of movie directors like D. W. Griffith and Cecil B. de Mille encouraged historians to become more actively involved in the making of films, and by the 1920s educational institutions in various parts of the world were embarking on projects to bring the power of the moving picture into the classroom. In the United States, the most ambitious of these projects was the *Chronicles of America Photoplays* series, launched by Yale University in 1921. The photoplays were very short films focusing on key moments in national history. *The Puritans*, for example, depicted 'early life in New England, 1630, contrasted with the court of Charles I', while *Jamestown* offered 'a faithful impression of the Jamestown settlement in 1612 under the stern rule of Sir Thomas Duke' and of 'the ever present menace of the Indians whose hostility is aggravated in part by Spanish intrigue' (Knowlton and Tilton 1929, 1–2).

Chronicles of America Photoplays were intended both for classroom use and for general cinema release, and became the focus of a number of interwar research projects designed to assess the impact of movies on children's understanding of the past. Educational researchers enthusiastically mobilized the new techniques of the social survey in their efforts to discover whether films helped or hindered children to recall particular types of historical fact (Knowlton and Tilton 1929, 90; see also Consitt 1931; Wise 1939). Elsewhere, even larger projects for the incorporation of film into education were underway. The Japanese Ministry of Education, for example, began sponsoring the making of educational films in 1923, and from then on developed a comprehensive nationwide programme of film production, which was soon accompanied by equally comprehensive efforts to survey the impact of movies on popular entertainment and public opinion (Inada 1962).

Debates on the value of film in history teaching, however, tended to concentrate on the viewers' recollection of facts. Surveys repeatedly probed the ability of audiences to recall particular events and details from movies. The capacity of the moving image to impress certain types of information on the mind was seen as a key to understanding the educational power of the movie. Where the content of the movies themselves was discussed, the main issue was generally the question of accuracy. One critic, for example, noted that 'much havoc has been wrought by dramatization utterly at variance with the facts established by historians', but went on to reassure teachers that

fortunately for history there are producers of historical films for theatres whose passion for historical veracity is as strong as that of the most exacting historical scholar. Of the best of their productions it may be said in high praise that in details of actor make-up, furniture, houses, landscape, and other externals, they are as accurate and exhaustive as critical investigation of all available sources can make them. (Johnson 1940, 171–172.)

These debates on memory and accuracy, though, seldom addressed the wider question of the way in which the structure of the movie frames an imaginative landscape of the past, and rarely confronted more profound issues of cinematic truth being raised by other interwar developments in the movie industry. Though educational films like the *Chronicles of America Photoplays* defined themselves as non-fiction, they were (like Griffith's facsimiles) reconstructions which used actors to perform dramatizations of the past. The 1920s, however, also witnessed the appearance of a different type of non-fiction film, the documentary, a term said to have been coined by British filmmaker John Grierson, whose work was to have a formative influence on the development of the non-fiction film around the world. For Grierson, an essential feature of the documentary was its rejection of dramatization in favour of recorded reality: 'We believe that the materials and stories thus taken from the raw can be finer (more real in the philosophic sense) than the acted article' (Grierson 1996, 97). Yet, while D. W. Griffith had envisaged reconstructed facsimiles as presenting audiences with 'what actually happened', Grierson saw the reality of the documentary as an act of imagination. The task of the documentary-maker was to work 'material taken from the raw' into a form which conveyed a social message. The documentary film, in other words, 'has given itself the job of making poetry where no poet has gone before it … It requires not only taste but also inspiration, which is to say a very laborious, deep-seeing, deep-sympathizing creative effort indeed' (Grierson 1996: 101–102).

Though Grierson's documentaries focused on contemporary social issues, the tension between reconstruction and 'material taken from the raw' also had ramifications for the presentation of historical truth on film. Grierson's early experiments with the documentary coincided with the period of Russian cinematic experimentation which followed the Revolution of 1917. For early Soviet filmmakers, one of the most important tasks was to capture on film the revolutionary origins of their own society. So recent Russian history became a central theme of their films. It was in this context that documentary filmmaker Esther Shub became the first director to grasp the potential of archival footage to bring the past to life. Shub discovered that Tsar Nicholas II had kept a private cameraman, who had recorded thousands of metres of film of court life. By combining this with other pre-Revolution newsreel footage, she was able to create the vivid historical documentaries, *The Fall of the Romanov Dynasty* (1927) and *The Russia of Nicholas II and Leo Tolstoy* (1928). For Shub, 'any available acting method for the historical film has only an ephemeral value in comparison with the chronicle film, which possesses a conviction which can never pale and can never age' (Leyda 1996, 56–61). Like the still photograph, the documentary film is a physical trace of the past, but a trace in motion, allowing the viewer an illusion of being present in the landscape of history. As Shub realized, however, using this landscape to *interpret* the past required the careful use of montage. Cutting back and forth between images of the gilded gaiety of a court ball and footage of toiling peasants or demonstrating workers, she was able to create a powerful and profoundly ideological narrative of Tsarist society and the origins of the Bolshevik Revolution.

Shub's friend and contemporary Sergei Eisenstein, on the other hand, chose to present similar events from the recent past through the medium of reconstruction rather than archival film, though his representation of the events leading up to the Revolution was influenced by the techniques of Shub as well as of D. W. Griffith (a director whom he deeply admired). The inspiration he received from Shub is evident particularly in his unforgettable representation of the St. Petersburg demonstrations of

July 1917 in the film *October* (1927). Here Eisenstein intercuts images of sneering, overdressed bourgeois revellers attacking a proletarian demonstrator with images of a young woman demonstrator in a pony cart mown down by government guns and left dying on the Neva bridge as it is (by order of the provisional government) raised to cut off the working-class districts from the centre of the city. In the climactic scene, the exultant representatives of the bourgeoisie fling copies of *Pravda* into the Neva as the dead pony dangles over the edge of the raised bridge and then silently falls into the river. Montage gives Eisenstein the means to create brilliantly reconstructed scenes through which he repeatedly counterposes, not only rich against poor, but also the massive power of technology – the vast wheels and girders of the rising Neva bridge – against the vulnerability of the human, or animal, body (Picture 4.3).

Unrepresentable Pasts: Testimony in *Shoah* and *Yuki Yukite Shingun*

These examples remind us that the distinction between fiction and non-fiction, in the historical film as well as in written history, is not a simple and absolute line. Some written histories, like Thomas Babington Macaulay's works, draw on the techniques of the novel to create vivid reconstructions of historical events, while others adopt a more sober documentary approach; some historical novels, like *Salammbô*, adopt a richly imaginative approach to the past while others, like *War and Peace* or *The Abe Family*, flow over the line between fiction and historical essay. Similarly, during the first decades of the twentieth century, a spectrum of differing techniques was developed for representing the past on film. These ranged from the documented presentation of material taken from the raw, via the would-be realistic reconstructions of the *Chronicles of America Photoplays* and the more consciously ideological reconstructions of a director like Eisenstein, to highly fictionalized visions of the past

4.3 Scene from *October*. Dir. Sergei Eisenstein, 1927.

like *The Birth of a Nation*, which, with its invented plot-line and main characters, still sold itself to viewers as a faithful representation of history.

At the same time, the realism of the documentary itself brought into sharp focus an issue which we have already encountered in the discussion of photographs. The power of photograph and film to convey graphic depictions of the past is so great that it raises its own problems of representation. At what point does the viewing of such a reality become an intrusion into others' privacy? At what point does it become an act of voyeurism, or a process that threatens to blunt rather than enhance the ability of the viewer to feel for the experiences of the viewed? These issues have become particularly contentious problems for documentary cinema in the second half of the twentieth century.

Alain Resnais, recalling the Holocaust in the 1950s, focused on the stark horror of its events, captured on the few remaining fragments of archival film and recalled by the decaying ruins of the camps. His film carried the viewer forward with a remorseless momentum into a confrontation with the visual evidence of indescribable acts. But in the 1980s Claude Lanzmann, seeking (like Resnais) eternally to engrave the reality of the Holocaust on the human memory, followed a very different course. For Lanzmann, the Holocaust is an occurrence beyond the realms of normal human history. Its events cannot be represented visually. He therefore deliberately refuses to use either documentary footage or reconstructions of the past, relying instead on contemporary film footage and above all on the spoken testimony of survivors, of those who 'speak for the dead'.

The audience of Lanzmann's 1985 film *Shoah*, like the audience of *Night and Fog*, is absorbed into a time-frame created by the director. But, rather than impelling the audience forward with accelerating speed, Lanzmann demands that the viewer's gaze inches very slowly across the landscapes of the Holocaust, dwelling on the facial expressions of survivors, experiencing silent journeys down the muddy forest tracks that lead to the places of death, listening to the sounds of everyday life which, almost incredibly, continue all around as victims and perpetrators speak of annihilation. As he has subsequently written:

> If I had found a real film – a secret film, because such things were strictly forbidden – made by an SS member and showing how 3,000 Jewish men, women and children died together, asphyxiated in the gas chamber of Auschwitz's crematorium 2, not only would I not have shown it but I would have destroyed it. I cannot explain why. That is the way it is. (Lanzmann 1994; see also Hansen 2000, 207.)

The same strategy is followed by Japanese director Hara Kazuo, whose 1987 film *Yuki Yukite Shingun* [*The Emperor's Naked Army Marches On*] similarly deals with the memory of mid-century atrocities. Filmed testimony, for Hara as for Lanzmann, is a way of confronting experiences so extreme that other forms of representation become impotent or grotesque. Film has a special role in preserving oral testimony because it allows us, not just to hear the voice of the witness to history, but to watch her or his face, to see those telling shifts of expression, the movements of hands or shoulders which can express as much as the words themselves. This role is all the more important in a world that has experienced total war. The film of testimony communicates the experiences which governments and armies carefully exclude or expunge from the official record. It is therefore also driven by a sense of urgency – a desperation to capture and pass on the voices of survivors and eyewitnesses before they are lost to time. Hence a sort of ruthlessness that suffuses both Lanzmann's and Hara's documentary style. In *Shoah*, it is the director himself who conducts the remorseless pursuit of truth, openly intruding on the lives of the perpetrators to reveal their secrets, and prodding reluctant witnesses with quiet but unrelenting interrogation: 'You must speak. You know you must describe this'.

Hara, meanwhile, follows the disturbing figure of Okuzaki Kenzô, a survivor of the Japanese Army's New Guinea campaign, as he – like an avenging angel – tracks down the people he believes to have been responsible for the deaths of his comrades-in-arms. Okuzaki's obsessive personality is matched by Hara's unrelenting documentary style. The camera becomes an unblinking eye, recording every moment of Okuzaki's increasingly violent pursuit of the truth. The only concessions made to viewers are occasional black-and-white captions conveying stark facts: 'There was an incident among the troops of the 37th Division left behind in Wewak where the corps commander ordered the shooting of subordinates'. Little by little, a story starts to piece itself together: a story of starvation, the murder of local civilians, the killing of fellow soldiers, cannibalism.

By avoiding the use of archival material and telling this story solely through the mode of testimony – through the interviews which Okuzaki extracts from his former comrades – Hara Kazuo forces the viewer to confront the relationship between past and present. Memories of violence are preserved in picturesque rural settings. Again and again, Okuzaki tracks down the officers responsible for wartime atrocities, only to be confronted by some mild-mannered elderly man who offers him tea and biscuits and introduces him to the grandchildren. Thus the audience is ultimately forced also to consider the link between the memories of violence and the surviving presence of the elderly Emperor Hirohito who, like Okuzaki's commanding officers, had never been called to account for his wartime role. At the same time, Okuzaki's increasingly unbalanced personality itself seems to bear witness to the unhealed wounds of war. The film ends with Okuzaki in prison after shooting the son of one his former wartime commanders. The unacknowledged violence of the past replicates itself in the present.

Film and the Grammar of Historical Time

At first sight, it seems easy to assume that the historical documentary is the film version of the written history text, while the historical feature film is the film version of the historical novel. Yet thinking through the films we have discussed, it seems clear that the relationship is more complex than this. Both historical films and history texts come in a variety of forms, embodying varying degrees of imagination. There are, however, certain inherent differences in the ways that the book and the film frame their presentations of historical truth. The written word is adapted to dealing with abstract phenomena. The text allows the writer to pull out certain threads from the totality of lived experience, and to follow those threads with relatively little reference to the surrounding texture of life. So it is rather easy to write books (or chapters in books) which focus on the history of ideas, ideologies or institutions, such as monarchies, parliamentary systems and so on. By comparison, as Robert Rosenstone observes, the codes of realism embodied in the mainstream film present life as a total process.

> The world on the screen brings together things that, for analysis, or structural purposes, written history often has to split apart. Economics, politics, race, class and gender all come together in the lives and moments of individuals, groups and nations. This characteristic of film throws into relief a certain convention – one might call it a fiction – of written history: the strategy that fractures the past into distinct topics, categories and chapters; that treats gender in one chapter, race in another, economy in a third. (Rosenstone 1995, 60.)

The popular film, Rosenstone argues 'emotionalizes, personalizes and dramatizes history'. It tends to offer an enclosed linear narrative covering a limited expanse of time and place. So 'there exist no broad film histories of nations, eras, or civilizations that provide a historical framework for specific films' (Rosenstone 1995, 50). But here Rosenstone is of course referring to film on the big screen, and his comments also remind us of an important reordering of the grammar of historical communication which occurred in the second half of the twentieth century. As we have seen, the coming of the motion picture at the beginning of the century led to the redefinition of still photography as a genre which specialized in 'reality' and 'aesthetic expression', while the movie took over the role of presenting fiction and recon-structed events. After the Second World War, a further reordering of media conventions redefined the cinema primarily as a space for the presentation of dramatized feature films, while television gradually assumed the role of presenting news and documentaries (while also, of course, offering its own historical and contemporary dramas). Films like *Shoah* and *Yuki Yukite Shingun* are unusual in being postwar historical documentaries made for the cinema screen, and neither was created with a mass audience in mind. (In the case of *Yuki Yukite Shingun*, the pusillanimous policies of the mainstream distribution houses meant that film showings were largely confined to art theatres, though in the end, with the help of video distribution, it is believed to have reached an audience of some one million (Ruoff and Ruoff 1998, 38).)

This shift of the documentary from large to small screen had profound consequences. The relationship between viewer and television programme is very different from the relationship between viewer and cinema film. In the cinema, we sit in darkness, overwhelmed by the vision and sound of the film. The television, by contrast, generally sits in a corner of the room, to be turned on and off at will, its volume adjustable and its sounds overlaid by the clatter of everyday life. We talk to friends or family members while we watch TV, sometimes commenting on the images we are seeing on the screen. In the cinema, however, comments are whispered if they are made at all, and we tend to watch in silence until we stumble out of the auditorium into the momentarily unfamiliar light of day. Television programmes are commonly broken up into episodes: by convention, usually six, seven, nineteen or twenty-six programmes of forty-five or fifty-five minutes each (Watt 1976, 172). Episodes may be repeated or, since the 1970s, recorded on video and watched in snippets whenever we want.

All of these things affect the way that we see the past on the small screen. While the mainstream feature film (like the realist historical novel) works in a limited temporal frame, usually covering at most the span of a couple of generations, television documentaries can cover large swathes of history, including the histories of nations or civilizations. The division of documentary series into episodes in some ways also mirrors the division of books into chapters, and allows a certain 'fracturing of the past into distinct topics'. A programme like the BBC's *The People's Century* (1997), for example, can divide twentieth-century history by theme, devoting one episode to population growth, another to communications media, another to the environment and so on.

Yet television documentaries share with feature films some peculiarities that distinguish them from the written text. They too have a particular capacity to synthesize rather than to analyse, to present life as an integrated whole. On the small screen, as much as the cinema screen, we see the past as a complicated texture. We simultaneously absorb images of costume and housing, landscapes and faces and movement. Documentaries, too, have the power to evoke intense emotion and identification by their weaving together of narrative, image and sound: a power vividly illustrated in the first episode of Ken Burns's immensely successful TV documentary *The Civil War* (1991), which concludes with the reading of a last letter written by a Confederate officer to his wife just before his death in battle. As Gary Edgerton points out, this scene provoked not only considerable criticism from some historians, but also an intense reaction from viewers, many of whom contacted Burns to convey their appreciation or to share with him accounts of their own family's role in the events of 130 years ago (Edgerton 2000).

The capacity of the documentary to evoke identification is made interestingly visible in the popular Japanese documentary series *Shitteiru tsumori ka* [*So You Think You Know About It?*]. This programme promises to shed new light on well-known incidents, mostly from the recent past. Its topics have ranged from deeply controversial historical events, such as the human experimentation performed on prisoners of war during the invasion of China by the notorious Unit 731, to well-known murders and political scandals. Here too, however, the narrative of historical events is often constructed around personal lives and experiences. The story of the famous 1970 hijacking of a JAL plane to North Korea by members of the Japanese Red Army, for example, is retold by focusing on the subsequent destinies of various participants in the events, including the hijackers and the plane's pilot. These past events are also linked to the present by a panel of celebrities – film stars, television personalities and others. As the documentary narrative comes to an end, the camera switches to the faces of the panel, capturing their expressions of shock, sorrow or remembrance. Their comments, and their shared reminiscences of particular events, seem to offer us, the viewers, suggestions as to the appropriate range of emotional reactions to the material we have just seen. A similar technique for linking documented events and the contemporary audience is used by the creators of the US series *500 Nations* (1995). In this account of the history of the Native American peoples, each episode opens and closes with a brief comment from Kevin Costner, whose role in the movie *Dances With Wolves* identifies him, in the minds of TV audiences, as an intermediary between the Native American world and 'majority' US society.

The popularity of individual anecdotes as a means of bringing the past to life has much to do with the inherent qualities of television as a medium of communication. In the words of TV documentary producer Jerry Kuehl, television

> offers its audience virtually no time for reflection. It is a sequential medium, so to say, in which episode follows episode, without respite. This clearly means that the medium is ideally suited to telling stories and anecdotes, creating atmosphere and mood, giving diffuse impressions. It does not lend itself easily to the detailed analysis of complex events; it is difficult to use it to relate coherently complicated narrative histories, and it is quite hopeless at portraying abstract ideas. (Kuehl 1996, 178–179.)

This brings us back to one of the recurring themes of earlier chapters: the relationship between history as identification and history as interpretation. Rosenstone, discussing the potential and limitations of the historical film, contrasts the views of US scholars R. J. Raack and Ian Jarvie (while also expressing his doubts about some of Jarvie's conclusions). Raack, who is an enthusiastic advocate of the filming of history, argues that the movie, with its ability to present the complex totality of life, is uniquely capable of presenting 'empathetic reconstruction to convey how historical people witnessed, understood and lived their lives'. The special quality of film is its capacity to 'recover all the past's liveliness'. Jarvie, by contrast, highlights the 'discursive weakness' of filmed treatments of historical debates. Though a historian might be able to express his or her view of the past in film, 'how could he defend it, footnote it, rebut objections and criticize the opposition?' Thus film lacks the capacity to capture a central feature of all historical enquiry: debate between historians about the causes, consequences and meaning of historical events (Raack 1983, 416–418; Jarvie 1978, 378; Rosenstone 1995, 25–26). In other words, Raack, like many commentators on filmed history, welcomes the power of film as a vehicle for history as identification; Jarvie echoes a common complaint in lamenting at its weakness as a medium for history as interpretation.

Who We Are is Who We Were: Personalizing the Amistad Case

To understand the impact of film on history as identification and history as interpretation, though, it is important to look, not only at the inherent qualities of film itself, but also at the way it coexists and interacts with other media of historical expression. We can explore this issue by considering the example of a major Hollywood historical production: Steven Spielberg's *Amistad* (1997). The film deals with a real event – an 1839 rebellion by Africans kidnapped into slavery by Spanish traders. After their ship, *La Amistad*, ran aground off the coast of Connecticut the Africans were put on trial for mutiny and murder, and their case, which involved questions of the rights of those illegally enslaved to resist their captors with force, eventually came before the US Supreme Court. *Amistad*, then, is a story which stands at the focal point of many intersecting pasts. It concerns the history of the Atlantic slave trade – a history whose worst horrors were as unrepresentable as those addressed by Claude Lanzmann and Hara Kazuo. It evokes memories of racial injustices whose legacy still tears at the fabric of US society, but also memories of the heroic struggle of some people in the US, West Africa and elsewhere against those injustices. At the same time, it also forms an integral part of the history of Sierra Leone, from whose Mendi language group the kidnapped Africans originated – a country whose continuing social suffering has roots going deep into the slave trade and British colonialism.

Not surprisingly, then, the Amistad affair has generated a multitude of written accounts. These range from fictional narratives like William Owens's 1953 novel *Slave Mutiny*, on which Spielberg's film is loosely based, and *Echo of Lions*, whose author, Barbara Chase-Ribout, sought to sue the film's makers for plagiarism, to scholarly studies like B. Edmon Martin's *All We Want is Make Us Free: La Amistad and the Reform Abolitionists* and Iyunolu Folayan Osagie's *The Amistad Revolt: Memory, Slavery and the Politics of Identity in the United States and Sierra Leone*, which includes a perceptive critique of the Hollywood version of the case (Owens 1953; Chase-Ribout 1989; Martin 1986; Osagie 2000). The written versions of the story vary greatly in their style, focus and interpretation of events. In the world of the mainstream movie, by contrast, Spielberg's account of the case is unique and dominant.

This reflects obvious differences between the economics of publishing and movie-making. It is, simply, far cheaper to produce a book or journal article than to produce a commercial movie. On the other hand, the average book or article reaches a far smaller audience than the average feature film. Book publishing has always been characterized by relatively small-scale production for a segmented and diversified market: movie-making, on the other hand, is even today dominated by a kind of Fordist mass-consumption of standardized models. Once a film like *Amistad* has been made, it is most unlikely that Hollywood filmmakers will produce alternative versions of the same story, at least for several decades. The written text generates a multiplicity of varied interpretations of the same event. Their diverse narratives can be compared by readers, but are likely to reach only a restricted audience. The movie, meanwhile, creates a single, unforgettable, widely influential narrative. Like the legends of oral societies, it embodies a moral and narrative structure which shapes popular images of the world in which we live. The movie provides modern society with its mythology.

One central feature of this mythology is its focus on a limited number of human actors, each with a clearly distinguishable personality. It is true, of course, that some experimental feature films have resisted this tradition. The most striking example is perhaps Eisenstein's *October*, where the film's central character is the proletariat rather than any specific individual. But not even Eisenstein's brilliant cinematography was able to make this depersonalized history appealing to cinema audiences. *October* was a critical success, but was shunned by moviegoers, who found it too abstract and complex.

The forward momentum of the movie (the fact that it is not possible, in a cinema, to reverse the narrative flow and refer back to earlier events to check names and details) generally makes it necessary to pare the story down to clear lines that the audience can readily follow. Even more than Owens's novel *Slave Mutiny*, then, Spielberg's *Amistad* focuses on a select handful of figures, including the leader of the mutiny

Sengbe Pieh, referred to in the film by the Hispanicized version of his name, Cinque; and the lawyers Roger Baldwin and John Quincy Adams, who defended the Amistad Africans before the US courts. In the process, a multitude of other figures who appear in the written accounts of the story fade from the scene. For example, much information survives about a number of the West Africans who arrived in Connecticut on the *Amistad*. During their incarceration and trial in New England, several learnt English, at least three wrote letters addressed to Adams, and one became a prominent missionary and educator on her return to Sierra Leone (Picture 4.4) (see Cable 1971; Osagie 2000; see also Chapter 6). The narrative structure of the Hollywood movie, however, encourages Spielberg to condense the personal experience of the African characters into the single readily identifiable figure of the leader, Cinque, and to focus on Cinque's relationship with the elder statesman Adams, who fills the role of the chief American hero in the drama. Most interestingly, in Spielberg's version, the rather dour white abolitionist Louis Tappan, who, according to most accounts, played a central role in the case, is upstaged by the benign and appealing figure of Theodore Joadson (played by Morgan Freeman), a wholly fictional character who incorporates elements drawn from the lives of various nineteenth-century Black abolitionists – but, as critics have pointed out, seems to lack some of the vigour and political energy of his historical counterparts (Osagie 2000, 128).

Like all myths, the commercial feature film draws on a repertoire of narrative structures familiar to its audience. *Amistad* makes a complex event in the nineteenth-century history of West Africa, Spain and the US readily comprehensible to a wide audience by casting it in the familiar pattern of the Hollywood courtroom drama. This dramatic structure requires that the seemingly unyielding face of the legal estab-lishment be brought into contact with the demands of humanity and justice, represented by the defence attorney: an outsider whose eccentric

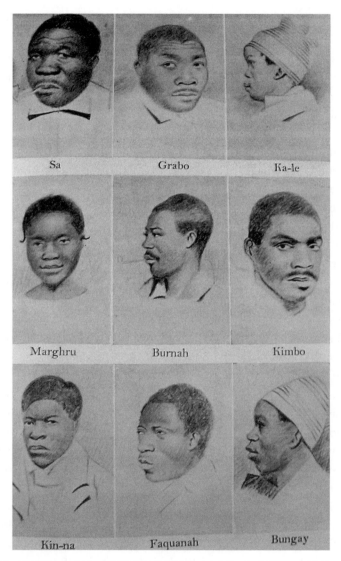

4.4 The many faces of Amistad. Sketches of the *Amistad* Africans by William H. Townsend. Source: William A. Owens, *Slave Mutiny*, London, Peter Davis, 1953.

personality highlights his (he is usually male) role as courageous individual confronting the system. As in most versions of this narrative, Spielberg's story ends with the triumph of the outsider's appeal for justice. The [US] legal system is thus shown as possessing, behind its stern exterior, a rationality and humanity capable of responding to the individual's assertion of his or her fundamental rights.

In the feature film, the personalization of the past is deeply influenced by a further factor: what Richard Dyer describes as 'the polysemic star image'. This image strengthens the empathetic link between past and present. Most of the main characters in the film are acted by movie stars whose faces are familiar to the audience, and whose lives themselves are the objects of popular consumption in the mass media. *Amistad* viewers, therefore, are attracted to the movie partly by the presence of stars like Anthony Hopkins, Morgan Freeman and Anna Paquin. As George Custen puts it, 'the moviegoer is drawn to resonant aspects of the impersonator as well as the life impersonated. In this light, perhaps one admires Queen Elizabeth I for her statecraft but also because she is Bette Davis'; or, one might add, Cate Blanchett. (Custen 2000, 68). Like the presence of the celebrity panel in *Shitteiru tsumori ka* and of Kevin Costner in *500 Nations*, the familiar face of the famous actor in the feature film brings history into the midst of our own lives. It assures us that the people of the past had recognizable emotions and motives that may be played out by the people of the present, and that the events of the past are considered sufficiently relevant to be addressed to us through the voices of the heroes of contemporary popular culture.

This interpretation of the past in terms that appeal to present-day viewers raises obvious problems of historical truth. Is Spielberg's invention of the amiable Theodore Joadson a justifiable way of redressing the long neglect of Black abolitionists in US historiography, or is it a misleading insertion of a fictional character into a film which advertises its own historical authenticity? More broadly, the historical meaning which Spielberg attributes to the Amistad case is also open to questioning at various levels. Both the kidnapping of slaves and the eventual return of the Amistad Africans to their homeland, where several of them engaged in Christian missionary activities, had profound implications for the history of Sierra Leone (see, for example, Cable 1971; Osagie 2000). The Hollywood version, however, focuses firmly on the US dimensions of the story. The kidnapping itself is reduced to a few moments of film, and the movie comes to a stop at the point where the freed slaves are about to step back onto African soil.

The way in which Spielberg locates his story in the broader narrative of American history has also invited controversy. As Simon Schama reminds us, the Amistad case was not actually about the morality or legality of slavery in the United States, but centred on a narrower argument about the legality of the slave trade on the high seas (Schama 1998). Spielberg, however, recasts Amistad into a key moment in the abolition of slavery in the US, and thus in the epic of an ongoing American quest for freedom and justice. John Quincy Adams's concluding address to the Supreme Court (which survives in print) consisted largely of relatively dry legal argumentation. In the movie, Spielberg therefore entirely rescripts this into a stirring speech about a national identity that transcends race. While preparing for the trial, Adams learns from Cinque the importance of summoning the spirits of one's ancestors in times of need. In his address to the court, Adams puts this into practice by invoking the memories of the American founding fathers (including his own literal father): 'Alexander Hamilton, James Madison, Benjamin Franklin, Thomas Jefferson, George Washington, John Adams'. Asking them to bestow their blessings on his quest for liberty and equality, he continues: 'We have been made to understand, and to embrace the understanding, that *who we are is who we were*'. If this realization leads to civil war, Adams concludes (with improbable prescience) 'then let it come, and may it be finally the last battle of the American Revolution'.

Even the sceptical viewer is likely to be moved by the closing lines of Adam's speech, rewritten by Spielberg and his production team. As actor Anthony Hopkins brilliantly delivers these lines to the crescendo of a haunting musical score, 'hearts around the theatre' (in Simon Schama's words) 'swell like popcorn' (Schama 1998, 38). But in evoking empathy for the reconstructed past, Spielberg is also implicitly offering an idiosyncratic reinterpretation of American history. The Spielberg version serves to present US history as a narrative in which freedom, justice and racial equality have *always* been the central themes, and support for slavery appears as a kind of temporary aberration.

This retelling of the Amistad case encourages viewers to identify with an inspiring narrative of liberation. But at the same time it erases or blurs a host of other historically significant narratives. The statement 'who we are is who we were' creates a cohesive American 'we' linking the founders of the nation, via the Amistad case, to an imagined contemporary national movie audience. But the 'we' thus constituted as the active subjects of this drama of liberty excludes the African participants in the story, who are implicitly defined as 'them', the beneficiaries of the liberty which 'we' have enshrined in law. In linking the founding father Thomas Jefferson to the Amistad case, and through this to contemporary notions of human rights, the narrative obscures the reality that Jefferson evolved from an impassioned critic of slavery to one of Virginia's largest slave-owners. In presenting the Amistad case as a triumphant turning point in the struggle for human rights in the US, Spielberg's narrative (as historian Eric Foner points out) ignores the fact that the majority of judges in the case were still on the Supreme Court in 1857, when it handed down the Dred Scott judgment, ruling that blacks had 'no rights which a white man was bound to respect' (Foner 1997). And in creating a national 'we' whose commitment to liberty stretches back to the founding fathers, *Amistad* comfortingly erases from Hollywood's memory intervening events like the making of *The Birth of a Nation*, and its enthusiastic reception in President Woodrow Wilson's White House.

The Cultural Economy of Memory and Interpretation

The myths created by the Hollywood movie are important not just because they are national myths, but also because they are global myths. The unequal exchange of historical visions that characterizes the historical novel is even more apparent in the realms of the mainstream historical movie. The landscapes of the historical imagination around the world have been shaped by Hollywood: whether by its epic depictions of ancient Rome, its portrayal of the colonial conquest of the American West, its versions of the American Civil War and the Second World War, or recent historical offerings like *Pearl Harbor* and *Amistad*. Subtitled or dubbed and distributed on video, the products of Hollywood reach widely across the face of the world. By contrast, movie accounts of historical events produced in Africa or Asia are far less likely to mould the historical imaginations of cinema and TV audiences in the North Atlantic nations. This unequal exchange of imagery is vividly illustrated by the case of Amistad. As Osagie points out, the Amistad case, long forgotten in Sierra Leone, was 're-remembered' there from the late 1980s onward, and incorporated into a new Sierra Leonean nationalist narrative associated with the rise of Valentine Strasser's National Provisional Revolutionary Council, which seized power in 1992. In the process it became, amongst other things, the subject of two acclaimed Sierra Leonean plays: Charlie Haffner's *Amistad Kata Kata* (1988) and Raymond Desouza George's *The Broken Handcuff or Give Me Free* (1994) (Osagie 2000, 98–118). But, though Haffner's play has been performed in New Haven, Connecticut (the town where the Amistad Africans were held in prison awaiting trial), Sierra Leonean dramas and paintings representing Sengbe Pieh as a national hero have rarely reached an audience outside the nation's boundaries. Spielberg's representation of Cinque as a central character in the narrative of American freedom, on the other hand, reaches audiences around the world, including those in urban centres through-out Africa.

Yet the very power of the Hollywood myth has another consequence which is crucial to interpreting the consequences of the filming of history. Mainstream movies and major TV documentaries are no longer single commodities consumed in isolation by their audiences. They generate a mass of other forms of historical representation: books of the film, reviews, magazine interviews, media debates, TV documen-taries on the making of movies, Internet websites, educational material and so on. A glance at a recent list of books and articles on the Amistad case shows that a large proportion have been published since the making of Spielberg's film, and many appeared in the months immediately after the film's release. Some, like Alexs Pate's novel *Amistad*, or the schoolkit on the Amistad case distributed by Spielberg's company Dreamworks, were part of the merchandise that accompanied the film (Pate 1997). Others, like Simon Schama's article, re-examined the Amistad case as part of a critique of the movie (Schama 1998; see also Foner 1998). Other writers again used the release of the movie as an opportunity to present their own perspectives on related historical issues. Gore Vidal, for example, greeted the release of the film with an article on the neglected significance of John Quincy Adams as a historical figure, while Cinqué Henderson (one of the film's technical advisors) used it as an occasion to reflect on the complexity of race relations and ethnic identity in the United States (Vidal 1997; Henderson 1997). The film also inspired much discussion on the Internet. Soon after its release, for example, Doug Linder, professor of law at the University of Missouri, added documentation on the Amistad case to his educational web site on famous trials (Linder 1998). Meanwhile the US National Records and Archives Administration developed an online educational programme on the case which, amongst other things, invites students to 'write a review of the *Amistad* movie, comparing the film to the actual events described in the documents' and to discuss 'the value of preserving the historical integrity of the story and the value of changing that story for a screenplay' (National Archives and Records Administration 1998). We shall return to this programme in Chapter 6.

Hollywood did not discover the Amistad case, but it certainly made it a focus of far greater interest, debate and research than it had attracted before. It helped to set the agenda within which this upsurge of remembering and reinterpretation took place, but it could not entirely determine the directions of the journey of memory initiated by the film. In the end, therefore, the relationship of film to historical truth cannot simply be understood by examining the content of films themselves. As we saw in the case of photography, it becomes important to think of the political economy of historical truthfulness generated by the film.

Jacques Aumont and others have observed that 'every film is a fiction film' (Plantinga 1997, 11). This statement is true in the sense that all films, including documentaries, involve acts of creation and imagination. In the representation of history on film, as we have seen, the line between fact and fiction is not a clear and absolute one. Rather, there exists a wide spectrum within the world of film, from highly imaginative reconstructions of the past to carefully documented works relying heavily on archival footage or recorded testimony. As filmmakers explore and combine new techniques to depict the past on film, the socially determined dividing line which bisects this spectrum into films seen as factual and those seen as fiction may shift.

But to say that every film is a fiction film does not take us very far in understanding how film can be used to deepen our knowledge of the past. As in the case of photography, so too in the case of the movie, the pursuit of historical truthfulness is a *relationship*: the relationship between past events, the people who record those events on film, and the viewer who sees, interprets and remembers the recorded images. Film has certain inherent properties: it draws the viewer into a totalized image of the past, it personalizes, it moves us to laughter and tears and leaves particular images indelibly engraved on our minds. It has a capacity to evoke intense identification with historical experiences, but in the process it casts that identification within the framework of a particular remembering community. The way that film frames the remembering community conveys certain implicit or explicit interpretations about the impact of past upon present. The film may invite the audience to see the people of a past age as part of a common national 'we', and to see this 'we' as striving for any one of a range of national goals. It may seek, as *The Birth of a Nation* did, to summon up a racialized 'we' by evoking feelings of hatred and revenge towards other racial groups. It may present the communities of viewer and viewed in class terms – evoking, as Eisenstein and Shub did, a proletariat who share a common history of struggle. Or it may work across national or class boundaries, recalling certain experiences as part of a past that defines the present of people in utterly different places and circumstances. It may reassure us of continuity – 'who we are is who we were' – or it may demand resistance to the amnesia induced by violent discontinuities: 'We pretend to believe that all this happened only once, at a certain time and in a certain place, and we refuse to look around us, we who do not hear the endless cry.'

Filmmakers choose from a range of techniques to create these remembering communities. Some draw on archival footage while others avoid it, relying instead on filmed testimony. Some use contemporary actors and imagined dialogue to reconstruct the past, and others take the act of imagination further, adding fictional figures to the narratives of historical events. Some, like Oliver Stone in *JFK*, mix archive and reconstruction. Film can contribute much to creating a richer, more comprehensive, more deeply thought-through knowledge of the past. But this requires, both from those who make and those who see films, a degree of reflection about the aims, techniques, possibilities and constraints of various movie genres. For viewers, reflecting on our own response to particular films, and on the images, techniques and narrative structures that evoke that response, can be a way of enlarging our understanding of the past and its hold on the present. This reflection will often take us beyond the world of film itself, to consider how the events brought to life by a particular movie are represented in other media, and how those media coexist, compete and resonate with one another. In a multimedia world, the process of historical imagining, debate and exploration may in fact begin at the point which the traditional movie firmly proclaims as 'The End'.

5

Angles of Vision:
Comic-Book Histories

In 1986, the year after Claude Lanzmann released his film *Shoah*, a very different form of testimony to the Holocaust appeared. This was the first volume of Art Spiegelman's *Maus: A Survivor's Tale*. Spiegelman's *Maus* retells the story of his parents' attempts to escape the closing jaws of genocide in wartime Poland, and their ultimate incarceration in Auschwitz. Though much of the story is told in the words – indeed, in the almost audible voice – of his father, Vladek, the work is also a meditation on Spiegelman's own troubled relationship with his father, and with the ghosts of his mother, who committed suicide in 1968, and of Richieu, the elder brother he never knew, who was poisoned by an aunt during the war to save him from the alternative forms of death which awaited in the concentration camps.

If *Shoah*, with its deliberate avoidance of reconstruction or documentary film, confronts the problem of representing the unrepresentable, *Maus* does so in an even more drastic way. For Spiegelman elects to tell his harrowing and profoundly personal story through a medium normally reserved for fantasy and fun: the medium of the comic book. Moreover, with conscious ironic reference to Mickey

Mouse, he depicts all the protagonists in the story as animals: the Jews as mice, Germans as cats, Poles as pigs and Americans as dogs.

The Comic Book as Testimony:
Nakazawa Keiji and Art Spiegelman

Maus highlights both the power and the problems of the comic book as a medium of historical expression. Unbounded by the codes of realism embodied in photography and film, the comic book can make visible images of the past that would otherwise be lost. No contemporary film of the gas chambers in operation survives, but Spiegelman can produce a detailed visual reconstruction of the chambers as they were in 1944, simultaneously interweaving a technical explanation of how the system worked with the voice of his father recounting the survivor's testimony: 'Special prisoners worked here separate, they got better bread, but each few months they also were sent up the chimney. One from them showed me everything how it was' (Spiegelman 1991, 70).

Similarly, Yamahata Yôsuke's photographs capture the devastation of Nagasaki after the atomic bomb, but the experience of the atomic explosion close to ground zero is not photographically recorded or even recordable, and efforts to reconstruct it on film confront the difficulty of creating visual meaning from a moment of chaos and blinding light and darkness. Yet works like Nakazawa Keiji's *Barefoot Gen* [*Hadashi no Gen*], and many other comic-book renderings of the atomic blast, have the capacity both to imagine and to rearrange the visual structure of the catastrophic event in a way impossible on film. Nakazawa's comic presents the bombing of Hiroshima from multiple angles simultaneously – as the ominously familiar mushroom cloud viewed from a distance, as the flash of light and infernal darkness experienced by those on the ground, and as the spectacle observed from the Enola Gay, whose crew are depicted exulting: 'We did it! It's a success! Wow, what a shock wave!' (Picture 5.1).

Barefoot Gen, like *Maus*, is a survivor's tale, a testimony to events which Nakazawa himself lived through as a six-year-old boy. But Nakazawa, writing his comic-book testimony in the 1970s, adopted a strategy of representation radically different from that chosen by Spiegelman in the 1980s. *Barefoot Gen* is a simple and relatively conventional, if unusually disturbing, comic-book narrative. The story follows Nakazawa/Gen's relentless battle to survive in the aftermath of the bombing, which killed all his household apart from his mother and a baby sister born the day the bomb was dropped. As the narrative unfolds, Gen's ordeal introduces the reader to a range of social issues: poverty and exploitation in post-defeat Japan, the fear and prejudice directed at sufferers of radiation sickness, the particular discrimination faced by Korean survivors of the Hiroshima bombing.

Spiegelman, by contrast, not only fantasizes his account by rendering the characters as animals, but also repeatedly unsettles his readers by breaking up the narrative. *Maus* operates in two time-frames at once. Events in wartime Poland are retold in the words of Vladek, but are counterpointed by a New York present, where Art Spiegelman coaxes (and sometimes bullies) his father to tell his story, while at the same time engaging in endless quarrels with the cantankerous Vladek over household trivia. The visual style alters subtly as the comic moves from present to past, and the comic-book format is disrupted by the inclusion of photographs, and of a previously published comic strip about the suicide of Spiegelman's mother, drawn in a totally different style from the rest of text. As Marianne Hirsch puts it, '*Maus* represents the aesthetic of the trauma fragment', where the survivor struggles to connect disjointed pieces of memory into a 'testimonial chain' (Hirsch 1997, 39). Spiegelman never allows the reader to be drawn into the illusions of his own comic for too long. He constantly directs our

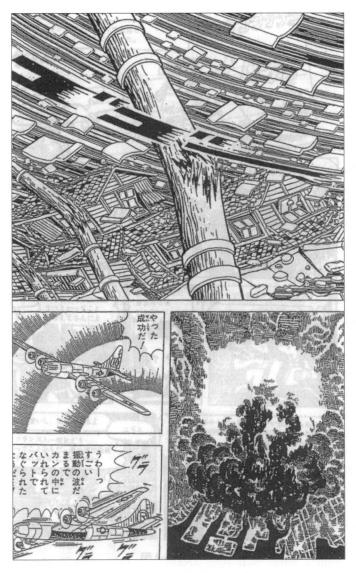

5.1 Image from Nakazawa Keiji, *Hadashi no Gen*, Tokyo, Shakubunsha, 1975, p. 251.

attention to the unreality of his representations. Volume 2 of *Maus*, for example, begins with Spiegelman and his wife Françoise (a French convert to Judaism living in the United States) debating whether Françoise should be shown in the comic as a mouse or as some other animal. The irony of the discussion is heightened by the fact that Françoise, even while debating her animal identity in the text, is already being depicted in the graphics as a mouse (Spiegelman 1991, 11; see also Witek 1989, 114).

But although their visual approaches differ so greatly, both Spiegelman and Nakazawa face a common dilemma of representation. The comic book can imagine and reorganize the visible past into unforgettable images, and can carry stories to new readers. Both *Maus* and *Barefoot Gen* were bestsellers, and, though addressed to rather different audiences, both undoubtedly expanded their readers' imaginative insight into profoundly important historical experiences. *Barefoot Gen* also became the first Japanese comic book to be published in English translation (the translation of comic books being made more difficult by the fact that Japanese and English comic books open from different ends, so that the layout of the pictures in translations has to be rearranged)

Yet the authors faced constant and troubling problems of imagery. *Barefoot Gen*, when it was serialized in the mass-circulation comic magazine *Shônen Jump* in 1973, was criticized by some as being too grim to be appropriate comic-book reading for the young. In response, Nakazawa admits, he was forced to exclude from his testimony some of the darkest images engraved on his memory: 'I gave in, and decided to shift to a visual style that was not my original intention. I thought that if people were dissuaded through revulsion from following important developments in the story, then there was no point in writing it, so I drew it in a rather soft style' (Nakazawa 1994, 213). Ultimately, he expresses disillusionment with the results of his efforts at representation:

When I reread my own work, my flesh crawled with loathing. I fell into a state of thinking "how could I have done it so badly?" And this was so painful that I could not bear it. I immediately hid the magazines in which my work was serialized in a drawer. The plot of Gen kept running through my head, but I spent half a year trying to alter my mood by writing entertainment comics. (Nakazawa 1994, 215.)

The difficulty is not simply the risk of negative reactions to excessively gruesome imagery. It is also that the graphic power of comic-book images – their instantly recognizable, unforgettable quality – means that the pictures themselves bear with them (often unintended) concealed memories: associations with other images that we have seen before. So, for example, seemingly horrendous comic-book depictions of death or injury may lack the capacity to move or shock – may even amuse or titillate – because we semiconsciously associate them with similar pictures which we have become accustomed to seeing in the context of adventure, horror or erotic comics. Conversely, some of Art Spiegelman's pictures are shocking precisely because they express horror through animal figures which we are more accustomed to see in cute and appealing poses. Yet for Spiegelman, as for Nakazawa, the process of comic-book creation remains troubling. Within the text of the comic itself he engages in repeated dialogues about his unease at the task he has undertaken and about his distress at the public response to his work:

[*Interviewer 1, depicted as a human wearing a dog mask*] Tell our viewers what message you want them to get from your book.

[*Spiegelman, depicted as a human wearing a mouse mask*] A message? I dunno … I – I never thought of reducing it to a message, I mean, I wasn't trying to to CONVINCE anybody of anything. I just wanted –

[*Interviewer 2, a human with a cat mask*] Your book is being translated into German – Many younger Germans have had it up to HERE with Holocaust stories. These things happened before they were even born. Why should THEY feel guilty?

[*Spiegelman*] Who am I to say … But a lot of the corporations that flourished in Nazi Germany are richer than ever. I dunno! Maybe EVERYONE has to feel guilty. **EVERYONE! FOREVER!** …

[*Interviewer 3, a human who appears to be wearing a human mask*] Artie, baby. Check out this licensing deal. You get 50 percent of the profits. We'll make a million. Your Dad would be proud.

[*Spiegelman*] HUH?

[*Interviewer 3*] So whaddya **WANT** – a bigger percentage? Hey, we can talk.

[*Spiegelman*] I want … ABSOLUTION. No … No … I want … I want my **MOMMMY!** (Spiegelman 1991, 16.)

The Rise of Sequential Art

The dilemmas faced by Nakazawa and Spiegelman highlight both the importance and the complexity of the comic book as a medium of historical expression. Historical comics not only reach a wide audience of people who may read few other history books. Their stark, dramatic images also have the power to burn themselves into our memories, influencing the way in which we see the present and re-remember the past. To understand how the comic book shapes our identification with and interpretation of history, then, it is important to consider the evolution of comic-book imagery. It is also necessary to think about the political economy of the comic book: the way that comics are produced and circulated, and how the production and ownership of their images influences the readers' power to interpret, to criticize and to imagine alternative accounts of the past.

The imagery of modern strip-cartoons and comic books – that genre that cartoonist Will Eisner called 'sequential art' – owes its shape to a wide variety of influences. An important source of inspiration for early European and North American comic strips was the German tradition of woodblock-illustrated children's tales, such as Heinrich Hoffmann's *Struwwelpeter* (1845), whose grotesque images of horrible punishments inflicted on children for minor pranks gave me nightmares when I read it as a child (Picture 5.2). The influence of works like *Struwwelpeter* and Wilhelm Busch's *Max und Moritz* (1865) can be clearly seen in the US newspaper comics which began to appear with the start of colour printing in the mass media in the late nineteenth century. A favourite figure in these comics was the mischievous child whose antics reduce the surrounding world to chaos (Blackbeard and Williams 1977).

By the first decade of the twentieth century, US newspaper comic strips were already featuring some of the classic elements of contemporary comic-book design, including speech bubbles. Though a few cartoonists experimented with more adventurous layouts, the typical comic strip was a single page spread with a story told in six or eight rectangular boxes. The weird and wonderful faces and human forms incorporated into newspaper comics also drew inspiration from the conventions of the political cartoon, whose origins go back at least to the seventeenth century, but whose popularity was enhanced by the rise of mass-circulation magazines like the British *Punch* (launched in 1841). Contemporary comics may owe something, too, to the Japanese tradition of woodblock printing, widely believed to be a factor behind the immense popularity and worldwide influence of Japanese comic-book art. They were certainly also influenced by the mid-twentieth-century Japanese *kamishibai* – the travelling 'theatres' where stories were

5.2 An early influence on the comic book – cover design from Heinrich Hoffmann-Donner, *Der Struwwelpeter*, Frankfurt, Literarische Anstalt Rutten & Loenig, ca. 1900.

narrated with the help of a series of illustrated cards displayed on a portable screen. Many of the leading pioneers of the postwar Japanese comic book (including Shirato Sanpei, whose work is discussed later) had a background as *kamishibai* artists (Schodt 1983, 62). Though the comic-book genre takes slightly different forms in different countries, the flow of visual influences is international. So early Japanese comic books were influenced by American strip cartoons (such as the 1920s favourite *Bringing up Father*) and by animated characters like Walt Disney's Mickey Mouse, while late twentieth-century comics in the US, Europe and much of Asia are influenced by the graphic innovations developed by the postwar generation of Japanese comic-book artists.

Sequential art, however, also owes much to the techniques developed by propaganda experts and advertising executives in the first half of the twentieth century. The spread of mass markets and the advent of total warfare, together with the emergence of the sciences of psychology and statistical sociology, brought a new sophistication to the use of visual images to communicate messages to wide audiences. The art of commercial advertising had a particularly close link to the rise of the comic book. Not only did artists move back and forth between the worlds of commercial design and comic-book production; the first comic books to be published included works like *Funnies on Parade* and *Skippies Own Book of Comics*, produced in the US in the early 1930s to be distributed free of change to customers as an advertising gimmick by the manufacturers Proctor and Gamble and Phillips Toothpaste (Wright 2001, 3). The comic book, indeed, was in every way a product of mass society. As Will Eisner recalled of the 1930s: 'We made comic-book features pretty much the way Ford made cars. I would write and design the characters, somebody else would pencil them in, somebody else would ink, somebody else would letter' (Wright 2001, 6).

Meanwhile, the First World War and the Russian Revolution, coinciding with the refinement of techniques for high-quality colour printing, encouraged an upsurge of poster art, whose stark imagery and caricatured faces were combined with simple slogans to convey social or political messages. Thus the rise of comic books derived impetus not just from mass markets and mass production methods, but also from the ideological techniques of mass mobilization. As Bradford Wright points out, the period of the Pacific War saw a boom in the US comic-book industry, and is still referred to by fans as 'the golden age of comics' (Wright 2001, 54). Comic-book producers cashed in on patriotic fervour, launching characters like 'Captain America', who fought for the nation against an array of grotesquely portrayed German, Japanese and other foes. Cheap, easily distributed and requiring little concentration, comics provided ideal reading matter for military forces at home and abroad.

In the ideological warfare of the mid-twentieth century, the comic book was mobilized in many countries and political contexts. In Franco's Spain, for example, the government fostered a boom in comics promoting national values and the glories of the Spanish race. Comics on historical themes enjoyed particular popularity. The Middle Ages were used as a metaphorical setting for countless tales of heroism, typically featuring a noble protagonist who fights to restore the true king after power has been seized by a wicked usurper (an unsubtle parable of the Franco regime's seizure of power from the republican government). Yet historical comics were also popular because, by locating an adventure in a remote period, writers could more freely explore themes which would attract the ire of the censor if discussed in a contemporary setting (Vazquez de Parga 1980, 91–107).

Early comic books focused on humour, fantasy, crime or adventures in exotic locations. By the 1940s, though, a growing number of publishers were beginning to harness the techniques of the comic for the presentation of 'real-life' stories (Picture 5.3). This was in part a reaction to criticisms from parents and political lobby groups who

5.3 The international rise of the non-fiction comic – A historical theme from the Canadian comic *Exploits Illustrés*, Vol. 3, No. 3, 1947. Source: Library and Archives of Canada.

attacked what they saw as the corrupting effect of comics on the minds of children. In the US, for example, *Parents' Magazine* launched a series of wholesome educational comics aimed at countering the escapism and violence of bestsellers like *Batman* and *Captain Marvel*. These included accounts of 'men and women who have made history by their courage, brilliance and perseverance', marketed under the slogan 'Truth is Stranger and a Thousand Times more Thrilling than Fiction'. Unfortunately, as one commentator points out, truth also proved to be 'a thousand times less saleable', and after a brief boom in the early 1940s the venture quickly collapsed (Gifford 1984, 172). A somewhat different destiny awaited Educational Comics launched by US entrepreneur Max Gaines in the mid-1940s. Gaines's series *Picture Stories from American History* (launched in 1945) and *Picture Stories from World History* (launched in 1947) were also commercial failures. However, after Gaines's death in 1947, his son William took over the company, which became known by the abbreviation EC, and turned it into one of America's most successful comic-publishing ventures by shifting from education to satire, fantasy and particularly lurid horror comics. But EC was also to publish some intriguingly iconoclastic representations of great moments in US history, to which I shall return shortly (Gifford 1984, 172; Witek 1989, 135).

Early English-language historical comics tended to be short (often four-to-five-page) accounts of the deeds of some 'real-life hero' whose virtues of patriotism and self-sacrifice are supposed to offer a model to their child readers. The style is exemplified by the historical sections in the British *Eagle* and *Girl* comics of the 1950s. Often set against the background of the colonial empire, these typically feature a British hero who brings order to the chaos of Africa or Asia. The local people ('natives') are generally anonymous, and appear in one of two guises: either as loyal subjects expressing humble gratitude for the deeds of the colonial master, or as unruly and rebellious 'savages'. Rereading these comics, which I read as a primary school child, I am struck not just by their racist ideology but also by their remarkably unimaginative graphic style. The page tends to be neatly divided into rectangular frames. The characters are shown in static poses with idealized faces as unconvincing as the leaden dialogue which fills the speech bubbles. The short format of the comics allowed no space for the development of character or plot, and the comic conveys little except a heavy-handed message about the glories of empire building. The stylistic limitations of the genre may help to explain why I find them less memorable than the romantic or humorous comics which filled other sections of the same magazines.

Escaping from the Frame: Harvey Kurtzman, Shirato Sanpei and Chiba Tetsuya

By the 1950s, however, innovations in content and style were opening up new possibilities for the comic as a medium of historical expression. In the postwar United States, a more adventurous approach, in every sense of the word, to the comic-book representation of history was pioneered by the EC comic magazines *Frontline Combat* and *Two-Fisted Tales*, edited by Harvey Kurtzman (later to become editor of *Mad* magazine). After its unsuccessful efforts at publishing educational comics, EC had by the 1950s become best known for its suspense and horror comics, which were characterized by their 'beautifully crafted and gleefully perverse transgressions of almost every imaginable cultural taboo, including thematic treatments of incest, bondage and sadomasochism, dismemberment and disembowelment, and family murders of every possible combination' (Witek 1989, 15). *Frontline Combat* and *Two-Fisted Tales*, though somewhat less lurid than the horror comics, were also firmly oriented towards a mass entertainment market, offering their readers what was then called 'he-man adventure'.

The comics produced by Kurtzman and his team of artists have been praised for their visual inventiveness and rich historical detail. By comparison with the visual techniques being developed simultaneously by Japanese comic artists like Tezuka Osamu, however, their style seems rather static. *Frontline Combat* and *Two-Fisted Tales* also stuck with the traditional format of the short comic (individual stories are usually seven to eight pages long) making the extended treatment of historical themes difficult. But within this format the writers developed some inventive approaches to reimagining the great events of past and present.

The publication of *Frontline Combat* and of earlier editions of *Two-Fisted Tales* coincided with the Korean War. Indeed, the demise of *Frontline Combat* in 1954 was advertised by its publishers as follows: '*Frontline Combat* ... Killed in Action! *Frontline* is dead, unhappily killed by the very happy ending of hostilities in Korea' (*Two-Fisted Tales* 36, January 1954). Both magazines therefore devoted a large amount of space to Korean War stories, but they also included tales of more remote conflicts: *Two-Fisted Tales* extending its range to the fall of the Roman Empire, the fifteenth-century Battle of Agincourt and the Spanish conquest of the Americas.

In many of these stories, an interesting ambivalence is at work. On the one hand, they are firmly located in the tradition of action comics: their graphics focus on exotic locations, blazing guns and the scowling faces of their he-man protagonists. But at the same time many of the comics reflect the fundamentally anti-war philosophy of their editor. Predictably enough, the comics made maximum use of the popular appeal of war action, and focused mainly on the bravery and suffering of the common US soldier. But within this conventional format, Kurtzman's team endeavoured to tackle some unconventional issues. Memorably, if not entirely persuasively, the comics 'Dying City!' and 'Rubble!' (most unusually for US comics) tell stories of the Korean War from the perspective of Korean civilians, just as the comic 'Atom Bomb!' tells the story of the bombing of Nagasaki from the perspective of Japanese civilians (Kurtzman et al. 1951a; 1951c; 1953). 'Atom Bomb!' is doubly unusual in that it also presents the story from a female perspective: through the eyes of an old woman waiting in vain for her son to return from a prison-of-war camp in Siberia.

Kurtzman's oblique view of history, indeed, was advertised on the opening page of the first issue of *Two-Fisted Tales*, where the Spanish conquest of the Americas is introduced as a tale of evil Europeans, driven by their lust for gold, inflicting rapine and pillage on indigenous American civilization (Kurtzman et al. 1950; confusingly, the first issue is numbered 18, as the magazine had previously been produced under other names). In the same iconoclastic vein, the Kurtzman version of 'Custer's Last Stand' is a story in which General Custer figures as a brutal, incompetent and unpopular commander, while the real heroes are the victorious 'Indians' and the ordinary soldiers who die as result of Custer's bungling (Kurtzman et al. 1952a).

The short and simple format of these comics means that their historical message often seems heavy-handed. At times, though, the images and words are combined into a more subtle commentary on the events of the past. One of the more interesting examples is the story 'Saipan!' (Kurtzman et al. 1952b). The text of this comic, which we are told is a true account told by 'a vet of World War II', seems at first to follow the conventional model of war stories. A group of US soldiers is cut off from their comrades. One is wounded, and his buddy, refusing to abandon his comrade, stays by him in a cane field awaiting a 'banzai attack' by the Japanese. In the end, the attack fails to materialize, and the trapped soldiers are rescued by their companions. The accompanying pictures, however, tell a second, counterpoint story, unannounced by the text. A local farmer comes out to harvest the fields; seen in the distance as he raises his machete, he is mistaken for a Japanese soldier with a

samurai sword, shot dead by the Americans and left lying in a field as
they move on to their next assignment. The point of the comic is made
precisely by the fact that the farmer's fate is not once mentioned in the
written text or dialogue: the local people, in this story, are the
unrecorded and unspoken victims of the great military encounter.

While Kurtzman and his team were venturing beyond the limits of
the historical comic as an edifying tale of nationalist heroism,
innovations were taking place in Japan which would transform the visual
potential of the comic as a medium of communication, not just in Japan
itself but internationally. A pioneer of these techniques was Tezuka
Osamu, whose *Shin Takarajima* [*New Treasure Island*, 1947] and later
Tetsuwan Atom [known in English as *Astroboy*] had an immense influence
on comic art in the second half of the twentieth century. A key to this
transformation of the comic was the introduction of long stories of
several hundred (indeed sometimes several thousand) pages. These
allow not just far greater scope for the development of narrative and
character, but also the extension of particular scenes across many
frames to produce stunning visual effects.

Tezuka is particularly well known for his application of cinematic
techniques to the comic. Other comic-book writers in the US and Japan
had in fact already begun to use some film-like techniques in their work.
In 'Saipan!' for example, the death of the farmer is depicted in a style
that resembles the frames of a movie sequence. But it was the length of
Tezuka's comics that allowed him to give free rein to these new possibilities (Schodt 1983, 62). His graphics draw the reader's eye into the
comic, offering a dramatic range of perspectives on landscapes and
human (or humanoid) figures. As he wrote in his memoirs, 'I experimented with close-ups and different angles, and instead of using only
one frame for an action scene or climax (as was customary), I made the
point of depicting a movement or facial expression with many frames,
even many pages' (Schodt 1983, 63).

If length was a characteristic of Tezuka's comics, it was to become an even more striking feature of the Japanese historical comics of the 1960s and 1970s. Shirato Sanpei's *Ninja bugeicho* [*Annals of Ninja Martial Arts*, first published from 1959 to 1962] ran to seventeen volumes, while Ishinomori Shôtarô's 'non-fictional' *Manga Nihon no rekishi* [*A Comic-Book History of Japan*] depicts the story of the Japanese past from the earliest times to the present day in fifty-five volumes totalling more than ten thousand pages.

The longer format allowed writers like Shirato to use the comic book to explore complex historical themes. His *Ninja bugeicho*, which recreates the struggles of the peasantry in sixteenth-century Japan through the adventures of the mythical ninja Kagemura, is famous for (allegedly) having introduced many of the 1960s generation of Japanese students to the concept of historical materialism (Lie 2001, 71). Shirato's comics, overflowing with movement, energy and violence, are concerned with philosophical and moral issues as much as with the events of history (Picture 5.4). His repeated return to themes of oppression, alienation and human folly are intended as metaphors for the present, as well as interpretations of the past. Yet, despite their far greater historical complexity, Shirato's comics embody ambivalences reminiscent of Kurtzman's *Two-Fisted Tales*. Shirato, whose work has frequently been criticized for its excessive focus on suffering and death, makes the most of the comic's potential for graphic depictions of violence simultaneously to appeal to a certain readership, and to convey a critical social message. Like Kurtzman's comic-book narratives, the epic conflicts of Shirato's stories often end with scenes reflecting the frailty of human life and the futility of violence – death awaits hero and villain alike; the boundless landscape overwhelms the fragile form of the human individual; the body of the defeated protagonist floats out on the tide into the oblivion of history.

The popularity and visual inventiveness of Japanese comics has allowed them to reach a huge audience and to have a profound effect on

5.4 Frames from Shirato Sanpei's *Akame*. Reprinted in *Shirato Sanpei Shû*, Tokyo, Chikuma Shobô, 1969, p. 93 (original published in 1960–1961).

the historical imagination of Japan's postwar generations. While a great deal has been written about the content of Japanese history textbooks, and above all about textbook treatments of Japan's military expansion in Asia, far less has been said about the treatment of history in Japanese comics. Yet comic-book versions of history – whether fictional or non-fictional – have probably shaped popular understandings of history at least as much as any textbook.

The comic's focus on action has meant that its presentations of history have inevitably centred on war, and particularly on the war in Asia and the Pacific. Japanese war comics range from the sternly critical depictions of Japan's aggression in Asia, such as the comic-book version of *Ningen no jôken* (*The Human Condition*, 1971 – a tale of the horrors of war in China which also appeared as a feature film), to escapist adventures of wartime heroism which began to win fans as Japan entered the period of high economic growth in the 1960s (Picture 5.5) (Ishiko 1983, 114 and 178).

A favourite figure in wartime adventure comics is the fighter pilot – a character whose individual daring and association with powerful machines appealed to young male readers. The aerial perspective on the conflict, it may be said, has the added advantage of avoiding confrontation with some of the more uncomfortable historical events taking place on the ground. Yet even the pilot adventures of the 1960s and 1970s often assume a cynical, if not whole critical, view of the war. Chiba Tetsuya's popular 1963–1965 serial *Shidenkai no Taka* (*The Hawk of the Shidenkai* – *Shidenkai* was a make of wartime fighter plane), for instance, attracted readers with its lovingly detailed drawings of wartime aircraft and its cinematic reconstructions of aerial dogfights. But its hero, *Shidenkai* pilot Taki Shôtarô (depicted in the classically cherubic model of the children's comic-book hero) repeatedly defies the commands of the military machine in his quixotic crusade against the (primarily American) enemy, and his final mission

5.5 Images of war from Gomikawa Junpei and Abe Kenji's *Ningen no Jôken* (1971); source: Ishiko Jun, *Manga ni miru sensô to heiwa no 90-nen*, Tokyo, Harupu Shuppan, 1983, p. 115.

as a reluctant suicide pilot provides a deeply ironic take on the meaning of the war.

Chiba here offers two conflicting visions of the suicide pilot story. One vision is represented by the hero Taki who, foreseeing Japan's imminent defeat, has begun to look forward to a peacetime future in which he plans to become a teacher, so that he can instruct children about the futility of war. The other vision is embodied in the hero's authoritarian commander, who, similarly sensing defeat, volunteers for a suicide mission in the hope of saving at least one Japanese life from US bombing raids. In the final frames, as the hero's beloved friend Nobuko travels happily towards his base for a long-awaited reunion, Taki takes off on his final mission 'abandoning his mother, abandoning Nobuko, abandoning his dreams of becoming a teacher, but trying his best to believe the statement that his own death will help to save his native land Japan' (Chiba 1985, 400).

Images of key events in Japanese history are shaped not just by adventure comics like Chiba's, but also by a host of educational non-fiction comics. While Max Gaines and others in the US struggled unsuccessfully to market educational comics to a reluctant youthful audience, the comic-book national histories of Ishinomori Shôtarô and others have been long-running bestsellers in Japan. Unlike the mid-century US educational comics, which offered edifying tales of heroic figures in an effort to tempt the young away from the antics of Superman and his associates, 'non-fiction' history comics in Japan serve as a more palatable supplement or alternative to school textbooks for a generation weaned on comics and television. Ishinomori's extended treatments of Japanese history are notable for their meticulously precise drawings, their relatively large amount of text and their inclusion of facts and figures (sometimes even graphs and tables) (Picture 5.6). Ishinomori moves repeatedly backwards and forwards from state to society – scenes of politicians debating key issues of the day are interspersed with images

5.6 Japanese comic book histories. This image from Ishinomori Shôtarô's 48-volume *Manga Nihon no rekishi* includes a chart showing the introduction of production control policies, alongside more conventional comic images. Source: Ishinomori Shôtarô, *Manga Nihon no Rekishi: Gendai Hen*, Vol. 5, Tokyo, Chûô Kôronsha, 1994, p. 97.

of anonymous 'people in the street' discussing the issues as they read their newspapers or eat their dinners. This allows him to offer detailed depictions of the landscape, costumes and customs of everyday life, while weaving an image of a national community that moves together through time, sharing in the great events of history (see for example Ishimori 1993–1994).

The Comic Eye

> In essence the critique of comics consists of nothing more than: 'It's interesting!!' 'It's not interesting!!' 'I love it!!' 'I hate it!!' Well, perhaps if we think about it we could add some other things: 'It's on my wavelength (it suits my feelings)'; 'It makes me feel good'; 'It's cute'; 'It's fun' ... In any case, words concerning historical significance or social criticism do not spring to mind, and we don't tend to think about problems of theme and construction. (Yonezawa 1987, 177–178.)

The successful comic uses the force of graphics to grab hold of the reader's attention and emotions. This is all the more important because of the speed with which comics are consumed. The average Japanese reader is said to consume comic books at a rate of approximately 3.75 seconds per page (Schodt 1986, 18). At that speed, the comic must transmit its message instantly through integrated packages of words and vivid images.

As a medium for communicating history the most striking characteristic of the comic is this inseparable interconnection of text and picture. Judgments about historical significance may not spring to the mind of the reader. But in the case of comic-book histories, the visual techniques which evoke those spontaneous cries – 'I love it!!' 'I hate it!!' – convey lasting messages about our relationship to the past. Photographs communicate historical messages not just by themselves but through their association with words and other images. In the case of the comic, though, the connection between words and image is far more profound. The text is built into the image, and generates its effects through its physical appearance as well as through the meaning of its words. Our response to the text depends on whether it is printed or written by hand, inserted in bubbles or boxes, inscribed in giant characters or in tiny, delicate script. Images, too, work their influence through their relationship with one another. 'Much of the action of a comic-book story', notes Joseph Witek, 'takes place *between* the panels, in the gutters, so to speak, which separate the panels' (Witek 1989, 22).

Photographs create a bridge between the self and the past because our own memories are so often embodied in photos, and historical photographs evoke memories preserved in family albums. Comic books prompt a process of identification in a rather different way. Drawing on the traditions of woodblock print, propaganda and political cartoon, the comic drawing's stark outlines and exaggerated features imprint themselves on our minds in the way that simple shapes imprint themselves on the mind of an infant. Uesugi Satoshi points out that once you have seen cartoons or caricatures of the face of a famous person, it becomes difficult to see the real face in a photograph or on a television screen without, as it were, superimposing the cartoon image upon it (Uesugi 1997, 15–16). The same thing happens with historical events. A vivid comic-book depiction of, say, a battle scene may permanently influence the way that the mind's eye recalls the scene any time it is discussed in subsequent encounters with history. The comic book thus evokes our emotions – our sense that 'I love it!!' 'I hate it!!' – not only in relation to its own images but also in relation to the events of history, and to the people who took part in those events.

Comic books, like novels, make certain historical landscapes visible while rendering others invisible. As we saw in the case of the EC comics *Frontline Combat* and *Two-Fisted Tales*, these landscapes may be spatially and chronologically remote from the readers – Kutzman's comics ventured into ancient Rome, mediaeval France and elsewhere. But the comic book, far more than the novel, thrives on the immediate visual impact of dramatic action. So it needs to present its readers not simply with historical landscapes to which they can form some imaginative connection, but also with landscapes that are visually exciting. Hence the appeal of war and exploration as topics for comic-book history. Hence too the enthusiasm in Japanese girls' comics (such as the works of Ikeda Riyoko) for stories set in seventeenth- and eighteenth-century Europe. Just as the expansion of British travel to the classical and Renaissance sites of Italy in the early nineteenth century encouraged (and was encouraged by) the creation of novels set in ancient Rome or in fifteenth-century Florence and Venice, so the expansion of Japanese tourism to the capital cities of Europe went hand in hand with the fashion for teenage girls' comics set in the age of the *Ancien Régime*, the French Revolution or the Napoleonic Wars. These settings offer scope for swashbuckling action of swordfights and duels, but also for scenes of the glamorous worlds of high-society Paris, Vienna or other European cultural centres, where lovingly depicted languorous young men engage in melodramatic romances in the picturesque surroundings of Versailles or the Tuilleries (see for example Ikeda 1972).

The visual quality of the comic book draws attention to a further crucial aspect of our imaginative landscapes of the past. What matters is not just *which* places and events we see, but also the angle that we see them from. The techniques of comic-book graphics developed by postwar artists like Tezuka Osamu, Chiba Tetsuya and others paid particular attention to angle of vision. By presenting a scene from a particular angle, the skillful comic-book writer can position the reader so that she or he sees events from a certain perspective: from the viewpoint, say, of a child or a fighter pilot, or (as in the case of Nakazawa Keiji's depictions of the atomic bombing of Hiroshima) from several points of view simultaneously. In this way the comic, even more than the museum, the novel or perhaps even the mainstream movie, has the capacity to define the collective 'we' of the viewing audience.

The positioning of the reader is especially significant because the comic book, far more than the novel, movie or television programme, directs its messages to specific audiences. The genre has evolved into sub-genres separated by gender, as well as by generation. Though some historical films may appeal more to men than to women (or vice versa), few are specifically produced for a male or a female audience only. Comic books, on the other hand, are typically targeted specifically at girls or boys, men or women, and include sub-divisions addressed to gay men, heterosexual men, lesbian or heterosexual women. The British 1950s comics *Eagle* and *Girl* were defined as being for boys and girls respectively, and their historical sections reflected this. Though both dealt with virtually identical imperial themes, *Eagle* normally offered male heroes in the role of conquerors, explorers and colonial governors, while *Girl* offered female heroes, typically nurses or missionaries narrowly escaping fates worse than death at the hands of rebellious colonials. While the Japanese fighter-pilot comics clearly defined their main readership as male, the comics of writers like Ikeda Riyoko are explicitly addressed to teenage girl audiences. Some artists, like Ishizaka Kei (whose work is discussed later) have indeed used a female perspective to develop comic-book critiques of the glorifications of war.

Studies of erotic comics point out how often they are drawn specifically from the viewpoint of the male gaze (for example, Allison 1996). Though there are obvious exceptions, particularly among the 'ladies' comics' – erotic comics for women – which proliferated in Japan from the 1970s onward, erotic comics are commonly drawn so that the reader sees most of the action from the standpoint of the male protagonist – either literally through his eyes or from a position looking over his shoulder at the woman who is the object of the comic's fantasy. In this way the comic clearly (though always implicitly) positions the reader both as male and as sharing with other males, including the protagonist and the author, in the communal consumption of the female body.

Historical comics also possess the power to position their readers on one side or the other of a key experience of the past. Joseph Witek has pointed out how, for example, differing comic-book depictions of the US Civil War construct their scenes so that the readers see events either from the Unionist or the Confederate perspective (Witek 1989, Ch. 1). As we shall see, however, the issue of viewpoint is not just a matter of choosing the side from which the reader will view a particular conflict or controversy. It is also concerns the ability of the comic-book writer to choose a particular line of vision as representing the totality of 'our side'.

From *Gômanism* to Chauvinism: Kobayashi Yoshinori Goes to War

The problems of the 'memories' carried by pictures, the imprinting of images on the mind, and the positioning of readers, are all vividly evident in the controversial historical comic books of Japanese writer Kobayashi Yoshinori. In 1992 Kobayashi, who had made his name as a comic-book writer with anarchic satires of Japan's exam-crazy education system, launched a series called *Gômanizumu sengen* [*A Declaration of Gômanism* – *Gômanism* being the ideology of *gôman*, which is arrogance or insolence]. Here, Kobayashi appears as the hero of his own comic – the embodiment of *gômanism* – gleefully giving the finger to the cherished values of politeness, corporate discipline, social harmony and so forth.

Gômanizumu sengen won many fans for its iconoclastic approach to social issues like safe sex and the influence of erotic comics. Looking back at the start of the series, though, it is already possible to see some of the themes that were to dominate Kobayashi's later comics on historical issues. One is a rather obsessive association of the nation with imperiled male sexual potency. Early issues, for example, repeatedly exhorted Japanese women to choose the 'domestically produced penis' as a protection from foreign contaminations such as AIDS (Kobayashi 1993, 22–23 and 26–27). At this stage, Kobayashi appears to be writing with his tongue firmly in his cheek, mocking the pretentions of bureaucratic nationalism and sententious health campaigns. As with many aspects of his comics, however, the theme remained constant while the irony was to fade over time.

As the series unfolded, Kobayashi used *Gômanizumu sengen* to focus attacks on a range of social targets including the Aum Supreme Truth religious group, discrimination against the *hisabetsu buraku* community, and the official bungling and indifference which led to the use of AIDS-infected blood in transfusions. At this point, Kobayashi's comic-book persona began to take on ironic overtones of the 'caped crusader' of 1930s US comics, fighting for the underdog against power, greed and corruption. After a widely publicized split with the campaign by victims of AIDS-infected blood transfusions, however, he shifted ground from being a leading voice in their campaign to being a vocal critic of his fellow campaigners. He began to present the movement as having been taken over by ideologically motivated activists who were pushing their own agendas. Most revealingly, as he later explained, Kobayashi was discouraged to discover that the pathetic child victims whose cause he had championed 'gradually turned into adults who became tainted by ideology and began to make statements about "having to change the world"' (Takeda, Kobayashi and Hashizume 1997, 36). This horror of victims who speak with their own voices, rather than waiting quietly for a benevolent media star to take up their cause, was to become even more sharply evident in his next crusade.

In the course of the 1990s, domestic and international attention began to focus on the wartime experiences of large numbers of women

who had been abducted or tricked into wartime Japanese military institutions – so-called 'comfort stations' – where they were held and forced to
have sex with soldiers. Although the existence of the 'comfort stations'
had been no secret, until the 1990s none of the so-called 'comfort
women' had spoken publicly of their experiences, but from 1988
onward the issue began to be raised by women's groups in South Korea,
and in 1991 Kim Hak-Soon became the first former 'comfort women' to
give public testimony of her ordeal. In 1994 the Japanese government
officially admitted that the military had initiated, and been directly or
indirectly responsible for running, the 'comfort-station' system.
Investigations by the International Commission of Jurists and the UN
Commission on Human Rights collected evidence which suggested that
thousands of young women from Korea, China, Taiwan, the
Philippines, Malaysia, Indonesia and the Netherlands had been drafted
into the 'comfort stations', often through force or deceit, and forced to
submit to sexual intercourse with soldiers. Testimony recorded by
survivors stated that many had had to endure beatings and other forms
of extreme physical and mental ill-treatment (Dolgopol and Snehal
1994; UN Commission on Human Rights 1996). It was this testimony
which now became the focus of attack by Kobayashi's comics. During
the latter part of the 1990s, *Gômanizumu sengen* and Kobayashi's other
publications propounded the view that the 'comfort women' were in fact
prostitutes who had been amply rewarded for their services, and that the
testimony presented by former victims was untrue. Kobayashi
meanwhile campaigned energetically against the inclusion of references
to the 'comfort women' in school history textbooks on the grounds
(amongst other things) that they were unsuitable reading material for
the young.

The shift from attacking corrupt bureaucrats and discrimination to
attacking the 'comfort women' was a move that brought Kobayashi into
association with the newly formed Japan Society for History Textbook

Reform. This society had been created in 1996 with the avowed aim of opposing the 'masochistic' views of the Japanese past, which it claimed were embodied in existing history texts; but a particularly large part of its efforts was devoted to discrediting the evidence of the 'comfort women' (Fujioka 1996; Japan Society for History Textbook Reform 1999). One of Kobayashi's main contributions to the Society's campaign to rewrite history was his best-selling 1998 special edition of *Gômanizumu sengen: Sensôron* [*On War*]. Here Kobayashi goes far beyond attacks on the 'comfort women', depicting Japan's wartime expansion as a 'race war' in which Asians, led by Japan, 'fought and defeated the Whites', only, alas, to fall victim to the overwhelming material might of the United States (Kobayashi 1998, 31–32). In the course of the 381-page comic, Kobayashi treats his readers to glorified accounts of the heroism and dedication of Japanese troops, as well as to gruesome tales of barbarities committed by Japan's enemies, particularly the Chinese. His vision of the war as a racial struggle between Asians and Whites does not deter him from using, amongst other things, stories of the 'Han [Chinese] race's tradition of cannibalism', complete with graphic illustrations of butchered bodies, to suggest that atrocities like the Nanjing Massacre were actually inflicted by Chinese troops on their own civilians (Kobayashi 1998, 134–135). At the same time he instructs the younger Japanese generation (to whom the book is clearly addressed) that 'war is not evil; war is policy', and urges them to ask themselves if they, in the same circumstances, would have been prepared to fight to protect their country from 'the power of US imperialism and Soviet and Chinese communism' (Kobayashi 1998, 33–34).

In the wake of the September 11 attacks in the United States, Kobayashi followed this up with a second volume, *Sensôron 2* [*On War 2*], in which he once again presents Japan's wartime role as having been that of victim rather than aggressor in the Asia-Pacific War, while also depicting himself as the victim of unpatriotic attacks from assorted

'left-wing' and 'postmodern' critics of his earlier volume. He also, inter-
estingly enough, interprets the events of September 11 as the start of a
Huntington-style clash of civilizations in which it will be necessary for
Japan to find its own non-religious 'Osama Bin Laden' who will rekindle
Japan's national spirit to fight the identity wars of the twenty-first
century (Kobayashi 2001, 9–31).

Kobayashi has also pursued related themes in *Taiwanron* [*On Taiwan*],
in which he applies his idiosyncratic view of the East Asian past and
present to contemporary China–Taiwan relations. *Taiwanron*'s comic-
book portrayal of Japan's colonization of Taiwan propounds the theory
that there have been three historical models of colonization practised by
great powers, 'the "plunder model", practiced by the Spanish in South
America, the "exploitation model", practiced by Britain etc. in India ...
and the "investment model" practiced by Japan in Taiwan and Korea'
(Kobayashi 2000, 146). Indeed Taiwan, according to Kobayashi, has not
only benefited from the blessings of Japanese colonization, but has
preserved intact key elements of 'the Japanese spirit' which are now
under threat in Japan itself (Kobayashi 2000).

These interpretations of the Japanese and East Asian past have
attracted fierce criticism from many Japanese historians and social
commentators, who have repeatedly pointed out the numerous mistakes,
omissions and distortions of historical fact in Kobayashi's comics (for
example, Miyadai et al. 1999; Higashi Ajia Bunshitetsu Nettowâku
2001). But the criticism itself highlights fundamental dilemmas of
debating history through the medium of the comic book. Written
critiques of Kobayashi's texts expressed in academic essays and
magazine articles, however valid their arguments, seem to have only a
rather limited power to reduce the impact of the comics on the
imagination of readers. As social commentator Ôta Masakuni points
out, it is important not just to examine the text of Kobayashi's comics
but also, as for example critic Uesugi Satoshi has done, to consider how

the visual layout of the comics works its effects (Ôta 2000; Uesugi 1997; Uesugi 2000). Looking closely at the combination of words and images in Kobayashi's comics sheds light both on the considerable influence of these comics in contemporary Japan, and on wider issues of the power of contemporary comic art to influence the landscapes of the historical imagination (see http://www.geocities.jp/pastwithin).

One obstacle to examining these images lies precisely in those visceral reactions – 'I love it!!' 'I hate it!!' – which the graphic force of comic books evokes. Just as I find it hard to watch Alain Renais's *Night and Fog* without feeling intense distress, so I find it hard to read Kobayashi's comics – to look at his quasi-pornographic representations of the 'comfort women', his depictions of Chinese cannibalism, or his grotesque images of the Japanese critics whom he labels 'lefties' [*sayoku*] – without feeling intense revulsion. These images are, after all, *designed* to produce loathing, and, if (as in my case) that loathing is not directed towards the subjects of the comics, it naturally tends to direct itself towards their creator. As in the case of other emotionally charged media, it is important to acknowledge this feeling, while at the same time trying to understand its source, and to imagine why the same comics prompt very different emotions in others.

Part of the popular appeal of Kobayashi's comics seems to come from the fact that, like Art Spiegelman (though to very different ends) Kobayashi makes use of the power of the comic to operate in two time frames – in past and present – simultaneously. His comics are not simply narratives of the past, but are always also commentaries on the present. Kobayashi's own face stares down on his representations of history, and the graphics depict him doing physical battle with a host of contemporary enemies – scholars and media figures with whose opinions he disagrees. With echoes of the caped-crusader imagery, these foes are typically presented as a massed array of drooling establishment authority figures (a.k.a. 'lefties') with whom our hero engages in single-handed combat. In the process, the past is always personalized. Interweaving his own biography into everything he writes, Kobayashi turns the great events of history, including Japan's military expansion in Asia and the Pacific, into metaphors for his personal quest for esteem. This constant counterpoint between past and present, and between national and personal, gives Kobayashi's renderings of history an immediacy absent from comics which simply relate a story within the self-contained landscape of a past time and place.

Kobayashi's *Gômanizumu sengen* series is characterized by the slow death of irony. In the earliest episodes, his pronouncements on the social issues of the day are always tongue-in-cheek, but by the time we reach *On War*, *On Taiwan* and *On War 2* much of the irony seems to have leached out of the comics, exposing the stark outlines of their underlying worldview. This gradual loss of irony is illuminated by a shift in the iconography of Kobayashi's self-portraiture. In the first volume of *Gômanizumu sengen*, Kobayashi pictures himself consistently as an outrageous comic figure, grimacing and yelling at his audience. The style with which he depicts his own face is almost indistinguishable from the style with which he depicts his critics and enemies. But the further the real Kobayashi advances into a rather flabby middle age, the more his eternally young comic-book alter ego is physically improved and idealized into the classic form of the youthful comic-book hero. By the end of *On War*, like some inverted portrait of Dorian Gray, the comic-book representation of Kobayashi is not only diverging drastically from its real-life counterpart; it is also becoming more and more sharply differentiated from the stylized representations of Kobayashi's enemies.

This shift in self-representation is part of a wider change in style which is central to Kobayashi's representation of history, and is important more generally to understanding the ideological potential of the comic book. The early *Gômanizumu* comics are drawn in energetic and crowded style, with heavily caricatured human faces and bodies dominating the page. But as time goes on the style becomes increasingly eclectic. Grotesque cartoon figures increasingly share the page with detailed drawings of buildings, highly realistic photo-like portraits and actual photomontage. Kobayashi also makes growing use of a graphic technique which has become one of his trademarks: the print collage, where a mass of cuttings from newspapers and books, or images designed to look like cuttings from newspapers and books, are jumbled together in apparently random order (though with certain sections enlarged or highlighted) to convey an overall impression of media reportage or academic opinion on a particular issue.

Each of the varied graphic styles comes bearing its own conspicu- ously imprinted messages. In *On War* and *On Taiwan*, 'good' figures are presented in a static, realistic style slightly reminiscent of the graphic conventions of the *Girl* and *Eagle* comics that I read as a child. 'Bad' characters, on the other hand (Chinese soldiers and Kobayashi's Japanese critics, for example), are drawn in grotesquely distorted form with bared teeth and ghoulish blank eyes.

As Uesugi Satoshi points out, Kobayashi's visual style in *On War* echoes the wartime propaganda techniques used by the Japanese military themselves (Uesugi 2000, 11–12). An even more striking parallel, though, is with the techniques of Soviet poster art. Wartime posters and cartoons, including the comic books of the Second World War and Cold War, have always drawn a sharp distinction between the appealing faces of 'us' and the exaggeratedly distorted features of 'them' – the enemy. But it was the Soviet poster artists who, in the decades following the 1917 Revolution, realized that this contrast could be intensified by combining radically divergent graphic styles within the same image. Their posters typically portrayed a handsome and muscular Soviet hero, drawn in the conventions of socialist realism, towering over a grotesquely caricatured enemy, depicted according to the conventions of the comic strip (Picture 5.7). A pioneering exponent of this approach

5.7 Poster by the Kukryniksy Group (1941).

was the artist Viktor Deni, of whose work a contemporary admirer wrote 'to make an enemy look ridiculous is to half kill him' (Baburina 1985, 3). Another much favoured technique was the combination of past and present in the same image. Thus, to give just one example, a well-known war poster by the Kukryniksy art group depicts resolute Soviet soldiers in the foreground, while behind them, like guardian spirits, stand the sketched outlines of the heroes of Russian history. The image presents a simple, stark message: the contemporary war machine is the bearer of an ancient and unbroken tradition of self-sacrifice to the nation. Kobayashi adopts an identical visual strategy when he depicts the wartime Japanese suicide pilots watched over by the spirits of the ancient Greek guardians of the polis.

Collage and photomontage were essential elements in the combination of styles refined by Soviet poster art. Cartoon-like drawings were combined with photographic or quasi-photographic images of towering buildings or machinery. Replicas of cuttings from newspapers or party documents were superimposed on one another or combined with cartoon or photographic images. Subtle distinctions of shading or highlighting were used to guide the reader's eye to key words or phrases in the collages (as in Rodchenko's well-known poster 'Peace, Bread, Land'). For Kobayashi, the advantage of the print collage is that it allows him to convey to readers the impression of there being archival source material for his statements, without having to resort to the tedium of actually reading the archives. A characteristic image in the first volume of *On War*, for instance, offers a jumble of virtually illegible cuttings from newspapers and magazines which purports to demonstrate how, during the postwar occupation period, the media brainwashed the Japanese public into feeling shame at Japan's wartime deeds. The viewer's eye is drawn to several highlighted phrases superimposed on the cuttings: 'the history of the Pacific War'; 'this is the truth'; 'the hidden truth is now revealed: know the guilt of the militarists'. The instantly conveyed message is that the entire content of occupation-period public discourse on the war can be reduced to these words.

Igor Golomstok, tracing the way in which the techniques of Soviet poster art were adopted by both the Nazi and Communist parties in Germany, observes how the images of totalitarian art achieved their effects through constant repetition: symbolic images of the worker's fist crashing down upon the head of the capitalist, a hand blocking an enemy hand, or the imperialist spider spinning its web of world control 'moved from poster to poster', reinforcing simple messages as they went (Picture 5.8) (Golomstok 1990, 173). As Hitler noted in *Mein Kampf*, 'Only constant repetition can finally bring success in the matter of instilling ideas into the memory of the crowd. The most important thing … is to paint your contrasts in black and white' (quoted in Golomstok 1990, 173). In an age when the power of the state propaganda poster is much diminished, this tradition remains alive in commercial advertising and in mass-marketed comic-book art. Kobayashi's comics return again and again to the symbolized imagery of the snarling faces of the 'lefties', the jabbing fist or accusatory finger of the author, and the outline image of the Japanese nation itself, bound in chains, pierced by spears or menaced by other graphic threats of emasculation.

But by the end of the twentieth century, the comic-book artist was able to draw not simply on the force of the images themselves, but on the memories they evoked of other comic-book imagery. This power is used to particularly powerful effect in Kobayashi's representations of the 'comfort women' issue. As we saw earlier, the visual depiction of exceptionally painful historical events involves the problem of representing the unrepresentable. Portrayals of extreme violence on film or in comics risk rendering the event banal or titillating, particularly when their imagery recalls that of erotica or fantasy entertainment.

5.8 'Capital'. Poster by Viktor Deni (1919).

Comic-book artists like Art Spiegelman struggle with this problem, extending their graphic imaginations in search of images which express past trauma without voyeurism or trivialization. Kobayashi does the opposite. He deliberately *exploits* this quality of unrepresentability in his efforts to half kill the former 'comfort women' with ridicule. If the weight of historical testimony cuts the ground from under his textual claims that the 'comfort women' were prostitutes, he can still draw on the conventions of the pornographic comic book to reshape the past according to his own imaginings. Even if his readers remain unpersuaded by his text, his sadistic sexual images are likely to remain in their memories, seeping into their own visualizations of the past.

A classic example appears in a 1997 comic where Kobayashi attacks an unnamed book on the history of the 'comfort women' issue. As he presents quotations from the text, Kobayashi accompanies these with his visualization of the events described, and, predictably, with an image of himself reading the book. The phrase 'women treated like draft animals', for example, is visualized by Kobayashi as group of naked women huddled in a wooden animal-pen, while the words 'we who were placed in the bestial Hades of sexual imprisonment' is envisaged in the form a naked woman in the classical pose of S-and-M, kneeling on all fours with her leg chained and her buttocks turned towards the reader, as a group of soldiers ogle at her through iron bars. The quoted text in these scenes is written in a grey and semi-legible font, allowing the words to be overpowered by Kobayashi's visual fantasies. The same page offers us the spectacle of the expressions on Kobayashi's face while he reads the book: his eyes pop and his mouth widens from sniggers into guffaws of laughter as he conjures up and hungrily devours his own images of the past (Kobayashi and Takeuchi 1997, 17).

What is striking about this comic is the obvious dissonance between the quoted text and the images. The quotations appear to be from the testimony of former 'comfort women' themselves. They speak of the 'comfort women' as 'us'. But in Kobayashi's comics 'we', the readers, are positioned so that we can see events only through the eyes of the male 'possessor' of the woman, or, to be more precise, through Kobayashi's eyes as he fantasizes himself into the position of their male possessor. This is the hallmark of Kobayashi's depictions of the 'comfort stations'. In scene after scene, 'we' are positioned as a soldier standing in the queue, and looking in through the door at the women within.

This positioning of the reader in relation to the 'comfort women', however, is just a part of a much wider positioning of readers in relation to history as a whole. Like most war comics in Japan, the US and elsewhere, *On War* and *On War 2* repeatedly place the viewer on 'our' side of the confrontation. The consumer of the comics sees events from a location in the line of marching Japanese soldiers, on the deck of the Japanese ship as it prepares to launch an attack on the enemy, or in the cockpit of the kamikaze plane. But Kobayashi also does much more than this. His interweaving of the personal and the national recreates the Japanese perspective in an extraordinary and revealing way.

Both volumes of *On War* offer their readers two parallel narratives: one of the victimization of Japan in the Pacific War and the other of the victimization of Kobayashi himself – a physically weak and bullied child who grows up to be an unappreciated teenager and then a media star assailed by assorted malicious foes. At each stage in this odyssey, the reader is drawn into Kobayashi's fantasies, as he restores his sense of potency by imagining himself into the role of the frontline fighter or kamikaze pilot: a role where his personal travails can be sublimated into trials undertaken on behalf of 'the public = the nation'. So the comic does not simply depict, for example, the heroism of the kamikazes: it depicts a downtrodden Kobayashi conjuring up memories of the heroism of the pilots as a tonic for his wilting virility. Rather than seeing the war through the eyes of the Japanese soldier, the reader in fact sees the war through the eyes of Kobayashi as he *imagines* himself at the controls of the fighter plane or the machine-gun, or in the squadron of departing kamikazes accepting the homage of a line of tearful young women. Meanwhile, the repeated images of the geo-body of the nation at the mercy of enemy weapons are interspersed with images of Kobayashi's own body (or, to be more precise, the slimmed-down Peter Pan version of his body) superimposed on the map of a victimized Japan – standing in the centre of the nation or cradling it lovingly in his arms.

Kobayashi's double story of victimization seems to appeal to some readers because it plays on rather deep-seated anxieties about contemporary social change. These anxieties emerge from the transformation discussed in Chapter 1 – the force of 'globalization', which erodes established political and economic structures – and are reinforced by the emergence of long-suppressed minority histories, which challenge conventional narratives of the national past. Japan is one among many countries where ingrained and intertwined images of gender and national identity are destabilized by contemporary trends. Technological change and shifts in employment patterns accompanying globalization, for example, undermine the certainties which many men felt about their career prospects. The collapse of lifetime employment and age-related seniority systems threatens the status of middle-aged, middle-class men, while at the same time undermining images of Japanese uniqueness. In this context, Kobayashi's personalized version of the war touches a nerve: it simultaneously constructs both a defensive patrimonial narrative of belonging to the aggrieved nation and a defensive patriarchal narrative of imperilled masculine identity.

But, by rather skillfully combining techniques reminiscent of prewar totalitarian art with the visual and marketing techniques of contemporary pop culture, Kobayashi succeeds in conveying this narrative to a surprisingly wide audience. His comics, while mobilizing readers' emotional identification with 'the nation', at the same time refashion 'the nation' in the author's image. So his readers – many of whom are in fact young, and some of whom are female – are induced by his graphics to identify themselves, not just with Japan, but with a particular Japan as male, middle-aged, and obsessively concerned with the task of reinflating its own imperilled ego.

Owning the Image

Works like Kobayashi's raise important questions about the comic book as a medium for historical debate, and particularly for addressing traumatic events like the war and the 'comfort women' issue. The problem, in other words, is how to counter the totalitarian capacity of some comic-book art to impose particular images of the past – images often laden with semi-conscious memories – on the minds of readers. One approach, of course, is to combat image with image, producing alternative comic-book renderings of the same past.

Totalitarian art was developed in the centralized, authoritarian states of the mid-twentieth century. Although some of its techniques still survive in the comic book, they now operate in the very different context of the contemporary mass-market for pop culture. In this context it is, at least in theory, quite possible to produce a wide range of alternative versions of past and present. As in the case of film, however, so too in the case of the comic book: the nature of the debate is powerfully influenced by the structure and the representational conventions of the media, as well as by those who control them.

Just as Harvey Kurtzman and his team confronted the glorification of events like Custer's Last Stand with their alternative comic-book depictions, so some writers in Japan have published comic-book counter-narratives to the Kobayashi version of the national past (Picture 5.9). Ishizaka Kei, for example, contests the glorification of the war and attacks on the 'comfort women' through comics such as *Aru hi ano kioku o koroshi ni* [*One Day to Kill that Memory*, originally published in the magazine *Young Jump* in 1996 (see Ishizaka 1999)]. This seeks to tell the story from the perspective of the 'comfort women' themselves, through the memories of an elderly Korean woman who is driven to the point of suicide in her efforts to seek an apology for the violence she experienced as a 'comfort woman' during the war. Here, therefore, the queue of soldiers at the 'comfort station' is viewed, not from the perspective of a person standing in the queue, but from the viewpoint of the women within as they face the approaching mob of war-damaged men (Picture 5.10).

5.9 This comic by war veteran and Kobayashi Yoshinori critic Mizuki Shigeru emulates Kobayashi's style in combining detailed realistic drawing with highly caricatured figures. Source: Mizuki Shigeru, 'Karankoron hyôhakuki sensôron', in Miyadai Shinji et al., *Sensôron môsôron*, Tokyo, Kyôiku Shiryô Shuppankai, 1999, pp. 85–92, image from p. 85.

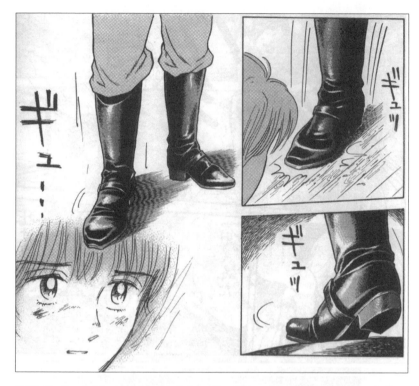

5.10 The 'comfort woman's' angle of vision. Frames from Ishizaka Kei, *Aru hi ano kioku o koroshi ni*, in Miyadai Shinji et al., *Sensôron môsôron*, Tokyo, Kyôiku Shiryô Shuppankai, 1999, pp. 155–184, image from p. 102.

Yet, drawing as it does on the conventions of the teenagers' comic, this depiction of the past also encounters some familiar problems of representing the unrepresentable. In terms of content, the need for a happy ending – or at least for an ending that is not overwhelmimgly bleak – threatens to soften the grim realities with which the story deals (just as Nakazawa Keiji found himself forced to soften the story of Hiroshima). In terms of style, the use of comic-book conventions in the depiction of violence and rape runs up against the problems of the concealed memory of images that we have already encountered earlier in this chapter. The dilemma for the writer, in other words, is not simply how to convey the past realistically, but how to find images to express unimaginable trauma without risking prurience.

The problem of communicative codes is compounded by problems of the control and marketing of the image. Comic books, like many other popular media, operate in a distinctive cultural economy. Though comic-book publishing is less oligopolistic than the world of the Hollywood movie, it has come to be increasingly dominated by relatively large firms working in close association with TV and film production. In Japan by the 1960s, as Frederick Schodt points out, 'television and comics were firmly intertwined in a symbiotic relationship' (Schodt 1983, 67). In the US, as intellectual property rights have been reinforced, comic-book publishers have moved in the direction of becoming 'creative rights companies', deriving much of their income from licensing their characters to movie makers, computer-game producers and so on (Wright 2001).

This market for characters and images thrives on, amongst other things, what might be called the 'economics of outrage'. The more extreme and controversial a product, the better it is likely to sell. A relatively careful and literal reconstruction of some historical event (such as the 'comfort women' issue) is rather less likely to attract a mass readership than an egregiously one-sided and offensive version. Truth may not always be a thousand times less saleable than fiction, but it is often a good deal less saleable than travesty.

A debate conducted through the comic book, then, demands not simply alternative comic versions of the same event, but also must encourage readers to look critically at the images they are consuming. But here too, the nature of the pop-culture market creates some challenges. The growing power of intellectual property rights can, as Japanese academic Uesugi Satoshi discovered, limit the opportunity to publish critical examinations of comic-book images of the past. Passages from written texts, provided they do not exceed a certain length, can usually be quoted by critics without the permission of the author (although even this is becoming more difficult in many societies). However, the ownership of images is more tightly policed. When Uesugi reproduced Kobayashi Yoshinori's comic-book images in his writings in order to subject them to critical scrutiny, he found himself on the receiving end of a law-suit for breach of intellectual property (though Kobayashi ultimately lost this court case) (Uesugi 2000, 92–106).

All the same, encouraging the critical consumption of images – whether specifically of Kobayashi's images or of comic-book imagery more generally – is a crucial task. Comic books are a very important medium of historical communication in many parts of the world, and, despite growing competition from electronic media, continue to play a vital role in shaping popular images of the past. The comic also reaches audiences who may seldom read academic history texts or historical novels. A look at the comic book highlights the importance, in a multimedia age, of imagination – particularly visual imagination – as an element in historical understanding. Above all, it highlights the importance of treating the visual imagination of readers as something that needs to be consciously nurtured – extended beyond passive consumerism to active and critical engagement with mass-marketed images. By extending their own visual imaginations, comic-book readers can recognize how the comic positions them in relation to a historical event, and can conjure up their own alternative images of that event as it might appear from other angles. In this way, they can begin to free themselves from the writer's sometimes totalitarian hold on their visualization of the past.

The visual imagination can also be utilized by comic-book writers, and other producers of historical representations to find oblique and unexpected counter-images capable of depicting traumatic events in the past without prurience or banality. Here the task may not simply be to draw conventional comics which tell the same story from a different point of view, but to think creatively (as Art Spiegelman, Claude Lanzmann, Hara Kazuo and others have done) about the way that unexpected images – or even blanks, gaps and silences – may be used to represent the unrepresentable.

This creative process may also involve moving across the boundaries of the various media of communication, or combining diverse media to tell a particular story. The contemporary range of popular media makes it possible for debates generated in the comic book (like those generated in the movie) to be pursued in other forums, including the emerging forums created by cyberspace. In the next chapter, we shall look at those forums, examine the ways in which their presentations of history intersect with those in comic books, documentaries, feature films and photographs, and consider some possibilities for multimedia approaches to experiencing and understanding history.

6

Random Access Memory: History in a Multimedia Age

My name is Dean … I am thirty-three years old and currently live in San Francisco. I am a third generation American of Japanese ancestry and had my uncles fighting on opposite sides of the war …

My earliest memory of the atomic bomb was from a Hanna Barbera cartoon, 'Beannie and Cecil'. In that episode, an atomic bomb was going to be detonated on 'No-Bikini-Atoll' and was stopped because of the existence of a prehistoric creature 'Sore'. At the time, I was too young to recognize all of the adult references in the cartoon but enjoyed it anyway. In the eighth grade, I had a very progressive Social Studies class which required us to do presentations on various social issues of the day. We were required to bring in film clips, get speakers and make handouts to accompany our presentations. After the presentations, we debated the pros and cons of the issues. In that class, I saw footage of the scenes from Hiroshima and Nagasaki before and after the bomb. I can recall that the most powerful image that remains with me today is the one of people's shadows imprinted on a wall. (Exploratorium 1995.)

In 1995 San Francisco's Exploratorium, a museum of 'science, art and human perception', commemorated the fiftieth anniversary of the end of the Pacific War by creating an Internet web site centred on Yamahata Yôsuke's photographs of the Nagasaki atomic bombing. The site presents seventeen of Yamahata's photographs, interspersed with quotations from his written recollections. The last picture in the series is the photograph of Tanaka Kiyo breastfeeding her dying baby Yoshihiro. The photographs, inlaid in an unadorned black background, are rather small, so that the details of the shots are not always readily visible, but their presentation conveys a vivid overall impression of utter devastation. The photographic images are reproduced alongside a variety of related documents, including a translation of Yamahata's eyewitness account of Nagasaki on the day after the bomb was dropped.

Like the editors and exhibition designers discussed in Chapter 3, the creators of the Exploratorium web site incorporate implicit interpretations into their choice and arrangement of Yamahata's photographs. The site focuses only on the experience of Nagasaki, not showing other scenes of war in the countries invaded by Japan, nor the land battles of Okinawa, nor the Japanese cities which were targets of conventional bombing raids. In this sense, the experience of the atomic bombings is implicitly represented as a unique and somewhat self-contained event.

But this site also differs in some important ways from other presentations of Yamahata's Nagasaki photographs. As part of the online exhibit, the museum opened Internet discussion groups, which allowed people from around the USA and beyond to respond to the photographs and to comment on the bombing. Contributors' comments are posted on the web site under four headings: telling history, the decision to use the bomb, war and peace, and nuclear science. In a separate section of the site entitled 'Atomic Memories', the museum also invited virtual visitors to share their recollections of first learning about the atomic bombings. The statement quoted at the start of this chapter is an extract from one of sixty-three responses to this invitation. Most of the written text in which the photos are embedded therefore comes not from an editor, curator or historical expert, but from the multitudinous voices of the discussion group participants. Rather than incorporating the photographs into a single narrative, the site confronts the viewer with the enormous diversity of responses which these images evoke.

The 'Atomic Memories' section of the web site tells us much about the way a knowledge of the recent past is transmitted from one generation to the next in a multimedia age. A small group of older contributors, born before the war, recall hearing about the atomic bombings at the time, from parents, newspapers or radio broadcasts. For the generation born immediately after the war, the first encounter with the existence of nuclear weapons generally came in the context of the civil defence drills held in US schools during the first decades of the Cold War. Their memories, in the words of one, include 'duck and cover' exercises for the classroom; daily tests of the Emergency Broadcast System on the radio; tests of air raid sirens; jokes about what to do if an atomic attack occurred …' (Exploratorium 1995). The generation born after about 1960, meanwhile, acquired their images of the atomic bomb and its effects in part from history lessons but above all – and most vividly – from popular media, whether Hanna Barbera cartoons, films like *The Day After*, museum exhibits, John Hersey's novel *Hiroshima* or Eleanor Coerr's account *Sadako and the Thousand Paper Cranes*, which retells the true story of a child's death from radiation sickness. In the words of a forty-five-year-old contributor from Sweden, 'Sadako wants to live, impressed my whole generation. The book made the whole thing real to us. It could have been [us], or our siblings, or cousins – and in a sense it [was]' (Exploratorium 1995).

At their extremes, the responses to Yamahata's images range from impassioned denouncements of the use of violence, to hate-filled statements justifying the bombings (and, in some cases, revealing the survival of curious myths about the war and its end). In some visitors to the site, however, the photographs stirred more complex and ambivalent feelings. A twenty-three-year-old Korean contributor to the 'Atomic Memories' discussion recalls that 'attending school in Korea I was taught only of the horrors of the Japanese occupation of Korea before and during WW2. Of the atomic bombings all I knew was that they had put an end to the war – and that the Japanese deserved it for all their sins in Korea and other places'. But growing up, he writes, he learnt about the bomb's effects not on 'an abstract evil nation but the daughter and the mother left clutching rice balls in burnt cities.' (Here I note with interest that the writer has assumed that the child with the rice ball is a girl, while I assumed this was a boy.) He continues,

> When I view these pictures or see shots from movies showing nuclear holocaust for a long time I've had trouble reconciling the lessons I was taught as a child and the conclusions I'm trying to arrive at as an adult. It's a difficult process and it's easy to pity these victims, it's easy to mourn or blame or feel sorry. I'm more interested in the thorny questions of relative justice, distortions or omissions of history, interested in what mix of feelings these images bring out in me. And I thank the exhibit for doing that, for providing an arena of burning ruin as it is for my thoughts to roam uneasily. (Exploratorium 1998.)

What impresses me in this statement is the way that it identifies the photograph as an image to which the viewer may return again and again, each time seeing it in a slightly different light. This process involves, but goes also beyond, the moment of recognition in which the viewer identifies with the unknown face on the photo. As our position in the present changes, and as we hear and compare diverse stories about the past, we come back to the image and pose new questions about its bearing on our interpretation of the event.

Hypertext History

The Exploratorium's online exhibition of Yamahata's photographs illustrates the capacity of media such as comics, novels, photography and the Internet itself to encourage us to keep on reshaping the stories we tell ourselves about the past. It also highlights the peculiarities of the Internet as a medium of historical communication. Far more than books, films, comics or conventional museum displays, this space is a babel of contending narratives, a space that readily flows across national boundaries.

Like most Internet sites, the Exploratorium's virtual exhibition sits rather literally at a point of intersection in a web of information. Starting from this point, the visitor to the site can quickly and almost effortlessly move in a variety of directions. The Nagasaki site, for example, is incorporated into a larger section of the Exploratorium web site dealing with questions of memory. Here the visitor can investigate other facets of the problems of remembering, such as the story of the artist Francesco Magnani, who feels compelled repeatedly to paint – in obsessive and extraordinarily accurate detail – scenes from the Italian village where he lived as a child. From this point one can move on to play memory games or read scientific articles on the functioning of the human brain. Following a different pathway, links from the Nagasaki site take the visitor to archives of information related to the development of nuclear science. Impelled by my own particular interests, meanwhile, I pursue the links from the Exploratorium's site in yet another direction: to the Hiroshima-based A-Bomb WWW Museum. From there I branch out to explore a couple of paths which take me, in less than a minute, to a site protesting the wartime use of Korean forced labour by Mitsubishi's Nagasaki shipyards and to the web page of the Yasukuni Shrine, the Shinto shrine dedicated to fallen soldiers (where I am informed that the page is currently overwhelmed by hits and experiencing severe delays).

In this chapter I want to reflect on the peculiarities and possibilities of the Internet as a means of communicating a knowledge of the past. More than any of the other media of communication discussed so far, these digital forums are in a state of rapid flux and evolution. This, on the one hand, makes predictions about their future use particularly difficult, but, on the other, also means that here, more than anywhere else, there is scope for users to shape the future by the creative application of their imaginations. As I have suggested earlier, though, the various contemporary media of historical communication exist not in isolation, but in constant interaction with one another. So it is important to consider, not just the potential of the Internet on its own, but also how it is interwoven with the other media we have discussed in earlier sections of this book.

Ironically, the Internet itself is the quintessential product of the threat of atomic holocaust. It first took embryonic shape in 1969 in the Advanced Research Projects Division of the US Department of Defense, and was designed as a network linking military command centres, defence contractors and universities so that communications could be maintained even in case of nuclear attack. By 1973, however, growing non-military use of computer networks had encouraged the Department of Defense to expand this into the more open Internetting project. During the 1980s, the development of new computer languages made networked activities increasingly accessible to non-specialists, creating the basis for the international explosion in public use of the Internet in the 1990s (Trinkle et al. 1997, 3–4).

The Internet came to be characterized by its anarchic quality. It is a realm to which anyone with a computer and a modem – and increasingly anyone with a mobile phone – can have access, a world where users create their own information as well as consuming information created by others. All of this has encouraged some utopian visions of cyberspace as an open and egalitarian forum for the exchange of ideas and information (Aizu and Kumon 1994; see also Stallabrass 1995). But during the 1990s, while scholars, including historians, were starting to make increasing use of the Internet, a rather different form of digital history was also taking shape. This was the CD-ROM. After Sony and Philips introduced audio compact disks in the 1980s, publishers began to turn their attention to the possibility of the CD as a medium for storing text, and in 1985 Grolier issued the first commercial text CD-ROM, a digital version of its Academic American Encyclopedia (Rosenzweig 1995, 1621).

The Internet and CD-ROM have much in common. As digital media, both have the ability to combine text, images and sound. Both are computer-based, and so the formats in which they present knowledge are constrained by the frame of the computer screen: images need to be trimmed to fit this frame; text works best when it is produced in short segments which can easily be read on the screen. At the same time, computer-based media have a special capacity to create links which allow users to jump from one document to another, and to choose their own paths through a maze of texts, sounds and images. This has important implications for the way that these digital media communicate knowledge, including a knowledge of the past. Their structure is quite different from the linear structure of the conventional text, or even of the movie or TV programme. Rather than a logical sequence determined by their creator, they present knowledge in the form that US computer visionary Theodore H. Nelson labelled 'hypertext': a multitudinous (though not unlimited) range of pathways through which the user navigates according to his or her own interests (Landow 1992; Nelson 1981; Rosenzweig 1995).

The explosion of these new media since the 1980s, like the birth of new media in earlier decades, has led to some extravagant claims about their potential. Just as D. W. Griffith was predicting in 1915 that children would soon be 'taught practically everything by moving pictures' and

'never be obliged to read history again', so by the 1960s Theodore
Nelson was predicting that books would be obsolete in five years, a
prediction which has repeatedly been echoed as computer technology
has evolved (Rosenzweig 1995). This history of futurology suggests an
obvious need for caution in assessing the implications of these new
media. In a sense, indeed, the very speed of the evolution of digital
technologies is one reason for hesitation in predicting events such as the
death of the book.

A good illustration of the issues at stake is provided by Art
Spiegelman's *Maus* comics. In the early 1990s, Spiegelman became a
pioneer of the use of CD-ROM. Although he bemoaned the problems
of adapting his comic-book graphics to the shape of the computer
screen, the new technology enabled Spiegelman to combine the
completed comics with early drafts of his drawings, documents on the
Holocaust and recordings of his father's voice recounting his
experiences in Auschwitz (Spiegelman 1994; Rosenzweig 1995). The
CD-ROM version of *The Complete Maus*, however, was designed in an
Apple Macintosh format that was overtaken by changes in computer
technology. As a result, while the book versions of *Maus* have survived
and continued to sell well, the CD-ROM version has not.

At the same time, the potential of digital history to cross boundaries
and to open up new knowledge of the past is also obviously circumscribed both by the boundaries of language and by the 'digital divide'
between rich and poor nations. Embarking on a journey of discovery
from the Exploratorium's Nagasaki Internet site, all of these limitations
quickly become visible. The potential paths leading out from this site are
often blocked in one of two ways. Some lead to dead ends created by
the ever-changing fluidity of information on the Net. Repeatedly,
promising-looking gateways open only onto a disappointing sign saying:
'This page cannot be found: The page you are looking for might have
been removed, had its name changed, or is temporarily unavailable'.

Other paths are blocked (for me) by barriers of language. Having followed a historical trail from San Francisco to Nagasaki and Hiroshima, I find trails leading on to Chinese and Korean sites which I cannot read. Lastly, there are also paths that are absent – whole regions of the world that are bypassed – because of inherent inequalities of wealth and power. So, while there is a relative abundance of web sites both criticizing and defending Japan's wartime activities in Asia, and these lead quite readily (for those who can read them) to sites in China and South Korea discussing similar issues, one looks in vain for readily accessible sites recalling the experience of wartime occupation from, say, a Vietnamese or East Timorese perspective.

As Roy Rosenzweig observes, however, a reaction against 'hyperpredictions' about the wonders of digital technologies should not lead us to a reactionary 'hypercynicism' (Rosenzweig 1995). As we saw in Chapter 1, a central element in the contemporary crisis of history is the problem of passing on a knowledge of the past in a globalized age. The interconnectedness of the contemporary world makes it more important than ever for people to have the capacity to find out about the past of societies geographically remote from their own. But at the same time, one response to globalization in some quarters is an alarming defensive retreat behind the reinforced walls of a narrowly nationalist view of the past. In this context, it seems particularly important to take a realistic look at the possibilities of digital history for opening up new perspectives on the past.

The Internet and the Landscapes of the Past

To consider the implications of digital history for our identification with and interpretation of past events, we might return to some of the historical narratives which we have already encountered: Steven Spielberg's retelling of the Amistad case; the story of the Williamite

Wars as recounted in John Banim's novel *The Boyne Water*; and revisionist accounts of the 'comfort women' issue.

As we have seen, the Amistad case has spawned a multitude of web sites, some of them inspired by the popularity of Spielberg's movie. The US National Archives and Records Administration (NARA), for example, includes the case as one of several topics covered by its educational Internet site, while the Museum of America and the Sea at Mystic Seaport, Connecticut, provides a detailed overview of the case linked to a collection of documents from the museum's library. A wide range of archival material related to Amistad is published on these sites: records from the trial itself; contemporary pamphlets and newspaper articles; the speeches and letters of politicians involved in the trials and of campaigners for the abolition of slavery. Both sites also suggest a range of activities which teachers can use with students to explore and assess the digital archive. For example, the NARA site encourages students not only to review Spielberg's movie, but also to compare and assess the role, motives and arguments of various participants in the case: the kidnapped Africans, the Spanish government, the US abolitionists, Charles van Buren (who was the US president at the time of the trial) and others (National Archives and Records Administration 1998).

Unlike Spielberg's movie, which creates a powerful sense of emotive identification with a particular version of the Amistad story, the web sites bring users into contact with the primary material related to the case, and force them to consider the multiple perspectives of the actors involved. The Mystic Seaport site introduces the voices of some of the Africans who, in the movie, are reduced to faces in the crowd. Kale, for example, a young man who was kidnapped into slavery while on his way to the market to buy rice, writes to John Quincy Adams, in a letter dated January 4, 1841, and digitized in the museum's archive: 'We want you to ask the Court what we have done wrong. What for Americans keep us in prison? Some people say Mendi people crazy, Mendi people dolt, because we no talk America language. America people no talk Mendi language. America people crazy dolts?'

In the movie, John Quincy Adams's concluding speech to the Supreme Court is recast into a form which readily appeals to a contemporary audience. But visitors to the Mystic Seaport web site find the original speech, complete with its rather archaic legal language and unmistakably nineteenth-century religious sentiments. The sense of distance between the world of the present and the world of John Quincy Adams is heightened, in the NARA site, by the fact that here the documents are reproduced as facsimiles – not a word-processed text but as photographic images of letters written in scrawling hands on faded and fraying paper. Rather than being drawn into a national narrative whose motif is that 'who we were is who we are', Internet users are confronted with the presence of multiple possible forms of 'we' – a complex landscape of diverse positions, interests and opinions through which they must navigate to discover the genealogy of their own ideas and thus their own identity.

This does not mean, of course, that the web sites simply present their visitors with the raw material of history itself, leaving them entirely free to make their own interpretations and draw their own conclusions. Certain implicit interpretations are already built into the choice of archives included in the site, the explanatory information and the questions that teachers are encouraged to pose to students.

The creators of the Mystic Seaport site explicitly address one recurrent problem of exposing the diverse views of historical actors to the scrutiny of contemporary students: the fact that these views may be couched in terms which many people today find unappealing, and some find deeply offensive. The museum therefore introduces the archive with its own editorial comment:

Warning: these documents reflect the racial and social attitudes of antebellum American popular culture. Some contain disturbing material. A few are extremely racist, and we are a little uncomfortable putting them on-line. But they are an important aspect of this history, part of the climate that surrounded the Amistad Africans as they made their way through the United States. (Mystic Seaport 1998.)

Nevertheless, these web sites, like the Exploratorium's 'Atomic Memories', illustrate a key characteristic of Internet history: unlike films or even conventional museum displays, digital hypertext is excellently suited to presenting a linked collection of short statements expressing diverse perspectives on the same event. As well as reading the radically different views of the Amistad case expressed by participants, such as the slave owners and the kidnapped Africans themselves, visitors to the Mystic Seaport site can also sample the varied opinions of present-day contributors to an Internet discussion group on Amistad, and, if they wish, add their own comments. Not all Internet presentations of history, of course, deliberately set out to offer such a diversity of opinion. Many, as we shall see, are devoted to publicizing a particular version of the past. But in looking for information on the Internet, the searcher almost inescapably becomes conscious of the presence of sites offering more than one view of history. Users may choose not read web pages whose views conflict with their own, but they can hardly fail to be aware of their existence.

As the Amistad sites also suggest, the Internet has the potential to reveal the cross-border implications of historical events. How far this potential is realized, of course, depends on the design of the site. Like film directors, web-site creators make choices about the chronological and geographical bounds which they set around their subjects. The NARA Amistad site resembles Spielberg's film in focusing heavily on the US dimensions of the Amistad case, while the Mystic Seaport's site acknowledges its international dimensions, presenting the case as a set of interlocked 'Atlantic Histories' which span West Africa, Cuba and the United States (Mystic Seaport 1998). But above all it is the existence of links between one site and another which creates opportunities for border crossing. Within a fraction of a minute of entering the Mystic Seaport site one can move from this point, via the Amistad Research Center at Tulane University, to a database of African archives where one can access everything from missionary records to contemporary debates on civil wars in West Africa. (It should be said, though, that a rather large share of this digital information on Africa is actually stored or generated in the United States. The Internet, like the world of the mainstream popular movie, remains dominated by the economic and informational power of the USA.)

Virtual Battlegrounds

In opening up a profusion of diverse historical accounts, the Web creates its own challenges. As a relatively anarchic forum for multiple voices, the Internet tends to become an arena for gladiatorial debates over contentious issues, among them aspects of history that have strong contemporary political resonances. A large proportion of the sites devoted to historical subjects deal with particularly controversial topics. Not all of these are recent events. The wars in the Balkans during the 1990s, for example, promoted a great number of sites in which incidents from the remote past (such as the fourteenth-century Battle of Kosova Polje) were claimed as justifications for a particular group's claim to a particular piece of territory.

Other conflicts of the past also resurface in the present with a vengeance, to be fought out on the Internet as rival groups contend for control over the historical imagination of the wider community. The 1690 Battle of the Boyne, for example, is commemorated not just in the family tragedy of *The Boyne Water* but also today in the annual triumphal parades by militant Protestant organizations through the streets of Northern Irish towns: parades which have become a key focus and source of ongoing communal conflict. As one Internet account puts it,

> It is hardly possible to mention the Battle of the Boyne without striking an emotional chord in the heart of anyone with Irish blood in his or her veins. The emotions, of course, will, vary. Are you Loyalist or Nationalist? Catholic or Protestant? Was William III the glorious victor? Or was James II the victim of a stolen throne? Perhaps the most amazing thing about the Battle of the Boyne is that it seems to live on more than 300 years after the original warriors moved on. (Friend 2001.)

These communal battles over Irish memory are reflected on the Internet, where various organizations contend for influence over the historical imagination of the present generation. Thus, for example, the militant Northern Irish Protestant Orange Order's site proclaims the anniversary of the battle as 'a great day for all the Irish and also for the entire democratic and free world!' and urges readers to celebrate by participating in the annual Drumcree march (a cause of repeated violence in recent years). Another Loyalist web site, meanwhile, provides a dramatic account of the Battle of the Boyne, complete with illustrations from seventeenth-century art, concluding that 'hope for a civilized Ireland has not yet been fulfilled' but that 'despite Roman Catholic persecution, contempt and propaganda Protestantism is a beacon of light in a world of darkness' (Kilpatrick n.d.).

In the Irish Republic, the landscapes of memory are rather different, and recollection of the battle itself tends to be over-shadowed by that of the betrayal of the Treaty of Limerick, and commemoration of the 'wild geese' – the defeated fighters who fled into exile in the 1690s. Here, then, memory is digitized in sites like the home page of the Wild Geese Heritage Museum and Library in Portumna, County Galway, which recounts a story of defeat and betrayal (complete with maps and biographies) and aims to 'provide a spiritual home and focal point for all persons of Irish origin who are scattered throughout the world and who yearn for some contact with their roots' (Ryan 1997). The theme is taken up by the electronic diaspora, in web sites like the US-based 'Wild Geese Today: Erin's Far Flung Exiles'. This links an account of the betrayal of the Treaty of Limerick to stories of the Irish soldiers who fought in the US War of Independence and Civil War, and thus to 'all those brave Irishmen who died for Irish freedom in Ireland and for those who died in exile far from the land they loved'. In the process, of course, it also simplifies the complex story of one of the largest mass-migrations of people in modern history, reinforcing a largely mythical (and masculine) bond which subsumes the many and diverse generations of Irish emigrants into the image of the exiled fighter devoted to the freedom of his ancestral nation.

The parallel presence of these radically divergent visions of the past on the Internet obviously creates difficulties for those who explore the Net in search of historical understanding: particularly for those who start off with little background information on the topic they are researching. The very nature of the Internet, then, draws our attention to the fact that the search for historical understanding always involves a set of relationships between people – a circuit of communication in which it is crucial to ask: 'Who is telling this story and why? Why do I respond to it as I do?' But the possibilities and difficulties of comparing varied versions of past events on the Web also raise more fundamental issues about the communication of historical knowledge in the contemporary world.

Hypertext and the Historiography of Oblivion

Examples like the Amistad web sites illuminate the value of the Internet as a space for encounter with a range of different perspectives on the past. Listening to the multiple voices of the participants in the case, and joining the present-day debate about the meaning of Amistad, we can gain a richer understanding of the heritage of ideas and actions that have created the world in which we live. We are also forced to expose our own preconceptions to critical scrutiny.

But there is also a risk that, without some compass-bearings for navigating this sea of ideas and opinions, users may simply become disoriented and drift inertly on its wind and waves. In other words, engulfed by a mass of divergent opinions, we may experience a kind of paralysis – a mental refusal to form any articulate opinion at all. There is some reason to think that this is an increasingly real problem in our multimedia age. Writing in the early 1970s, Edmund Carpenter was already suggesting that the proliferation of media had created a world where the young in particular regarded different media as 'self-contained environments, having little correspondence with other realities or environments'. As a result, they found nothing incongruous about encountering conflicting reports in the press, radio or TV, and felt no need to attempt to reconcile or make judgments between contradictory representations of the past in books and film (Carpenter 1972, 44–45).

At the beginning of this book I discussed the notion that there is a connection between the spread of 'postmodern' skepticism about historical truth and the rise of certain sorts of historical 'revisionism' – for example, of writings which seek to deny the reality of the Nazi Holocaust. I suggested there that skepticism about the possibility of representing the total truth of a historical event is nothing very new. However, I also think it possible that, confronted with a great diversity of representations of history, we may be tempted to suspend judgment, adopting a kind of detached cynicism which creates an open field for all forms of ideological re-interpretation or denial of the past. This cynicism is not necessarily a product of a thoroughgoing postmodern scepticism about the nature of reality: it may simply reflect a sense of being overwhelmed by so much conflicting information that the recipient loses the courage to take on the burdens of judgment, preferring to leave the expression of opinions to 'the experts'.

The problem, I would argue, is compounded by some of the inherent qualities of hypertextual media. Consider, for example, the large range of Internet sites which address the issue of the 'comfort women'. Many of these have great value as sources of historical knowledge. They contain a mass of archival material to which most people would otherwise have little access, including documents like the 1996 report by the UN Commission on Human Rights on the 'comfort women' issue, collections of testimony by former 'comfort women' (as well as by former soldiers and others), and research papers by academics. Since the issue is one which generates passionate feelings and wide-ranging opinions, visitors to these sites quickly find themselves confronted with a diversity of conflicting information. The Saesparam group's *Jûgun ianfu mondai jôhôshitsu* [Information Room on the 'Comfort Women' Issue], for example, opens onto a mass of discussion groups and opinion forums offering radically divergent perspectives on the issue. Some of these are created by academic researchers, others by NGOs and lobby groups, others by individuals with a particular view to air. They include statements by Kobayashi Yoshinori fans, material posted by critics of Kobayashi's comics (including Uesugi Satoshi), pages produced by the Society for History Textbook Reform and by discussion groups refuting their views. Using the Internet to develop an understanding of the problem therefore obviously involves, first and foremost, an effort to identify authors and assess the positions from which information and opinions are offered.

But the 'comfort women' sites also raise other broader issues of 'hypertext history'. Let us look, for a moment, at two web sites which adopt a revisionist approach to the 'comfort women' issue. One is an English language site created by one Kakichi Shinji. The information posted here tells us nothing about the author or his reasons for creating the site. However, it includes English translations of some newspaper articles and the testimonies of four former Japanese soldiers, the managers of two 'comfort stations', and two former 'comfort women', together with a statement questioning the accuracy of the account given by one of these women. The second web site is a series of questions and answers on the 'comfort women' issue attached to the site of the Institute for Liberal Historiography [*Jiyûshugi Shikan Kenkyûjo*], one of the alter egos of the Society for History Textbook Reform. Here, the answers to correspondents' questions are supplied by two members of the Institute, Tanihara Shigeo and Noguchi Hakaru.

Both sites approach the issue in a very similar way. Their first step is to redefine the terms of the debate. Rather than considering broader issues of historical context, cause and meaning, they deliberately shrink the discussion to a focus on a specific question: the question of whether the 'comfort women' were or were not forcibly abducted by members of the Japanese armed forces. Having redefined the question in this way, the sites then move on to a second step, the selection of particular pieces of historical evidence or testimony, whose credibility they subject to sustained attack. Like other revisionist approaches to the issue, both are particularly critical of testimony about the recruitment of 'comfort women' given by a former Japanese soldier, Yoshida Seiji (Tanihara and Noguchi n.d.; Kakichi 1997). This process of reduction serves an important rhetorical function. By raising doubts about evidence that *particular* women were forcibly recruited by the military, the web-site creators seek to create doubt that *any* women were recruited in this way. And by evoking doubt about the issue of forcible recruitment, they seek implicitly to negate the whole image of the 'comfort women' as victims of military violence.

This rhetorical structure is characteristic of contemporary historiographies of oblivion. Whether applied to the Nazi Holocaust, the Nanjing Massacre or the 'comfort women', or to other historical events like the massacres of Aboriginal Australians by colonists, these repeatedly follow the same two-stage strategy. First, they shift the arena of discussion away from the overall meaning, causes and effects of the historical event, towards a more narrow matter of definitions; and second, they subject a small number of selected pieces of evidence to sustained critical scrutiny. Thus in relation to the Holocaust, the Nanjing Massacre and massacres of Australian Aborigines, the historiography of oblivion begins by shifting the debate to the question of the numbers killed, and then moves on to a critical discussion of particular pieces of documentary or testimonial evidence, with the intention of minimizing the number of people who are recognized as victims of that event (for a good discussion of this approach, see Yang 2000).

This strategy is one that is rather easily adapted to hypertextual media like the Internet. The Internet can of course be used to post long and complex documents such as academic articles or the UN Commission of Human Rights' report on the 'comfort women' issue. But these are difficult to read on the screen and sometimes cumbersome to handle in the Internet format. As we have seen, then, web sites seem particularly well adapted to presenting a linked maze of short pieces of fragmented data. This often makes it difficult to use them as a starting point for creating an overall sense of the historical origins and meaning of an event. Debate rather readily becomes channelled into a focus on very specific and factual issues. (Is a particular document credible? Can this fact or figure be believed?)

The Internet, in other words, is a realm where a knowledge of the past comes to us, literally, in bits. It is immensely useful in giving many people access to primary documents and testimony that they would otherwise be unlikely to find. It is also an excellent forum for exposing people to a wide range of conflicting views on controversial issues. But it provides a rather less useful forum for assembling those pieces of the puzzle into sustained interpretive narratives. Many crucial and contentious issues of modern history (including the 'comfort women' issue and issues of sexual violence in other wars; including too the sexual violence inflicted on women in Okinawa and other parts of Japan by the US military) cannot be understood simply through a detailed assessment of the reliability of one or two specific pieces of evidence. Our knowledge of such issues is created by confronting the presence of a very large and complex body of oral and written evidence, few pieces of which, by themselves, provide any clear overall picture of events. Only when this body of evidence is brought together and assessed as a whole can we begin to perceive patterns through which we can pursue the task of understanding the past. Hypertext tends to fragment rather than synthesize, and cannot easily be used to address wider conceptual questions raised by these histories: what political, social and ideological structures sustain the systematic sexual abuse of women in war? How do victims deal with their trauma and how do those involved in the maintenance of the system (whether as the paid procurers of women, managers of 'comfort stations', common soldiers or commanders) deal with their memories? What can we learn from the past to relieve the sufferings of survivors in the present and prevent the repetition of such violence?

Multimedia Pasts

At the same time, the worldwide emergence of historiographies of oblivion, and the signs of a growing reluctance to form independent opinions about the past, make it all the more important to think creatively about new media as means to communicate a knowledge of history. As we have seen in earlier chapters, all the media of historical expression have certain inherent advantages and limitations. With a growing diversity of media, though, it becomes easier to combine various forms of communication so as to make use of of their unique potential. This may, for example, mean using the power of the Internet to introduce users to archival material, multiple voices and cross-border linkages, but using it in conjunction with other media which present a broader narrative of the background to events, and to evoke a stronger sense of the texture of past lives and societies (see http://www.geocities.jp/pastwithin, which provides further material on the themes of this book).

This, for example, is the approach taken by the documentary series *Africans in America: America's Journey Through Slavery*, shown on the US Public Broadcasting Service in 1998. Unlike Spielberg's *Amistad*, which focuses on a particular moment in the story of slavery and abolition, the TV series *Africans in America* creates a documentary narrative of the social history of African Americans from 1450 to 1865. Its narrative, like that of many documentaries, is woven around the lives of individuals: historical figures like Antonio Johnson, a Black indentured servant who became a plantation owner in the seventeenth century, before race-based slavery made such achievements impossible; figures like Olaudah Equiano and Venture Smith, both of whom wrote memoirs recounting their experiences as slaves transported to America in the eighteenth century. But the documentary form also allows these biographies to be punctuated by comments from contemporary historians and the programme's narrators, giving interpretations of background events – changes in policy, social trends, shifts in popular ideas. Film also offers a visual sense of the landscapes and material environments in which the traumas of slavery were played out.

One particularly interesting feature of the PBS documentary is that it is linked both to a book and to a web site containing an unusually rich array of archives on the experience of African Americans, as well as statements by historians (Johnson, Smith and Morris 1998; WGBH Educational Foundation 1998). By linking the three media, *Africans in America* creates a coherent narrative of the history of slavery, and also opens a window onto resources which its audience can use to explore aspects of the story further. After watching the documentary, which, for example, outlines the life of Olaudah Equiano, kidnapped into slavery in Benin in the 1750s, placing his life in the wider context of the slave trade, TV viewers can then move to the Internet to read extracts from Equiano's autobiography. They can also read a letter by George Washington setting out his views on slavery, look at posters advertising rewards for the return of runaway slaves, or make use of a large archive of other primary material, as well as browsing through the views of contemporary commentators on the issue of slavery, ranging from historian Thomas Davis to general-turned-politician Colin Powell. All this can help them to develop their own views on the narrative that they have watched on the TV screen, and to define their own positions in relation to the history of slavery. The high cost of producing this multimedia history, it must be said, has made it necessary for the producers to rely heavily on corporate sponsorship, so that the documentary episodes are prefaced by disconcerting advertisements for McDonald's and Bankers Trust. But *Africans in America* nevertheless suggests some interesting possibilities for making the most of the Internet's potential as a medium of historical communication.

At a time when the past, like a repressed memory, returns to haunt the politics of the present, such creative uses of media may become more important than ever as a means of opening up the borders of memory which resurgent nationalisms seek to barricade. Though language is one of the barriers that restrict movement through the pathways of cyberspace, a growing number of Internet sites are finding ways around those barriers. Many sites (like the web site of the

Independence Hall of Korea, discussed in Chapter 1) now operate in two or even three languages at once, while others use translated material as an integral part of their archives. One interesting instance is the Teachers' Virtual School in the UK, whose educational material for teaching the history of the First World War includes a substantial section of translated material from the early twentieth-century German satirical magazines *Simplicissimus* and *Kladderadatsch*, introducing students to the diversity of opinion which existed in Germany at the time of the war (Teachers' Virtual School 2001). Developing online sites which use translated media material in this way can help to bridge the enduring trench that often runs through historical knowledge, maintaining hostilities between former enemies as each learns an inward-focused version of the national past.

Meanwhile, addressing the crisis of history involves developing a sensitivity to the way that media like the Internet shape our perceptions of the past. The teaching of history needs to empower students to use these media with creativity and imagination, but also with a critical awareness of their potential biases and limitations. The paths of the Net are sometimes dead ends, and sometimes filled with pitfalls, but navigated with care they can provide avenues for expanding the imagination. They enable us to cross boundaries, to hear and assess contesting stories.

And sometimes (for this too is an important part of the encounter with history) they simply create a space for our thoughts to 'roam uneasily'.

7

Towards a Political Economy of Historical Truthfulness

June 28, 1989 was the six-hundredth anniversary of the Battle of Kosova Polje, the conflict in which the Serbian forces of Prince Lazar were defeated by the Ottoman Empire. The commemorative ceremony marking the anniversary was attended by the entire leadership of what was then the Yugoslav Federation, but – in a carefully scripted media event – the central role was played by Serbian Communist leader Slobodan Milošević. As one account describes it:

> The commemoration had all the trappings of a coronation staged as a Hollywood extravaganza. Milošević descended by helicopter from the heavens into the cheering crowd; the masses were the extras. The cameras focused on his arrival. In some vague way, the commentator placed Slobodan Milošević at the center of the Serbian ancestral myth of Prince Lazar, the hero of the Kosova battle. (Milošević 1995, 107.)

The anniversary celebrations marked 'the crowning of Milošević as the strongman of Serbia', and launched the irrevocable slide of the former Yugoslavia into war and genocide (Curuvija and Torov 1995, 85).

The 1389 Battle of Kosova Polje was not the only historical event to be seized on by the media during the break-up of Yugoslavia. Franjo Tudjman, who became president of Croatia in 1990, had previously been a professor of history known for his controversial views on the Second World War (during which the Croatian regime of Ante Pavelić had collaborated with Nazi Germany). Tudjman did not deny the horrors of the Holocaust, but he sought to relativize them by emphasizing 'the timeless universality of genocidal acts' (Tudjman 1996, 121). His particular contribution to the historiography of oblivion was an account of the Second World War which claimed that the number of deaths in the Jasenovac camp in Croatia, where many Serbs and Yugoslav Jews had died, was greatly exaggerated (Tudjman 1996; Tanner 1997, 152–153 and 205). As Tudjman's political influence grew, Serbian television responded by broadcasting programmes which argued, on the contrary, that official history had concealed the extent of wartime massacres of Serbs by Croats. Television cameras recorded the opening-up of mass graves of the victims of Second World War massacres, and the reburial of their remains. Reminders of the gruesome killings of Serbs at Jasenovac and elsewhere rekindled old hatreds and intensified Serb fears of resurgent Croat nationalism. Meanwhile, Croatian television also began demonizing the wartime behaviour of the Serbs and presenting the Croats as the true victims – victims of Communist propaganda (Milošević 1995, 109–110; Tanner 1997, 233).

The Lessons of Kosova Polje

I cite these examples from the Yugoslav tragedy because they illustrate, in rather extreme form, key concerns of this book. One is the fact that, in a multimedia age, people's knowledge of the past is framed not just by formal history education, but also by representations of history in photographs, film, television, the Internet and so on. These media of historical representation often have great power to evoke a sense of identification between past and present, but in so doing they may also offer potent implicit interpretations of the relationship between history and contemporary society. The televised spectacle of Slobodan Milošević descending by helicopter onto the spot where Prince Lazar was slain in battle, for example, not only cast Milošević in the role of heir to the hero of Serb history, but also, in the minds of many viewers, linked fourteenth-century Christian Serb resistance to the Muslim Ottoman empire with the contemporary conflict between Christian Serbs and Muslim Kosovar Albanians. Revived memories of wartime atrocities evoked a mistrust of neighbouring communities, and encouraged people to respond more violently than they might otherwise have done to emerging political tensions, for fear of the violence which they anticipated from their old enemies. In the case of Serbia and Croatia, the power of television to disseminate two radically different versions of history was particularly great because television in both places was heavily influenced by the state, and worsening economic conditions made it difficult for people to afford other sources of information. The situation provoked Serb student protestors in 1992 to coin the slogan 'Turn off your TV and open your eyes!' (Milošević 1995, 121).

Even in situations where the media are less open to obvious manipulation, their impact on the way the past is understood, for better or worse, is both subtle and profound. As we saw in Chapter 6, for example, many people in the United States know of the atomic bombing of Hiroshima and Nagasaki primarily from media such as novels, comic books, films or TV. My argument here, however, is that it makes little sense to deny or lament the impact of media upon memory. Rather, what matters is that history education should empower people to use the varied media of twenty-first-century society critically and creatively to develop their own understanding of the past. The message, in other words, might be rephrased as 'Turn on your TV but open your eyes'. That is to say, understanding the possibilities, limitations and communicative codes of various media – including of course, conventional history textbooks, and including this book itself – is an essential part of learning to understand the past. In a multimedia age, this involves not simply looking at separate media in isolation (as part of literary studies, film studies and so on) but also considering how they interact and resonate with one another to shape our visions of history.

The example of the former Yugoslavia reminds us just how important this is. History has shaped all the social patterns in which we live: family, school, work, community, state, global order, as well as shaping the ideas which we have about these patterns. Without understanding something of how such things have come into being, we cannot begin to imagine how they might be changed. Contemporary political decisions around the world are based upon conceptions of history. All wars are fought over differing interpretations of the past. In the former Yugoslavia thousands of people were killed by their former neighbours, driven to hatred and revenge by one-sided interpretations of history, and by fears that their nightmare vision of the past would repeat itself.

The Yugoslav example also reminds us of another crucial feature of history in the twenty-first century. In an age of complex global interaction, historical knowledge can no longer simply be contained within national boundaries. The wars in the former Yugoslavia evoked international responses, ranging from diplomatic pressure and humanitarian aid to military intervention. So, during the 1990s, voters in France, the United States, Australia, Japan, the Philippines and a host of other countries were suddenly expected to have an opinion about their government's response to the complex Balkan conflict, a conflict of whose origins most knew virtually nothing. Yet meaningful decisions about appropriate responses to the conflict were impossible without some knowledge of the history of Ottoman colonization, previous

Balkan wars, German occupation and the postwar federation, which had shaped the present of the region. Knowing very little of Yugoslavia's history, many people's emotional responses to the crisis were guided by memories of other, better known historical events. Photographs and film of desperate refugees huddled in farm carts as they fled from genocide were seen by many viewers around the world through the interpretive lens of the memory of similar images from past wars. Thus the NATO military intervention which followed acts of genocide in Kosova was clearly influenced by memories in Western Europe and the United States of the prewar failures of governments to respond to the genocide of the Jews in 1940s Germany.

It is, of course, impossible for history education to provide students with a detailed knowledge of the history of the whole world. History teaching in schools almost inevitably concentrates most on the issues which are of most obvious relevance to students: the history of their own country and neighbouring countries, of the most powerful nations and the most dramatic events of recent centuries. But the study of the past can also do something else – something of crucial importance in the contemporary world. It can nurture curiosity about history, and give students the ability to use diverse media to explore the past: and to keep on exploring long after they have left formal education behind them. In this way, even if they have been taught nothing about the background to an event like the Balkans war, people in many countries will be better equipped to ask questions, to acquire knowledge about its causes, and to develop informed opinions about how governments and international organizations should respond.

History and Truth

The notions of questioning and informed opinion are intimately connected to the problem of historical truthfulness. The wide range of

ideas loosely summed up under the heading 'postmodernism' has
provoked much debate about the problem of historical truth, not all of
it particularly helpful. Both some enthusiasts and some critics of
postmodernism are too quick to draw a sharp dividing line between a
pre-postmodern age, when facts reigned supreme and historical truth
was unproblematic, and a postmodern age, when all history is narrative
and all narratives are equal. As I have argued earlier, though, there is
nothing new about the idea that history involves the representation of
the past, and that this representation can never be 'the truth, the whole
truth and nothing but the truth'. What various forms of postmodern
thought have done is to make us more sensitive than before to the
complexities of representing the past in words or images. They remind
us that the very words used to speak about the past ('civilization',
'progress', 'century', 'society', 'memory') carry their own burden of
history. Postmodern writings illuminate the fact that the lines we draw
around particular pasts – the spatial lines around national, regional or
civilizational history and the temporal lines around eras like the Middle
Ages or modernity – are mental constructions, and that the texture of
the past looks very different when the lines are redrawn. And they
remind us that the same events can generate many different narratives,
each with its own internal 'regime of truth'.

All this should challenge us to deeper thought about the relationship
between representation and truth, rather than (as sometimes seems to
happen) evoking a detached and casual cynicism about the possibility of
truthfulness. Such cynicism, I think, is only possible when we forget the
fact that thought, feeling and action are irrevocably interconnected. Our
knowledge of the past is of course made up of representations, which
include 'narratives' in the conventional sense of the word, as well as
non-narrative images such as photographs. But it is not *just* representation. It is knowledge which shapes feelings and actions, and which is
itself shaped by the experience of acting in the world.

My grandfather may tell me a story about the past, according to which the people in the village down the road were responsible for mass murder. The people in the village down the road may believe another story about the past, according to which it was actually my grandfather and his neighbours who were responsible. These are just two different narratives. Either or both can be recorded as oral traditions, treated as texts for doctoral research, incorporated into school textbooks or children's comic books. Historians may reasonably insist that neither story tells the whole truth of what really happened, and that it is no longer possible to reconstruct the truth with perfect accuracy. But if they stop at that point – if they conclude that it does not matter which story I hear and believe, that only the social location of the narrator, the strength of narrator's convictions or the internal coherence of the narrative matters – then I think they misconstrue the nature of historical knowledge.

For when I walk down the road with a machine gun in my hands to exact revenge on the people of the next village, because I have heard my grandfather's story of the past but not theirs, I step across the limits of the notion that history is merely narrative. I also step across the same limits if, without wielding a gun, I neither care nor act when disaster overtakes the people of the next village, because I have heard only my grandfather's story, and believe that they are mass murders who deserve no sympathy.

We are implicated in the events of the past because we live within the institutions, beliefs and structures that the past has created. But we are also implicated in the past because the past lives in us. The knowledge of history we have absorbed consciously or unconsciously through a host of media determines who we feel sympathy for, which contemporary events stir us to joy, compassion or anger, and how we respond to those events.

But if historical knowledge is embedded in feeling and action, then it matters profoundly how people absorb, interpret and compare different representations of the past, and how these representations relate to past events. In recent years, a number of scholars have come back to this question of the relationship between representation and event, searching for an approach to history which acknowledges the complexity of language and the impossibility of perfect representation, without lapsing into that detached scepticism where all narratives are seen as equally fictional. Philosopher Takahashi Tetsuya, for example, criticizes the view that the value of historical narratives can be judged without reference to the outside events that they describe. Efforts to assess the value of narratives by, for example, favouring the suppressed narratives of marginalized communities over the dominant narratives of majorities are inadequate: in the contemporary European context, Takahashi observes, Holocaust denial might be described as being the suppressed narrative of a minority, but this does not make it a valuable form of historical knowledge. Without some sense of 'truth and untruth' or 'justice and injustice', historical knowledge is incomplete (Takahashi 2001).

In their book *Telling the Truth About History*, Joyce Appleby and others call for a 'qualified objectivity', which they define as an 'interactive relationship between an inquiring subject and an external object'. Historians, they argue, cannot recapture the totality of the past. All they can do is create interpretations of the past based on the traces left in documents, material evidence, oral tradition and so on. The questions historians pose about these traces, and the answers they supply, will inevitably be influenced by the historian's position in the present. However, certain ways of enquiring about the past are likely to produce a clearer and more meaningful picture than others. A key element of this 'qualified objectivity' is open debate between scholars of different backgrounds and persuasions (Appleby, Hunt and Jacob 1994).

The vision of 'qualified objectivity' offered in *Telling the Truth About History* is open to various criticisms. As Dipesh Chakrabarty points out, it too easily assumes that ideas and experiences from diverse historical settings can, without much distortion, be translated into the common language of contemporary academic history (Chakrabarty 2000, 75). It also seems to take the nation state for granted as the framework for historical knowledge, and, at times, treats open historical enquiry as though it were some uniquely American virtue. Besides, the authors of *Telling the Truth about History* are mainly concerned with the way professional historians theorize the past. By contrast, in these pages I have been interested in thinking about the place of historical knowledge in everyday life, and I am therefore particularly concerned with the way in which public knowledge of the past infuses, and is infused by, feeling and action.

However, the issues raised in *Telling the Truth about History* are important, and some of the ideas put forward are useful. One of these ideas is the emphasis on openness to multiple perspectives on the past. Learning about the varied perspectives of different participants in a past event gives us a fuller understanding of what happened and why, and helps us to understand the genealogy of our own ideas. Listening to, and participating in, present-day debates about historical events exposes our own preconceptions to challenge, and so makes us think more deeply about our conceptions of history – indeed, often makes us refine or change them.

In Relation to the Past

The notion of the search for historical knowledge as a 'relationship' is also a valuable one. In earlier chapters I have used the idea of 'historical truthfulness' as something that is expressed (more or less fully) through a series of relationships between participants in historical events, the people involved in recording and representing the events, and the people who consume the accounts that are subsequently produced. Historical truthfulness begins, I would argue, with *an attentiveness to the presence of the past within and around us*: the recognition that we ourselves are shaped by the past, and that knowing the past is therefore essential to knowing ourselves and others, and indeed to knowing what it is to be human. Whatever else it may impart, history education which does not stimulate this attentiveness serves very little useful purpose.

As we saw in the discussion of photography and film, our relationship with the past is complex and multilayered. Most people do not learn about history by studying primary evidence in the archives or at archaeological sites. Instead, what we encounter are representations of the past which reach us through the filter of other people's interpretations and imaginations: through the words of the novelist, the lens of the photographer, the graphics of the comic-book artist. Attentiveness to the presence of the past implies paying attention to these representations: a desire to know why this person tells the story in this way, and what other stories are, or could be, told about the same event. Central to historical truthfulness, then, is the willingness and capacity to pay attention to the differing representations of the past created by people who view (or viewed) the same set of events from different places, social backgrounds and ideological perspectives.

An attentiveness to diverse representations of the past is important for many reasons. At the most obvious level, it helps to prevent an unquestioning acceptance of slanted propaganda about the past. It would have been better for people in the former Yugoslavia to have had a chance to hear and assess both nationalist Serbian and nationalist Croatian versions of the events of the Second World War, rather than, as many were, simply being exposed to one or the other. It would have been better still had they had more ready access not just to two counterposed nationalist narratives of the past, but to the multiple alternative narratives put forward (often at considerable personal risk) by dissenters, minorities and fringe media on both sides of the ethnic divide, as well as by those who viewed the Serbian and Croatian past from outside the frontiers of the former Yugoslavia.

Listening to multiple voices encourages critical awareness and enriches our knowledge of the events of the past. It also helps us to think imaginatively about the spatial and temporal frameworks that we draw around events. As we saw in the case of the Amistad incident, whether one sees this as an event in the history of US abolitionism, an event in the history of slavery in Sierra Leone, or an event that spans and connects the histories of both countries, has important implications for an understanding of the past. A new spatial framework – for example, one that sees the incident as part of Sierra Leonean history as well as of US history – opens up a new temporal framework. Now the story no longer begins on the slave ship *Amistad*, and ends at the moment when the Amistad Africans return home; now we begin to be curious about the lives of the Amistad captives before they were kidnapped, and what happened after they returned.

To understand and compare different representations of the past, it is essential not just to ask *who* is telling this story, but also to ask *how*. A key theme of this book has been the way that differing media of historical expression influence the way that the past is represented. Those media possess their own codes of representation, their own possibilities and limitations. Some readily evoke emotion and identification, while others encourage abstract explanation; some tend to present the life of past ages as an interwoven texture, while others encourage us to separate the threads for analytical purposes. In a multimedia age, the same event is represented in many forms, and representations in one medium resonate with representations in another. The impulses to compare multiple representations, to understand the relationship between medium and message, and use varied media creatively to find out about the past are crucial aspects of historical truthfulness.

Attending to diverse representations of a past event does not give us a perfect picture of what happened. Nor can it be a purely relativist process, where all accounts are treated with equal scepticism. Our knowledge of the past determines who we are and how we live in the present. It is therefore inevitable that some representations will influence us more than others. Living at the beginning of the twenty-first century, I cannot fully enter into the mental world and lived experiences of a nineteenth-century English factory worker, a 1930s Japanese farmer, or the precolonial Aboriginal families whose territory once encompassed the piece of land that is now my back garden. It is unlikely, too, that I can fully enter into the mental world and experiences of some contemporary Aboriginal communities, such as those whose accounts of the past (drawing on quite different 'regimes of truth' from those which dominate Australian academic history writing) are documented by Deborah Bird Rose and Hokari Minoru (Rose 1990; Hokari 2001, 2004). This should not prevent me from exercising my imagination to the full in the effort to understand their experience and vision of the world. But in the end historical truthfulness also demands an acknowledgement of the fissures and silences that run through all knowledge.

While recognizing its own limits, though, historical truthfulness above all involves an effort to *make sense* of the past. Listening to the multiple voices of history must also be a process through which we try to gain a broader picture of past events, judge the reliability of conflicting accounts, assess the meanings of different forms of testimonies and evidence, and search for patterns that explain the relationship between past and present. In a complex information age, it is easy to feel overwhelmed by a mass of contradictory narratives. But the temptation to abdicate opinion – to leave the conclusions to 'the experts' – is dangerous because it creates a vacuum which can all too readily be filled by the latest or most appealingly presented ideology. In relation to historical understanding, as in relation to politics, amorphous apathy and a frenzied enthusiasm for media-manipulated public performance are two sides of the same coin.

Historical truthfulness, then, is an ongoing conversation through which, by engaging with the views of others in different social and spatial locations (across and within national boundaries), we shape and reshape our understanding of the past. It is therefore also a process of self-reflection. As we enter into a dialogue with varied representations of the past, we do not only create our own interpretations and our sense of identity by accepting some representations and rejecting others. We are also forced to think about our position in the present, and how it influences our interpretations and choices. My reactions to a particular novel or photograph or film – whether it moves me, how I relate it to the wider stories I tell about the past, whether and how it influences the way I live my life – depends on many factors: amongst other things on my background knowledge of the past, on my current social position and views of the world, and on the way in which I have experienced historical events.

I grew up in England in the 1950s and 1960s, learning school history in a framework which, at least in the early years, was intensely nationalistic and often imperialist. But in writing this book I have found myself looking back at the wide range of other stories and images that influenced my sense of the past. These included highly jingoistic films about the Second World War, which characteristically presented the war as a conflict in which good (=Britain) confronted evil (=Germany), and good triumphed, as well as imperialist comic books in which heroic British explorers and missionaries brought the blessings of 'civilization' to suitably grateful 'natives'. But they also included more complicated accounts of the past. As a teenager I was deeply impressed by R. C. Hutchinson's now long-forgotten novel *Joanna at Daybreak*, which deals with the issue of the Holocaust from the perspective of a

German woman struggling to come to terms with her sense of responsibility in the chaos of the immediate postwar years. Re-reading this in
middle age, I find its power as a novel marred by excessive moral and
religious overtones, but it still suggests the potential of the novel to
extend the historical imagination into unfamiliar landscapes which offer
a new vantage point on the past. Going to school in the Netherlands for
two years I also discovered that the events of the Western European
past looked surprisingly different in Dutch textbooks and museums
from the way they looked in British textbooks and museums. This gave
me a clearer understanding of the stories my mother had told me of
her own childhood experiences, moving between schools in England,
where she was taught about the glorious reign of 'Good Queen Bess'
(Queen Elizabeth I), and schools in the newly independent Ireland,
where she was taught about the misery inflicted on the Irish people by
'Bad Queen Bess'.

As an adult I have spent most of my time studying and researching
Japanese history, and in the process defining and redefining my own
relationship to that history. Studying key events of the recent Japanese
past, including the experiences of prewar imperial expansion and of the
war, have made me look in new ways at the past of Britain, where I grew
up, and of Australia, where I now live. I cannot, for example, reflect on
problems of war responsibility in Japan without also reflecting on
problems of British responsibility for colonialism in Australia and
elsewhere. At the same time, I have found myself increasingly involved
in intense and ongoing debates about the teaching of history in Japan.
As time has gone on, I have been forced to reflect on a notion that once
seemed straightforward: the notion of my history. The idea that some
parts of the past are ours, and some are not, no longer seems so simple.
The historical events that took place in particular geographical spaces
(like Britain and Ireland) may be parts of my past because they have in
some way helped to shape who I am, but the historical events that took

place in others (like Australia and Japan) have also in a sense become parts of my past because my life is caught up in their future.

It is absurd and illusory to imagine that we can view the past from any vantage point but the present, or to pretend that we can project ourselves back into the minds and bodies of participants in past events. All we can do is endeavour to be honest about our position in the present, and about the way our vision of the past relates to our vision for the future. If we recognize that we view the past from the present, acknowledge the limits of that viewpoint, and compare our vantage with those of our contemporaries, learning about the past can, I think and hope, become part of an ongoing effort to create for ourselves a meaningful position in the present.

Historical Truthfulness as a Social Issue

Lastly, historical truthfulness is not just a psychological relationship between an individual and the past. It is also a social matter. In the twenty-first century, our knowledge of the past is deeply influenced by the unequal power and reach of various media, and by the unequal access of different groups of people to those media. Political and economic power translates into the capacity to shape the landscapes of the historical imagination. The economics of publishing and the communicational codes of the comic book have had a decisive impact on Japanese people's access to knowledge regarding key events of the recent Japanese past. The global reach of Hollywood allows certain images of the past to be exported around the world, moulding many people's unconscious sense of the structure and meaning of world history.

Historical truthfulness, then, requires a shared effort to make history more accessible, both by using the potential of existing media to the full and, at times, by attacking the systems of privilege that generate unequal exchanges of knowledge. The emergence of new media like the Internet can open up new ways to overcome existing monopolies of knowledge. But at the same time, the legally enforced private ownership of knowledge is increasingly used to prevent the critical examination of certain versions of history. History teaching and research comes under growing pressure from the worldwide tendency towards the privatization of higher education. Yet those of us who engage in the creation of historical knowledge have perhaps greater opportunities than ever before to combine the uses of varied media and to explore new ways of communicating that knowledge beyond the narrow confines of the lecture theatre.

In this sense, we need to work not just towards a discourse of historical truthfulness but also towards a political economy of historical truthfulness – a society which creates space for the critical under-standing and open exchange of multiple interpretations of the past, an understanding and exchange which extends across national boundaries. Without this we risk one of the most pernicious forms of impover-ishment: the self-inflicted poverty that human beings, for fear of one another, create within their own minds.

Bibliography

Achebe Chinua. 1994 (first published in 1959). *Things Fall Apart*. New York: Doubleday.

Aida Yûji. 1986. *Rekishi shôsetsu no yomikata*. Tokyo: PHP Kenkyûjo.

Aizu Izumi and Shumpei Kumon. 1994. 'Co-Emulation: The Case for a Global Hypernetwork Society'. In *Global Networks: Computers and International Communications*. Ed. Linda M. Harasim. Cambridge Mass.: MIT Press. 311–326.

Akutagawa, Ryûnosuke. 1995. 'Rashômon'. In *Akutagawa Ryûnosuke zenshû*. Vol. 1. Tokyo: Iwanami Shoten. 145–154.

Akutagawa Ryûnosuke. 1996 (first published in 1915). 'Toshishun'. In *Akutagawa Ryûnosuke zenshû*. Vol. 6. Tokyo: Iwanami Shoten. 254–271.

Allison, Anne. 1996. *Permitted and Prohibited Desires: Mothers, Comics and Censorship in Japan*. Boulder: Westview Press.

Anderson, Benedict. 1991. *Imagined Communities* (Second Edition). London: Verso Press.

Appleby, Joyce, Lynn Hunt and Margaret Jacobs. 1994. *Telling the Truth About History*. New York: W. W. Norton & Co.

Asahi Shinbunsha ed. 1960. *Arubamu: sengo 15-nen shi*. Tokyo: Asahi Shinbunsha.

Baburina, Nina. 1985. *The Soviet Political Poster – 1917–1980*. (Trans. Boris Rubalsky.) Harmondsworth: Penguin Books.

Baker, Ernest A. 1914. *A Guide to Historical Fiction*. London: George Routledge.

Banim, John. 1976 (first published in 1826). *The Boyne Water*. Lille: Université de Lille III.

Barkan, Elazar. 2000. *The Guilt of Nations: Restitution and Negotiating Historical Injustices*. New York: W. W. Norton & Co.

Barmé, Geremie. 1993. 'History for the Masses'. In *Using the Past to Serve the Present: Historiography and Politics in Contemporary China*. Ed. Jonathan Unger. Armonk, NY: M. E. Sharpe.

Barsam, Richard M. 1992. *Nonfiction Film: A Critical History* (Revised Edition), Indianapolis: Indiana University Press.

Berlier, Monique. 1999. 'The *Family of Man*: Readings of an Exhibition'. In *Picturing the Past: Media, History and Photography*. Ed. Bonnie Brennen and Hanno Hardt. Urbana and Chicago: University of Illinois Press. 206–241.

Blackbeard, Bill and Martin Williams. 1977. *The Smithsonian Collection of Newspaper Comics*. Washington: Smithsonian Institution Press.

Bluestone, George. 1961. *Novels into Film: The Metamorphosis of Fiction into Cinema*. Berkeley: University of California Press.

Bourdieu, Pierre. 1990. *Photography: A Middle-Brow Art*. (Trans. Shaun Whiteside.) Stanford: Stanford University Press.

Bowring, Richard. 1979. *Mori Ôgai and the Modernization of Japanese Culture*. Cambridge: Cambridge University Press.

Brecht, Bertolt. 1993. *Bertolt Brecht Journals*. (Trans. Hugh Rorrison.) London: Methuen.

Burgoyne, Robert. 1996. 'Modernism and the Narrative of Nation in *JFK*'. In *The Persistence of History: Cinema, Television and the Modern*

Event. Ed. Vivian Sobchack. New York and London: Routledge.

Cable, Mary. 1971. *Black Odyssey: The Case of the Slave Ship* Amistad. New York: Viking Press.

Cahalan, James M. 1983. *Great Hatred, Little Room: The Irish Historical Novel*. Syracuse NY: Syracuse University Press.

Carpenter, Edmund. 1972. *Oh, What a Blow that Phantom Gave Me!*. New York: Holt, Rinehart and Winston.

Chakrabarty, Dipesh. 2000. *Provincializing Europe: Postcolonial Thought and Historical Difference*. Princeton: Princeton University Press.

Chang, Iris. 1997. *The Rape of Nanking: The Forgotten Holocaust of World War II*. New York: Basic Books.

Chase-Ribout, Barbara. 1989. *Echo of Lions*. New York: William Morrow.

Chiba Tetsuya. 1978. *Chidenkai no taka – dai 3 shû*. Tokyo: Kôdansha.

Coe, Brian and Paul Gates. 1977. *The Snapshot Photograph: The Rise of Popular Photography 1888–1939*. London: Ash and Grant.

Consitt, Frances. 1931. *The Value of Films in History Teaching*. London: G. Bell and Sons Ltd.

Cowart, David. 1989. *History and the Contemporary Novel*. Carbondale and Edwardsville: Southern Illinois University Press.

Croce, Benedetto. 1949. *History as the Story of Liberty*. London: Allen and Unwin.

Crompton, Dennis, David Henry and Stephen Herbert. 1990. *Magic Images: The Art of Hand-Painted and Photographic Magic Lantern Slides*. London: The Magic Lantern Society of Great Britain.

Ćuruvija, Slavko and Ivan Torov. 1995. 'The March to War (1980–1990)'. In *Yugoslavia's Ethnic Nightmare: The Inside Story of Europe's Unfolding Ordeal*. Eds. Jasminka Udovićki and James Ridgeway. New York: Lawrence Hill Books. 73–104.

Custen, George F. 2000. 'Making History'. In *The Historical Film: History and Memory in Media*. New Brunswick: Rutgers University Press. 67–97.

Deane, Seamus. 1996. *Reading in the Dark*. London: Jonathan Cape.

Dilworth, David A. and J. Thomas Rimer. 1977. *The Historical Literature of Mori Ogai*. Honolulu: University of Hawaii Press.

Dolgopol, Ustinia and Snehal Paranjape. 1994. *Comfort Women: An Unfinished Ordeal*. Geneva: International Commission of Jurists.

Dower, John. 1999. *Embracing Defeat: Japan in the Wake of World War II*. New York: W. W. Norton and Co.

Doyle, Roddy. 1999. *A Star Called Henry*. London. Jonathan Cape.

Dreamworks. 1998. Amistad: *A Celebration of the Film by Steven Spielberg*. New York: New Market Press.

Escabelt, Bernard. 1976. 'Introduction'. In *The Boyne Water*. John Banim. Lille: Université de Lille III. 8–31.

Edgerton, Gary. 2000. 'Ken Burns's Rebirth of a Nation: Television, Narrative and Popular History'. In *The Historical Film: History and Memory in Media*. New Brunswick: Rutgers University Press. 303–315.

Eisenstein, Sergei. 1949. 'Dicken, Griffith and the Film Today'. In *Film Form*. Ed. and trans. Jay Leyda. New York: Harcourt Brace and Co.

Exploratorium. 1995. 'Remembering Nagasaki, a website commemorating the 50th anniversary of the bombing of Hiroshima and Nagasaki'. © 1995 Exploratorium, www.exploratorium.edu/Nagasaki, cited by kind permission of Exploratorium.

Faurisson, Robert and Harry Elmer Barnes. 1985. *Is the Diary of Anne Frank Genuine?* Newport Beach: Institute for Historical Review.

Fitzgerald, Alan. 1995. *1945: War and Peace*. Canberra: Australian War Memorial.

Flaubert, Gustave. 1886. *Salammbô*. (Trans. M. French Sheldon.) London: Saxon and Co.

Foner, Eric. 1997. 'Hollywood Invades the Classroom'. *New York Times*. 20 December.

Fowles, John. 1969. *The French Lieutenant's Woman*. Boston: Little Brown.

Friedländer, Saul. 1988. 'Historical Writing and the Memory of the Holocaust'. In *Writing and the Holocaust*. Ed. Berel Lang. New York and London: Holmes and Meier. 66–77.

Friend, Patricia K. 2001. 'The Battle of the Boyne'. irishculture. about.com/library/weekly/aa070501a.htm

Fujioka Nobukatsu et al. 1996. *Kyôkasho ga oshienai rekishi*. Tokyo: Fusôsha.

Fujioka Nobukatsu. 1999. 'Shashin netsuzô, abareta teguchi: kakute "shôko shashin" wa, ichimai mo sonzai shinai'. In *'The Rape of Nanking' no kenkyû*. Eds. Fujioka Nobukatsu and Higashinakano Shudô. Tokyo: Shôdensha.

Fujita Masayuki. 1997. *Eiga no naka no Nihonshi*. Tokyo: Chirekisha.

Gessner, Robert. 1968. *The Moving Image: A Guide to Cinematic Literacy*. London: Cassell and Co.

Gifford, Denis. 1984. *The International Book of Comics*. Adelaide: Rigby.

Gifford, Henry. 1982. *Tolstoy*. Oxford: Oxford University Press.

Golomstok, Igor. 1990. *Totalitarian Art in the Soviet Union, the Third Reich, Fascist Italy and the People's Republic of China*. (Trans. Robert Chandler.) London: Collins Harvill.

Griffith, David Wark. 1971 (first published in 1915). 'Some Prophecies: Film, Theatre, Screenwriting and Education'. Reprinted in *Focus on D. W. Griffith*. Ed. Harry M. Geduld. Englewood Cliffs: Prentice Hall Inc. 34–35.

Grindon, Leger. 1994. *Shadows on the Past: Studies in the Historical Fiction Film*. Philadelphia: Temple University Press.

Hansen, Miriam Bratu. 2000. '*Schindler's List* is not *Shoah*: The Second Commandment, Popular Modernism, and Public Memory'. In *The Historical Film: History and Memory in Media*. New Brunswick: Rutgers University Press. 201–217.

Heibonsha ed. 1960. *Warera Nihonjin 5: seikatsu no rekishi*. Tokyo: Heibonsha.

Heiwa Kinenkan o Tsukuru Kai ed. 1994. *Shashin monogatari: Ano hi, Hiroshima to Nagasaki de.* Tokyo: Heiwa no Aterie.

Henderson, Cinqué. 1997. 'Making a Name: A Personal *Amistad* Voyage'. *The New Republic.* 22 December. 16–18.

Henderson, Robert M. 1972. *D. W. Griffith: His Life and Work.* New York: Oxford University Press.

Henisch, Heinz K. and Bridget A. Henisch. 1994. *The Photographic Experience 1939–1914: Images and Attitudes.* Pennsylvania: Pennsylvania State University Press.

Higashi Ajia Bunshitetsu Nettowâku ed. 2001. *Kobayashi Yoshinori 'Taiwanron' o koete.* Tokyo. Sakuhinsha.

Hillgruber, Andreas. 1993. 'No Questions are Forbidden to Research'. In *Forever in the Shadow of Hitler? Original Documents of the Historikerstreit, the Controversity Concerning the Singularity of the Holocaust.* Ed. and trans. James Knowlton and Truett Cates. Atlantic Highlands: Humanities Press. pp. 155–161.

Himmelfarb, Gertrude. 1992. 'Telling It as You Like It: Post-modernist History and the Flight from Fact'. *Times Literary Supplement.* 16 October. 12–15.

Hirsch, Marianne. 1997. *Family Frames: Photography, Narrative and Postmemory.* Cambridge Mass.: Harvard University Press.

Hobsbawm, Eric. 1997. *On History.* London: Weidenfeld and Nicolson.

Hokari, Minoru. 2001. *Cross-Culturalizing History: Journey to the Gurindji Way of Historical Practice.* Unpublished PhD thesis. Australian National University.

Hokari Minoru. 2004. *Radikaru Ôraru Hisutorî.* Tokyo: Ochanomizu Shobô.

Hong Alvin Tan Peng. 1999. 'Two Imaginings: The Past in Present Singapore'. In *Our Place in Time: Exploring Heritage and Memory in Singapore.* Eds. Kwok Kian-Woon et al. Singapore: Singapore Heritage Society. 111–128.

Hugo, Victor. 1902. *Notre Dame de Paris*. (Trans. Jessie Haynes.) New York: P. F. Collier and Son.

Ienaga Saburô. 2001. *Japan's Past, Japan's Future: One Historian's Odyssey*. (Trans. R. Minear.) Lanham: Rowman and Littlefield.

Iizawa Kôtarô et al. 1998. *Nihon shashinka 23: Yamahata Yôsuke*. Tokyo: Iwanami Shoten.

Iizawa Kôtarô et al. 1999. *Nihon shashinshi gaisetsu*. Tokyo: Iwanami Shoten.

Ikeda Riyoko. 1972. *Berusaiyu no bara*. Vol. 1. Tokyo: Shûeisha.

Inada Tatsuo. 1962. *Eiga kyôiku undo sanjûnen no kiroku to kaisô*. Tokyo: Nihon Eiga Kyôiku Kyôkai.

Inoue Yasushi. 1981a (first published in 1963). *Rôran*. In *Inoue Yasushi rekishi shôsetsu shû*. Vol. 2. Tokyo: Iwanami Shoten. 3–53.

Inoue Yasushi. 1981b (first published in 1963). *Fûtô*. In *Inoue Yasushi rekishi shôsetsu shû*. Vol. 5. Tokyo: Iwanami Shoten.

Irving, David. 1990. *Hitler's War*. London: Avon Books.

Ishiko Jun. 1983. *Manga ni miru sensô to heiwa 90-nen*. Tokyo: Horupu Shuppan.

Ishinomori Shôtarô. 1993–1994. *Manga Nihon no rekishi gendai hen* (7 vols). Tokyo: Chûô Kôrônsha.

Ishizaka Kei. 1999. 'Aru hi ano kioku o koroshi ni'. Reprinted in *Sensôron, môsôron*. Miyadai Shinji et al. Tokyo: Kyôiku Shiryô Shuppansha. 155–184.

Iwakami Junichi. 1942. *Rekishi bungaku ron*. Tokyo: Chûô Kôronsha.

Japan Society for History Textbook Reform. 1998. *The Restoration of National History*. Tokyo: Japan Society for History Textbook Reform.

Japan Times and Mail. 1937. *The Truth Behind the Sino-Japanese Crisis*. Tokyo: Japan Times and Mail.

Jarvie, Ian C. 1978. 'Seeing Through Movies'. *Philosophy of the Social Sciences* 8 (4). 374–397.

Jenkins, Rupert. 1995. *Nagasaki Journey: The Photographs of Yosuke Yamahata, August 10 1945*. Tokyo: Charles E. Tuttle Co.

Jenks, Tudor. 1908. *Photography for Young People*. New York: Frederick A. Stokes.

Johnson, Charles, Patricia Smith and Iona Morris. 1998. *Africans in America: America's Journey Through Slavery*. New York: Harcourt Brace.

Johnson, Henry. 1940. *Teaching of History in Elementary and Secondary Schools with Applications to Allied Studies*. New York: Macmillan.

Kajiyama Toshiyuki. 1995. *The Clan Records: Five Stories of Korea*. (Trans. Yoshiko Dykstra.) Honolulu: University of Hawaii Press.

Kakichi Shinji. 1997. 'Comfort Women: Were They Really Abducted by the Japanese Army?' coralnet.or.jp/kakichi/index.html

Kalaw, Maximo M. 1964. *The Filipino Rebel: A Romance of American Occupation in the Philippines*. Manila: Pilipiana Book Guild.

Kamei Hideo. 1999. *Shôsetsu ron: Shôsetsu shinzui to kindai*. Tokyo: Iwanami Shoten.

Kanamaru, Shigemine, Eiichirô Ishida and Kenzô Nakajima. 1956. 'Jinrui no jojishi: The Family of Man ten o miru'. *Kamera Mainichi*. 4 (6). 122–129.

Kang Sangjung. 2002. 'Nihon no Ajiakan no tenkan ni mukete'. In *Nihon no rekishi*. Vol. 26. Ed. Amino Yoshihiko et al. Tokyo: Kôdansha. 63–100.

Kilpatrick, Cecil. n.d. 'The Battle of the Boyne, July 1 1690'. members.nbci.com/_XMCM/orangeorder/boyne.htm

King, Edward. 1886. 'Introduction'. In *Salammbô*. Gustave Flaubert. (Trans. M. French Sheldon.) London: Saxon and Co.

Knowlton, Daniel C. and J. Warren Tilton. 1929. *Motion Pictures in History Teaching: A Study of the Chronicles of America Photoplays as an Aid in Seventh Grade Instruction*. New Haven: Yale University Press.

Kobayashi Yoshinori. 1993. *Gômanizumu sengen 1*. Tokyo: Fusôsha.

Kobayashi Yoshinori and Yoshikazu Takeuchi. 1997. *Kyôkasho ga oshieka-nenai jigyaku*. Tokyo: Bunkasha.

Kobayashi Yoshinori. 1998. *Gômanizumu sengen spesharu: Sensôron*. Tokyo: Gentôsha.

Kobayashi Yoshinori. 2000. *Gômanizumu sengen spesharu: Taiwanron*. Tokyo: Shôgakukan.

Kobayashi Yoshinori. 2001. *Gômanizumu sengen spesharu: Sensôron 2*. Tokyo: Gentôsha.

Komagome Takeshi. 1996. *Shokuminchi teikoku Nihon no bunka tôgô*. Tokyo: Iwanami.

Koyama Eizô. 1942. *Senji senden ron*. Tokyo: Sanseidô.

Kuehl, Jerry. 1976. 'History on the Public Screen II'. In *The Historian and Film*. Ed. Paul Smith. Cambridge: Cambridge University Press. 177–185.

Kumon, Shumpei and Izumi Aizu. 1994. 'Co-Emulation: The Case for a Global Hypernetwork Society'. In *Global Networks: Computers and International Communications*. Ed. Linda M. Harasim. Cambridge Mass.: MIT Press. 311–326.

Kurtzman, Harvey et al. 1950. 'Conquest'. *Two-Fisted Tales*. 18 November–December.

Kurtzman, Harvey et al. 1951a. 'Dying City!' *Two-Fisted Tales*. 22 July–August.

Kurtzman, Harvey et al. 1951b. 'Kill!' *Two-Fisted Tales*. 23 September–October.

Kurtzman, Harvey et al. 1951c. 'Rubble!' *Two-Fisted Tales*. 24 November–December.

Kurtzman, Harvey et al. 1952a. 'Custer's Last Stand'. *Two-Fisted Tales*. 27 May–June.

Kurtzman, Harvey et al. 1952b. 'Saipan!' *Two-Fisted Tales*. 28 July–August.

Kurtzman, Harvey et al. 1953. 'Atom Bomb!' *Two-Fisted Tales*. 33 May–June.

Kyôdô Tsûshin. 2000. *Shashinshû: 20 seiki no kioku: Shimbunsha ga tsutaeta Nihon no 100 nen, sekai no 100 nen*. Tokyo: Kyôdô Tsûshin.

Lalvani, Suren. 1996. *Photography, Vision and the Production of Modern Bodies*. Albany: State University of New York Press.

Landow, George P. 1992. *Hypertext: The Convergence of Contemporary Critical Theory and Technology*. Baltimore: Johns Hopkins University Press.

Landy, Marcia ed. 2001. *The Historical Film: History and Memory in Media*. New Brunswick: Rutgers University Press.

Lanzmann, Claude. 1994. 'Holocauste, La Représentation Impossible'. *Le Monde*. 3 March.

Le Goff, Jacques. 1988. *Histoire et Memoire*. Paris: Editions Gallimard.

Lie, John. 2001. *Multiethinic Japan*. Cambridge Mass.: Harvard University Press.

Linder, Douglas. 1998. 'Famous American Trials: *Amistad* Trials 1839–1840'. www.law.umkc.edu/faculty/projects/ftrials/amistad/AMISTD.HTM

Litwack, Leon F. 1995. 'Birth of a Nation'. In *Past Imperfect: History According to the Movies*. Ed. Mark C. Carnes. New York: Henry Holt and Co. 136–141.

Lowenthal, David. 1985. *The Past is a Foreign Country*. Cambridge: Cambridge University Press.

Lukács, George. 1983 (first published in 1937). *The Historical Novel*. (Trans. Hannah and Stanley Mitchell.) Lincoln and London: University of Nebraska Press.

Lytton, Edward Bulwer. 1879a (first published in 1834). *The Last Days of Pompeii*. Leipzig: Bernhard Tauchnitz.

Lytton, Edward Bulwer. 1879b. *Kisô shunshi*. Japanese version of *The Last Days of Pompeii*. (Abridged and translated by Tamba Jun'ichirô.) Tokyo: Takahashi Gengorô.

Macaulay, Thomas Babington. 1986 (first published 1848–1861). *History of England*. Ed. and abridged by Hugh Trevor-Roper. Harmondsworth: Penguin.

Macdonald, Kevin and Mark Cousins. 1996. *Imagining Reality: The Faber Book of the Documentary*. London: Faber and Faber.

McCormack, Gavan. 2000. 'The Japanese Movement to "Correct" History'. In *Censoring History: Citizenship and Memory in Japan, Germany and the United States*. Eds. Laura Hein and Mark Selden. Armonk, NY: M. E. Sharpe. 53–73.

McCourt, Frank. *Angela's Ashes: Memoirs of a Childhood*. London: Harper Collins.

Mainichi Shinbunsha ed. 1998–1999. *Mainichi Shinbun hizô: Fukyoka shashin 1*. Tokyo: Mainichi Shinbunsha.

Mainichi Shinbunsha ed. 1999. *1945-nen. Nichi-Doku zentaishugi no hôkai*. Tokyo: Mainichi Shinbunsha.

Manzoni, Alessandro. 1984 (first published in 1850). *On the Historical Novel*. (Trans. Sandra Bermann.) Lincoln and London: University of Nebraska Press.

Martin, B. Edmon. 1986. *All We Want is Make Us Free: La Amistad and the Reform Abolitionists*. Lanyon, NY: University Press of America.

Martinez-Sicat, Maria Teresa. 1994. *Imagining the Nation in Four Philippine Novels*. Diliman: University of the Philippines Press.

Milošević, Milan. 1995. 'The Media Wars'. In *Yugoslavia's Ethnic Nightmare: The Inside Story of Europe's Unfolding Ordeal*. Eds. Jasminka Udovićki and James Ridgeway. New York: Lawrence Hill Books. 105–122.

Miyadai Shinji et al. 1999. *Sensôron, môsôron*. Tokyo: Kyôiku Shiryô Shuppansha.

Monaco, James. 1981. *How to Read a Film* (Second Edition). New York and Oxford: Oxford University Press.

Morita Ichirô. 1985. *Garasuban no shashinten: Meiji no Nihon*. Tokyo: Habitat Seibu (exhibition poster).

Morris-Suzuki, Tessa. 1998. 'Gurôbaru na kioku, nashonaru na kijutsu'. *Shisô*. No. 890. 35–56.

Morris-Suzuki, Tessa. 2001. 'Hihanteki sôzôryoku no kiki'. *Sekai.* January. 80–92.

Moses, Michael Valdez. 1995. *The Novel and the Globalization of Culture.* New York and Oxford: Oxford University Press.

Museum of Modern Art. 1955. *The Family of Man.* New York: Museum of Modern Art.

Mystic Seaport. 2003. Discover Amistad. www.mysticseaport.org/discover/do-Amistad.htm.

Nakazawa Keiji. 1994. *'Hadashi no Gen' jiden.* Tokyo: Kyôiku Shiryô Shuppankai.

Narita Ryûichi. 1998. 'Shiba Ryôtarô no rekishi no katari: "Saka no ue no kumo" o megutte'. In *Nashonaru hisutorî o koete.* Eds. Komori Yôichi and Takahashi Tetsuya. Tokyo: Tokyo Daigaku Shuppankai. 69–84.

Narita Ryûichi. 2001. 'Rekishi' o kyôkasho ni egaku to iu koto'. *Sekai.* 689. June. 69–77.

Narita Ryûichi. 2001. *'Rekishi' wa ika ni kataru ka: 1930 nendai 'kokumin no monogatari' hihan.* Tokyo: NHK Books.

Nash, Gary B., Charlotte Crabtree and Ross E. Dunn. 1997. *History on Trial: Culture Wars and the Teaching of the Past.* New York. Alfred A. Knopf.

National Archives and Records Administration. 1998. *The Amistad Case.* www.nara.gov/education/teaching/amistad.html

National Archives and Records Administration. 1998. 'The Amistad Case: Teaching Activities'. www.nara.gov/education/teaching/amistad/teach.html

Nelson, Theodore H. 1981. *Literary Machines.* Swarthmore: Ted Nelson.

NHK. 1995. *NHK supesharu: Nagasaki – Eizô no shôgen.* TV documentary, broadcast 9 August.

Nishio Kanji et al. 1999. *Kokumin no rekishi.* Tokyo: Fusôsha.

Nishio Kanji et al. 2001. *Atarashii rekishi kyôkasho.* Tokyo: Fusôsha.

Nolte, Ernst 1993a. 'Between Historical Legend and Revisionism? The

Third Reich in Perspective'. In *Forever in the Shadow of Hitler? Original Documents of the Historikerstreit, the Controversy Concerning the Singularity of the Holocaust*. Ed and trans. James Knowlton and Truett Cates. New Jersey: Humanities Press. 1–15

Nolte, Ernst. 1993. 'The Past That Will Not Pass: A Speech That Could Be Written But Not Delivered'. In *Forever in the Shadow of Hitler? Original Documents of the Historikerstreit, the Controversy Concerning the Singularity of the Holocaust*. Ed. and trans. James Knowlton and Truett Cates. New Jersey: Humanities Press. 18–23.

Nora, Pierre. 1998. 'The Era of Commemoration'. In *Realm of Memory: The Construction of the French Past*. Vol. 3. Ed. Pierre Nora. (Trans. Arthur Goldhammer.) New York: Columbia University Press. 609–637.

Nozaki Yoshiko and Hiromitsu Inokuchi. 2000. 'Japan's Education, Nationalism and Ienaga Saburô's Textbook Lawsuits'. In *Censoring History: Citizenship and Memory in Japan, Germany and the United States*. Eds. Laura Hein and Mark Selden. Armonk: M. E. Sharpe. 96–126.

Ogawa Kazumasa. 1892. *Scenes from the Chushingura and the Story of the Forty-Seven Ronin*. Tokyo: privately published.

Ôgoshi Aiko. 2000. 'Rekishi shûseishugi no kansei'. Paper presented to the DIJ International Symposium: 'Contested Historiography – Feminist Perspectives on World War II'. Tokyo. 13–14 April.

Ônishi Shirô. 1960. *Nihon hyakunen no kiroku*. Tokyo: Kôdansha.

Ôoka Shôhei. 1974. *Rekishi shôsetsu no mondai*. Tokyo: Bungei Shunjûsha.

Orel, Harold. 1995. *The Historical Novel from Scott to Sabatini: Changing Attitudes toward a Literary Genre, 1814–1920*. New York: St. Martin's Press.

Osagie, Iyunolu Folayan. 2000. *The Amistad Revolt : Memory, Slavery and the Politics of Identity in the United States and Sierra Leone*. Athens and London: University of Georgia Press.

Ôta Masakuni. 2000. "'Teki' ha waga uchi ni ari: "Nihon nashonar-izumu" o kaitai suru"". *Tosho shinbun.* 2510. 18 November. 1–3

Owens, William A. 1953. *Slave Mutiny: The Revolt on the Schooner* Amistad. London: Peter Davis.

Pate, Alexs. 1997. *Amistad.* New York: Penguin.

Perry, Jos. 1999. *Wij Herdenken, dus wij Bestaan.* Nijmegen: Sun.

Petrov, Sergei Mitrofanovich. 1960. *Russkii Istoricheskii Roman 19 Veka.* Moscow: Khudozhestvennaya Literatura.

Plantinga, Carl R. 1997. *Rhetoric and Representation in Non-Fiction Film.* Cambridge: Cambridge University Press.

Plumb, J. H. 1969. *The Death of the Past.* Harmondsworth: Penguin.

Pollack, Peter. 1958. *The Picture History of Photography from the Earliest Beginnings to the Present Day.* New York: Harry N. Abrams.

Price, David. 1999. *History Made, History Imagined: Contemporary Literature, Poiesis and the Past.* Urbana and Chicago: University of Illinois Press.

The Queen's Empire: A Pictorial and Descriptive Record. 1897. London: Cassell and Co.

Raack, R. J. 1983. 'Historiography as Cinematography: A Prolegomenon to Film Work for Historians'. *Journal of Contemporary History.* 18.

Rayne, Godfrey and Peter Jackson. n.d. 'Cecil Rhodes: Patriot and Pioneer'. *Eagle Annual.* 9. London: Hulton Press.

Reynolds, Henry. 2000. 'The Public Role of History'. *Dissent.* Spring. 2–5.

Rogers, Agnes and Frederick Lewis Allen. 1947. *I Remember Distinctly: A Family Album of the American People in the Years of Peace: 1918 to Pearl Harbor.* New York: Harper and Brothers.

Rosaldo, Renato. 1993. *Culture and Truth: The Remaking of Social Analysis* (Second Edition). Boston: Beacon Press.

Rose, Deborah Bird. 1991. *Hidden Histories: Black Stories from Victoria River Downs, Humbert River and Wave Hill Stations.* Canberra: Aboriginal Studies Press.

Rosenstone, Robert A. 1995. *Visions of the Past: The Challenge of Film to our Idea of History*. Cambridge, Mass. and London: Harvard University Press.

Rothstein, Arthur. 1956. *Photojournalism: Pictures for Magazines and Newspaper*. New York: American Photographic Book Publishing Co.

Rosenzweig, Roy. 1995. "'So, What's Next for Clio?'" CD-ROM and Historians'. *Journal of American History*. 81. 4 March. 1621–1640.

Ruoff, Jeffrey and Kenneth Ruoff. 1998. *The Emperor's Naked Army Marches On*. Trowbridge: Flick Books.

Ryan, Sean. 1997. *Wild Geese Heritage Museum and Library*. indigo.ie/~wildgees/

Saesparam. 2000. *Jûgun ianfu mondai jôhôshitsu*. www.saesparam.com/jugun/

Sakamoto Takao. 1994. *Nihon wa mizukara no raireki o katariuru ka*. Tokyo: Chikuma Shobô.

Sasabuchi Tomoichi. 1990. *Shôsetsuka Shimazaki Tôson*. Tokyo: Meiji Shoin.

Schama, Simon. 1998. 'Clio at the Multiplex: What Hollywood and Herodotus have in Common'. *The New Yorker*. 19 January. 38–43.

Schippers, Donald, J. 1968. 'The Literature of Oral History'. In *Second National Colloquium on Oral History*. Ed. Louis M. Starr. Arden house, NY. 18–21. Nov. 1967, Oral History Association, NY.

Schodt, Frederik L. 1983. *Manga! Manga! The World of Japanese Comics*. Tokyo: Kodansha International.

Scott, Walter. 1829 (first published in 1814). *Waverley, or 'Tis Sixty Years Since*. Edinburgh: A. C. Black.

Scott, Walter. 1962 (first published in 1819). *Ivanhoe: A Romance*. New York: New American Library.

Scott, Walter. 1879. *Shunpû jôwa*. Japanese version of *The Bride of Lammermoor*. (Abridged and translated by Tsubouchi Shôyô.) Tokyo: Nakajima Seiichi.

Scott, Walter. 1910. *Aibanhô*. Abridged Japanese version of *Ivanhoe*. Tokyo: Naigai Shuppan Kyôkai.

Seiberling, Grace, with Carolyn Bloore. 1986. *Amateurs, Photography and the Mid-Victorian Imagination*. Chicago: University of Chicago Press.

Sekula, Alan. 1984. 'The Instrumental Image: Steichen at War'. In *Photography Against the Grain*. Halifax: Press of the Nova Scotia College of Art and Design.

Sekula, Alan. 1999. 'Reading an Archive: Photography Between Labour and Capital'. Reprinted in *Visual Culture: The Reader*. Eds. Jessica Evans and Stuart Hall. London: Sage Publications. 181–192.

Seton, Marie. 1978. *Sergei M. Eisenstein: A Biography*. London: Dennis Dobson.

Shiba Ryôtarô. 1999 (first published in 1968). *Saka no ue no kumo* (8 vols). Tokyo: Bunshun Bunkô

Shimazaki Tôson. 1981 (first published in 1929–1935). *Yoake mae*. In *Shimazaki Tôson zenshû*. Vols 8 and 9. Tokyo: Chikuma Shobô.

Simmon, Scott. 1993. *The Films of D. W. Griffith*. Cambridge: Cambridge University Press.

Simpson, Moira. 1996. *Making Representations: Museums in the Post-Colonial Era*. London: Routledge.

Sobchack, Vivian ed. 1996. *The Persistence of History: Cinema, Television and the Modern Event*. New York and London: Routledge.

Soh, Chunghee Sarah and Jerry D. Boucher. 2001. *The Comfort Women Project*. online.sfsu.edu/~soh/comfortwomen.html/

Sontag, Susan. 1973. *On Photography*. New York: Farrar, Straus and Giroux.

Spiegelman, Art. 1986. *Maus: A Survivor's Tale I – My Father Bleeds History*. New York: Pantheon Books.

Spiegelman, Art. 1991. *Maus: A Survivor's Tale II – And Here My Troubles Began*. New York: Pantheon Books.

Spiegelman, Art. 1994. *The Complete Maus*. (CD-ROM). Irvington: Voyager Co.

Staiger, Janet. 1996. 'Cinematic Shots: The Narration of Violence'. In *The Persistence of History: Cinema, Television and the Modern Event*. New York and London: Routledge. 39–54.

Stallabrass, Julian. 1995. 'Empowering Technology: The Exploration of Cyberspace.' *New Left Review*. 211 (May/June). 3–32.

Sturken, Marita. 1997. *Tangled Memories: The Vietnam War, the AIDS Epidemic and the Politics of Remembering*. Berkeley: University of California Press.

Suh Kyung-sik and Tetsuya Takahashi. 2000. *Danzetsu no seiki, shôgen no jidai*. Tokyo: Iwanami Shoten.

Takahashi Tetsuya. 2001. *Rekishi/Shuseishugi*. Tokyo: Iwanami Shoten.

Takeda Seiji, Yoshinori Kobayashi and Daizaburô Hashizume. 1997. *Seigi, sensô, kokkaron*. Tokyo: Michi Shobô.

Tanaka, Masaaki. 2000. *What Really Happened in Nanking: The Refutation of a Common Myth*. Tokyo: Sekai Shuppan.

Tanihara Shigeo and Hikaru Noguchi. n.d. 'Jûgun ianfu ni tsuite'. www.jiyuu-shikan.org/frontline/noguchi/ianfu.html

Tanner, Marcus. 1997. *Croatia: A Nation Forged in War*. New Haven and London: Yale University Press.

Teachers' Virtual School. 2002. *History Department*. www.spartacus.schoolnet.co.uk/TVS.htm

Thorpe, Adam. 1993. *Ulverton*. New York: Farrar, Straus and Giroux.

Time-Life Books. 1969. *This Fabulous Century*. New York: Time-Life Books.

Time Life Books. 1975. *Life at War* (Japanese edition). Tokyo: Time Life Books.

Tolstoy, Leo. 1978 (first published in 1869). *War and Peace*. (Trans. Rosemary Edmonds.) Harmondsworth: Penguin.

Tomiyama Ichirô. 2002. *Bôryoku no yokan: Iha Fuyu no okeru kiki no mondai*. Tokyo: Iwanami Shoten.

Trevor-Roper, Hugh. 1986. 'Lord Macaulay: Introduction'. In *History of England*. Thomas Babington Macaulay. Ed. and abridged by Hugh Trevor-Roper. Harmondsworth: Penguin.

Trinkle, Dennis A., Dorothy Auchter, Scott A. Merriman and Todd E. Larson. 1997. *The History Highway: A Guide to Internet Resources*. Armonk: M. E. Sharpe.

Trumpener, Katie. 1997. *Bardic Nationalism: The Romantic Novel and the British Empire*. Princeton: Princeton University Press.

Tudjman, Franjo. 1996. *Horrors of War: Historical Reality and Philosophy*. (Trans. Katarina Mijatovic). New York: M. Evans and Co. (A revised English version of Tudjman's 1989 book *Bespuca Povijesne Zbiljnosti.*)

Udovićki, Jasminka. 1995. 'The Rise and Fall of the Balkan Ideal'. In *Yugoslavia's Ethnic Nightmare: The Inside Story of Europe's Unfolding Ordeal*. Eds. Jasminka Udovićki and James Ridgeway. New York: Lawrence Hill Books. 17–36.

Uesugi, Satoshi. 1997. *Datsu Gômanizumu Sengen: Kobayashi Yoshinori no 'ianfu' mondai*. Osaka: Tôhô Shuppan.

Uesugi Satoshi. 2000. 'Ko' to kokka o koeru'. In *Datsu Sensôron*. Ed. S. Uesugi. Osaka: Tôhô Shuppan. 10–23.

United Nations Commission on Human Rights. 1996. *Report on the Mission to the Democratic People's Republic of Korea, the Republic of Korea and Japan on the Issue of Military Sexual Slavery in Wartime*. http://heiwww.unige.ch/humanrts/commission/country52/53–add1.htm

Vardac, A. Nicholas. 1971 (first published in 1949). 'Griffith and *The Birth of a Nation*'. Reprinted in *Focus on D. W. Griffith*. Ed. Harry M. Geduld. Englewood Cliffs: Prentice Hall Inc. 84–87.

Vazquez de Parga, Salvador. 1980. *Los Comics del Franquismo*. Barcelona: Editorial Planeta.

Vidal, Gore. 1997. 'Reel History: Why John Quincy Adams was the Hero of the *Amistad* Affair'. *The New Yorker*. 10 November. 112–120.

Vidal-Naquet, Pierre. 1993. *Assassins of Memory*. (Trans. Jeffrey Mehlman.) New York: Columbia University Press.

Wallace, Michael. 1986. 'Visiting the Past: History Museums in the United States'. In *Presenting the Past: Essays on Public History*. Ed. Susan Porter Benson, Stephen Brier and Roy Rosenzweig. Philadelphia: Temple University Press. 137–161.

Watt, Donald. 1976. 'History on the Public Screen I'. In *The Historian and Film*. Ed. Paul Smith. Cambridge: Cambridge University Press. 169–176.

Weyman, Stanley J. 1894. *Under the Red Robe*. London: Methuen.

WGBH Educational Foundation. 1998. *Africans in America: America's Journey Through Slavery*. www.pbs.org/wgbh/aia

White, Hayden. 1973. *Metahistory: The Historical Imagination in Nineteenth Century Europe*. Baltimore: Johns Hopkins University Press.

White, Hayden. 1996. 'The Modernist Event'. In *The Persistence of History: Cinema, Television and the Modern Event*, Ed. Vivian Sobchack. New York and London: Routledge.

Windschuttle, Keith. 2000. 'The Myths of Frontier Massacres in Australian History'. Parts 1–3. *Quadrant*. Oct–Dec.

Wise, Arthur Harry. 1939. *Motion Pictures as an Aid in the Teaching of American History*. New Haven: Yale University. Press.

Witek, Joseph. 1989. *Comic-books as History: The Narrative Art of Jack Jackson, Art Spiegelman and Harvey Pekar*. Jackson and London: University Press of Mississippi.

Wright, Bradford W. 2001. *Comic-book Nation: The Transformation of Youth Culture in the United States*. Baltimore and London: Johns Hopkins University Press.

Yamada, Eikichi. 1934. *Shashinkan haneisaku*. Osaka: Osaka Shishin Shinbunsha.

Yamahata, Yôsuke. 1959. 'Genbaku satsuei memo'. In *Kiroku shashin: Genbaku no Nagasaki*. Ed. Kitajima Muneto. Toyko: Gakufû Shoin.

Yanagida Izumi. 1961. *Meiji shoki honyaku bungaku no kenkyû*. Tokyo: Bunshunsha.

Yang Daqing. 2000. 'The Challenges of the Nanjing Massacre: Reflections on Historical Inquiry'. In *The Nanjing Massacre in History and Historiography*. Ed. Joshua Fogel. Berkeley: University of California Press. 133–179.

Yang Daqing. 2002. 'Regime of truth and possibilities of Transnational History in Japan and China'. Paper presented at the conference 'Can We Write History: Between Postmodernism and Coarse Nationalism'. Meiji Gakuin University, Tokyo, March 19.

Yoneyama Lisa. 1999. *Hiroshima Traces: Time, Space and the Dialectics of Memory*. Berkeley: University of California Press.

Yonezawa Yoshihiro. 1989. 'Manga no kairaku – fûkei, sen, jotai, gurotesuku'. In *Manga hihyô sengen*. Ed Y. Yonezawa. Tokyo: Aki Shobô. 177–199.

Yoshikawa Eiji. 1981. *Musashi*. (Trans. Charles S. Terry.) New York: Harper and Row/Kodansha International.

Yoshimi Yoshiaki. 1995. *Jugun ianfu*. Tokyo: Iwanami Shinsho.

Yuson, Alfred A. 1988. *Great Philippine Jungle Energy Café*. Cubao: Adriana Printing Co.

Index